GRAMMAR AND PRACTICE

Jimmie Hill

with

Rosalyn Hurst
Senior Lecturer in Education, West Sussex Institute of Higher Education

Grammar Consultant
Michael Lewis
Grammar Summaries
Celia Blissett and Katherine Hallgarten

THOMSON
HEINLE

Australia Canada Mexico Singapore Spain United Kingdom United States

THOMSON

HEINLE

Grammar and Practice

Jimmie Hill with Rosalyn Hurst

Publisher/Global ELT: *Christopher Wenger*
Executive Marketing Manager/Global ELT/ESL: *Amy Mabley*

Printed in Croatia by Zrinski d.d.
2 3 4 5 6 7 8 9 10   09 08 07

For more information contact Heinle, 25 Thomson Place, Boston, MA 02210 USA,
or you can visit our Internet site at http://www.heinle.com

ISBN: 978-0-906717-74-5

Acknowledgements
We are grateful to Michael Berman for permission to adapt several exercises for this book, to
James Slater for a number of illustrations, and Ann Hunt for preparing the artwork.

CONTENTS

CONTENTS

START HERE

You are going to do extra study and practice on your own. Before you start the units of this book, study this section and do the exercises. They are specially designed to help you study more efficiently. If you have any problems, ask your teacher to help you.

How Grammar Helps You

Grammar provides you with a map of English. Like all good maps it helps you to get somewhere more quickly.

- **Grammar shows you the patterns of English so that you can learn more quickly.**
- **Grammar helps you to think about English clearly.**
- **Grammar gives you the terminology to think about English in a useful way.**
- **Grammar gives you a quick way of checking what is correct.**
- **Grammar shows you that most English is regular.**

Patterns of English

There are two patterns in the following 10 sentences. Can you sort them into two groups — then say what the two patterns are.

a. We knew the Taylors a long time ago.
b. They used to live in the same street as us.
c. They didn't have a very big house.
d. They moved when their first son was born.
e. They don't live very far away now.
f. I met them last week in the supermarket.
g. Mr Taylor looked very well.
h. Mary didn't look well at all.
i. She said she'd been in hospital.
j. I don't think they are happy.

Now stop and decide on the two groups before you read on.

Did you choose one group as c, e, h and j (the negative sentences)? They have special patterns.

Thinking about English

The present continuous can be used to talk about:

a. the time of speaking
b. things true now, but not always
c. plans for the future

Decide which of these descriptions fits the following:

1. We're flying to Canada next week. ....
2. Sorry? Who's calling? ....
3. Who is Mary speaking to? ....
4. We're looking for a new secretary. ....
5. I'm studying. ....
6. You know I'm learning to drive, don't you? ....

As you will see, grammar is something to help you. There is no point in just knowing Grammar. Grammar is only there to help you organise your learning more effectively. You should have just noticed the patterns a 2,3,5; b 4,6; c 1. Organising and naming similar sentences helps!

START HERE

Studying Grammar Effectively

Learning Grammar has four stages:

examples — sentences which show us the natural use of a structure and which allow us to see patterns

patterns — regular features which are always the same

rules — descriptions of the patterns

practices — activities to help you to make the patterns yourself

Read the following comments. Write **I agree** beside the ones you agree with and **I don't agree** beside the others. After you have done that, read the comments below.

a. I find it helpful to see patterns in English. ....

b. I like to learn rules. ....

c. I think of rules when I speak. ....

d. Most rules have lots of exceptions. ....

e. Thinking about natural examples is helpful. ....

f. I only learn by practising. ....

a. Most people find patterns helpful. **b.** Some people do, some don't. Rules alone do not help. They are only one small part of good learning. **c.** Impossible! If you try to think of the rules when you speak, you will speak very slowly and sound unnatural. **d.** Good rules have no exceptions. A rule with exceptions is not a rule! **e.** Most people agree. **f.** Yes, you learn by practising, but you also learn by reflecting quietly.

- **Try to learn in different ways. Study rules, think about examples, look at patterns, do practices.**

- **Rules are abstract, examples are concrete. Most people find concrete things more helpful. Rules are only to guide you. Do not spend a long time worrying about them.**

- **You will learn best if you study in a variety of different ways.**

Mistakes

Mistakes are a natural part of learning. Unless we make mistakes, we will never learn. When you make a mistake, how do you react?

> **Oh dear, I got it wrong. I failed.**
> **Oh good, I almost got it right. I almost succeeded.**

The first is negative and unhelpful. The second shows a much more positive attitude.

Nobody wants to make mistakes, but everybody makes them. They are an important part of learning English. Experimenting helps learning — but you cannot expect every experiment to work first time. Don't be afraid of mistakes. Don't worry about them.

START HERE

Terminology

You will find it easier to study grammar if you understand the special words used to talk about it — the terminology. The words on this page give you all the most important terminology.

Match the words and terminology

1. better		a.	modal auxiliaries
2. quickly		b.	auxiliaries
3. does, am, has		c.	second forms of the verb
4. the		d.	third forms of the verb
5. singing		e.	comparative
6. house		f.	superlative
7. can, must		g.	adverb
8. up, during		h.	adjective
9. cheapest		i.	conjunctions
10. wasn't it		j.	definite article
11. began, took		k.	the **-ing** form
12. white		l.	tag
13. although, or		m.	passive
14. chosen, gone		n.	prepositions
15. were told		o.	noun

1	2	3	4	5	6	7	8	9	10	11	12	13	14	15

In this book the verb form ending in **. . . ing** is called **the . . . ing form.** The **first, second,** and **third** forms are used to talk about the three parts of the verb (**go, went, gone; take, took, taken**).

Name the tense

Match up the names of the structures with the sentences below:

1. the present simple		a.	Watch your head.
2. the present continuous		b.	I've never been there.
3. the past simple		c.	We're thinking of leaving.
4. the past continuous		d.	They're French, aren't they?
5. the present perfect		e.	What had they done about it?
6. the present perfect continuous		f.	I'm going to resign.
7. the 'going to' future		g.	We were each given a book.
8. the 'll future		h.	He lives on his own.
9. the passive		i.	I was thinking of ringing you.
10. the imperative		j.	He died alone.
11. a tag question		k.	I'll see you later.
12. the past perfect		l.	I've been thinking about it.

1	2	3	4	5	6	7	8	9	10	11	12

You will find it difficult to use any grammar book until you know the most important terminology. The answers to the problems on this page are given on page 11. If you found these difficult, ask for help with the terminology before you try to use the book alone.

START HERE

Finding What You Want

How do you start to look up a piece of information about grammar? You can only look something up if you have a key word, for example, **future, irregular, plural.**
There are four ways to find things in a grammar book:

- Decide on a key word.
- Look it up in the Index.
- Look for it in the Contents page.
- Flick through the book.

What is the **key word** you will look up to find answers to these questions? Which pages of this book answer the questions?

1. What is the difference between **He's going to write to you.** and **He'll write to you?**
2. What is the past tense of the irregular verb **catch?**
3. Can we use both **some** and **any** in questions?
4. What is the difference between **We must leave now** and **We have to leave now?**
5. What is the natural way to answer **You're going to London, aren't you?**
6. What's the difference between **I have studied** and **I have been studying?**
7. Is there a difference between **I lived in Leeds** and **I was living in Leeds?**
8. Does **It's** mean the same as **It is?**
9. What is the difference between **will** and **shall?**
10. Is the present perfect only used for the **recent** past?

(The words to look up are: **1.** going to, 'll, future **2.** irregular, past simple **3.** some, any **4.** must, have to **5.** tags, question tags **6.** present perfect, present perfect continuous, have **7.** past simple, past continuous **8.** it's, is has **9.** will, shall, future **10.** present perfect, have)

What's the word?

What grammatical word will you look up to find out more if you have a problem with the words in **bold** print in these examples:

1. **Do** you come here often? ....
2. He built it **himself.** ....
3. I'll meet you **at** the station. ....
4. We really **shouldn't** leave yet. ....
5. I **slept in** this morning. ....
6. **What's** the matter? ....
7. Who **was told?** ....
8. They**'ve** just **arrived.** ....

(The answers are: **1.** auxiliary, do **2.** reflexives **3.** prepositions — where **4.** modal auxiliaries, should **5.** phrasal verbs **6.** question word questions **7.** passive **8.** present perfect)

Both of those exercises are easier if you have learned the most important terminology.

START HERE

Correct English

It is very often possible to say that something is correct or incorrect.

> *The woman **comed** in with two **mans**.* is incorrect.
> The woman **came** in with two **men**.   is correct.

Mark the following sentences **C** if they are correct. If you think they are incorrect, mark them **INC** and write the correct form.

1. We really enjoyed ourselves. ....
2. The bus leave soon, so we'd better hurry. ....
3. We leaved this morning very early. ....
4. What are you thinking about? ....
5. I caught a very bad cold. ....
6. There's a lot of persons outside. ....
7. We met that girl who knows you. ....
8. You don't have to go, if you don't want to. ....
9. It's been done, isn't it? ....
10. That's the man which did it. ....

There were 5 correct and 5 incorrect. All were of the same kind. Each was a mistake of form:

2. leave — **leaves**	3. leaved — **left**
6. persons — **people**	9. isn't it — **hasn't it**
10. which — **who**	

In those examples there was no choice. Only one answer was correct. These are the facts of English. You simply have to learn them. For example, **left** is the past tense of **leave.** We can not "explain" this. It is a simple fact which you have to learn. Here are other areas of English grammar where you simply have to learn the facts:

spelling   irregular verbs   phrasal verbs   prepositions

Mark the correct form in these pairs.

1. **a.** in 1937
   b. on 1937

2. **a.** their books
   b. thier books

3. **a.** the three next years
   b. the next three years

4. **a.** happyly
   b. happily

5. **a.** worse
   b. badder

6. **a.** He plays guitar.
   b. He plays the guitar.

Often you use your grammar book to check the difference between correct and incorrect English. But there is another important part to English grammar too. It is discussed in the next section.

START HERE

Choosing Your Meaning

When we speak or write, we make lots of choices. For
example, we choose one word rather than another:

> We can say: She's very good-looking.
> She's very attractive.

These are very similar in meaning, but not exactly the same.
We choose one to show more exactly what we want to say.
We also choose grammar. We choose one structure rather than
another — not because one is right and the other is wrong,
but because one expresses our meaning better than the other.
For example:

She **lived** there.	I've **waited**.
She **was living** there.	I've **been waiting**.

**In this book you will find practices which ask you to decide which structure
is more likely,** or **more natural** — in other words, which structure best expresses
the meaning of a certain situation. Try the following examples:

1. There is a notice in the window of a local department store, giving information
about opening times. Which is more likely:

> **a. This store will be closed on 25th Dec, 1st Jan.**
> **b. We will close this store on 25th Dec, 1st Jan.**

2. You have just met a friend. Last night you tried six times to telephone your
friend, first about 7 o'clock and finally about 10 o'clock. Which is more likely:

> **a. I tried to ring you all evening. Where were you?**
> **b. I was trying to ring you all evening. Where were you?**

3. You have lost your wallet. A friend suggests you go to the police station
immediately. Which is more likely:

> **a. Somebody there will be able to help you.**
> **b. Anybody there will be able to help you.**

4. You are planning to have a party and have just met a friend. You want him to
come and bring his girlfriend. Which is more likely:

> **a. You must bring your girlfriend. I'd love to meet her.**
> **b. You have to bring your girlfriend. I'd love to meet her.**

5. Most children at school in Britain learn French for two years at least. You are
speaking to a 17-year-old English friend. Which is more likely:

> **a. You haven't studied French, have you?**
> **b. You've studied French, haven't you?**

The most likely choices were: 1a, 2b, 3a, 4a, 5b. When you do the practices in this
book, you sometimes have to choose between correct and incorrect, and sometimes
between **more likely** and **less likely** answers. These practices help you to show
your **exact** meaning.
You will find that it can also be unhelpful to translate examples into your own
language. You will learn best if you think about English and compare an English
example with another English example, like the examples above rather than trying to
translate, and comparing English with your own language.

START HERE

Important Grammar Points

Most of the units of this book are two pages. The left hand page gives the grammar explanation and the right hand page contains the practices.

Some of the units contain extra pages of practices. This is because these points are particularly important or difficult. You still need to follow the same approach: examples — patterns — rules — practices. But we think that for these important points you will need more practice. Do not work through five pages of practices all at the same time!

Grammar is not something to be afraid of. It is interesting, sometimes a challenge, but also extremely helpful. Relax, and enjoy using **Grammar and Practice!**

The Authors.

Grammar Summary

These words, called the modal auxiliaries, are used *only* as auxiliaries:

can could may might will would shall should must ought to

The modals add extra meaning.

Auxiliaries used to make structures

(be)	am	is	are	was	were	been	being
(have)	has	have	had	having			
(do)	do	does	did	done	doing		

(be) always behaves like an auxiliary. Its patterns are on page 102.
(have) is sometimes an auxiliary and sometimes a main verb. The main verb patterns are on page 100.

Important structures using auxiliaries:

1. Making negatives:

Add **n't** at the end of the first auxiliary; if there is no auxiliary use **(do)**.

He could drive.	He **couldn't** drive.
He drives.	He **doesn't** drive.

2. Making questions:

Change the order of the subject and the first auxiliary; if there is no auxiliary use **(do)**.

We should try to ring her.	**Should** we **try** to ring her?
He drives.	**Does** he **drive?**

Grammar Comment

1. Auxiliaries are one of the most important parts of English Grammar. They are particularly important in spoken English. You cannot use English naturally unless you can use auxiliaries.

2. The regularity of English structure depends on auxiliaries. If a sentence has a full verb and no auxiliary, we use the special auxiliary **(do)** to keep the structure regular.
   For example:

   You can come.   —   **Can you** come?
   You live here.   —   **Do you** live here?

   This makes English different from many other languages where the word order *Live you here?* might be possible. In English, main verbs need part of **(do)** to make negatives and questions in a regular way.

3. If there is more than one auxiliary in a sentence, it is the first one which is used in negatives and questions. For example:

   He **could** have come.   —   He **couldn't** have come.
                                  Could he have come?

4. Although auxiliaries are small words, they are very important for the meaning of a sentence. Look at the differences between:

   It**'s** raining.   It **could** have been John.
   It**'s been** raining.   It **must** have been John.

   This means it is very important to hear exactly what people say, even though the auxiliary often does not have a strong stress.

5. Notice that **will** + **n't** = **won't**.

UNIT 1

Practice 1.1

Underline the auxiliary in each of these sentences.

Example: She **can't** come till after 8 o'clock.

1. What will he think?
2. Are you going on Friday?
3. We must leave in ten minutes.
4. Would you like another cup?
5. Does your brother live with you?
6. What were you doing yesterday?
7. Have you heard the news?
8. I won't be there tomorrow.
9. Is John learning French as well?
10. Do you really think so?
11. How soon can you come round?
12. What will your parents say?
13. We didn't know what to think.
14. How much did it cost?
15. Should we arrive early?
16. We are thinking of going.
17. It may be Peter.
18. Won't you have some more?
19. What has Jill done to her hair!
20. He drives, doesn't he?

Practice 1.2

Underline all the auxiliaries in this text. Be careful, sometimes there is more than one in a sentence, and sometimes there isn't one at all.

I have always liked learning foreign languages, but I'm not very good at them. I always have a lot to say, but I make a lot of mistakes. People can usually understand me, but my teachers are always telling me that people could understand me more easily if I didn't make so many mistakes. I would like to speak better — it would be nice if I didn't make so many mistakes. People might understand better, but I don't want to speak slowly and carefully. I don't want to be boring. Have you noticed how boring it can be when people are worrying all the time about their mistakes? "You must be more careful" my teachers say. But when I am trying to say something interesting, I can't worry too much about getting it correct as well!

Do you agree with what the author says?

Practice 1.3

Fill in the auxiliaries in this text.

You are walking along a street one day. You look down and see a wallet which someone h............. dropped. You pick it up and open it. Inside you find £500. "Who c............. it belong to?", you think to yourself. The real question is what a............. you going to do with the money?

"S............. I take it to the police station?" It m............. belong to a poor old lady. She m............. be very upset. So, if I take it to the police I w............. make an old lady very happy. Something tells me that is what I s............. do. Then I think to myself, "Why d............. I keep it?"

Think of everything I c............. buy! First of all, I w............. buy a new tape deck. That m............. cost as much as £200, I w............. have at least £300 left. I h............. always wanted a cordless telephone — the kind you c............. use wherever you are in the house. But then what a..... I going to do with the rest of it? And then I start to think of the old lady. She d............. have enough to eat. Perhaps she w............. coming from the bank when she dropped the money. Perhaps she w............. going to pay her rent. I d............. know. S............. I take it to the police station after all? And if nobody claims it in 12 months, I c............. have it!

UNIT 1

Practice 1.4

Make these sentences negative.

1. He could drive.   *He couldn't drive.*
2. It's raining.
3. I can play tennis.
4. You should go.
5. We were thinking of going.
6. They are waiting outside.
7. John drives to work.
8. I believe you.
9. I like cheese.
10. They came to the party.

Practice 1.5

Make these into questions.

1. We can go early.   *Can we go early?*
2. She is getting married.
3. You were speaking to John.
4. He would like to go.
5. Bob gets the 7.55 train.
6. I know Chris.
7. Britain still uses miles not kilometres.
8. Banks usually close in the afternoon.

Practice 1.6

Make questions from these statements. In all of these you will need **do**, **does** or **did**.

1. We need some more milk.   *Do we need some more milk?*
2. He plays for Liverpool.
3. It looks like rain.
4. They said it was going to rain.
5. She took her umbrella.
6. School starts again next Monday.
7. It takes longer by train.
8. Money makes people happy.

14

UNIT 1

Practice 1.7

Make the following into questions. Sometimes there is an auxiliary; sometimes you need (do).

1. You've met Ann before. ....
2. You know my colleague, Ann Carson. ....
3. John would lend us one. ....
4. They sell them in the market. ....
5. We could borrow one from John. ....
6. It looks like rain. ....

Practice 1.8

Make the following negative. Sometimes there is an auxiliary, sometimes you need (do).

1. I think I understand exactly what you mean. ....
2. I want to have an early dinner this evening. ....
3. I would ask Paul if I were you. ....
4. We'll see him before the weekend. ....
5. The boss understands the problem. ....
6. I sleep very well nowadays. ....

Practice 1.9

Look at these two dialogues.

A Is Jane taking her driving test tomorrow?
B It isn't tomorrow. It can't be tomorrow — it's Saturday.
A Has she been worried about it?
B Not really. I told her she mustn't worry.
A Has she got a good chance of passing?
B No. She hasn't done enough driving. She won't pass, but at least she isn't worried about it.

A Does Jane take her driving test tomorrow?
B No, she doesn't take it until Monday. They don't work on Saturdays.
A Does she worry about it much?
B Not really. I told her worrying doesn't help.
A Does she have a good chance of passing?
B No. She doesn't do enough driving. They don't pass people who drive as badly as Jane, but at least she doesn't worry about it.

There are nine examples of negatives and questions in each dialogue. Underline them. Notice how they use the patterns which are given on page 12. Notice how (do) helps to make the patterns more regular.

Grammar Summary

1. Making a tag:

Use the first auxiliary; if there is no auxiliary use (**do**).

It's a lovely day.   It's a lovely day, **isn't** it.
He drives.   He drives, **doesn't** he?

2. Making a short answer:

Use the first auxiliary; if there is no auxiliary use (**do**).

Have you heard from Paul?	▷ Yes I **have.**	▷ No I **haven't.**
Will Jill be there?	▷ Yes she **will.**	▷ No she **won't.**
Do you know where it is?	▷ Yes I **do.**	▷ No I **don't.**

3. Making an interested response:

Use the first auxiliary in the answer; if there is no auxiliary use (**do**).

I've been there before.	▷ Oh, **have** you?
He was looking for you.	▷ Oh, **was** he?
She drives an old Fiat.	▷ Oh, **does** she?
We caught the early train.	▷ Oh, **did** you?

4. Emphasis, to show special emotion:

Stress the first auxiliary; if there is no auxiliary use (**do**).

I've been waiting 10 minutes.	I can come tomorrow.
→ I **have** been waiting 10 minutes.	→ I **can** come tomorrow.
I know the way.	I waited more than an hour.
→ I **do** know the way.	→ I **did** wait more than an hour.

Grammar Comment

1. The four auxiliary patterns in this unit are very important in conversation. It is impossible to have a natural conversation without them. You will only start to use them naturally if you:
   — understand why they are important
   — notice when other people use them
   — practise them a lot

2. They are important because they help you to be more friendly:
   — Tags make you sound friendly and easy to talk to.
   — Short answers are friendlier than using 'Yes' or 'No' alone.
   — Interested responses help the other person to say more.
   — Stressed auxiliaries help you to show how you feel.
   So the auxiliaries are not only important grammatically, they are also essential to make us sound friendly and helpful in conversation.

3. The patterns in this unit remind you of a general rule of spoken English:
   If a pattern uses an auxiliary, and the sentence does not have an auxiliary, use part of (**do**) — **do, does, did** — and follow the same pattern.

UNIT 2

Practice 2.1

Add tags to these.

1. They were there, *weren't they?*
2. It wasn't very nice ....
3. He can swim ....
4. They live near you ....
5. He knows the way ....
6. You speak some German ....
7. The film starts at 8 o'clock ....
8. Paul comes to school by bus ....

Practice 2.2

Make short answers to follow the pattern.

1. Have you heard from Dad?
   — Yes, ...*I have*........................
2. Did you go to the show?
   — No, ...
3. Does she know him well?
   — Yes, ...
4. Do you come here often?
   — No, ...
5. Are they from here?
   — Yes, ...
6. Will they let me in without a ticket?
   — No, ...

Practice 2.3

Make an 'interested response' to follow the pattern.

1. I've been to the zoo today.
   — Oh, ..*have you*........................
2. It's going to snow.
   — Oh, ...
3. He owns two Rolls Royces.
   — Oh, ...
4. I got back early.
   — Oh, ...
5. Mary was there on her own.
   — Oh, ...
6. There's going to be a demonstration.
   — Oh, ...

Practice 2.4

Emphasise the auxiliary to show special emotion. Write the sentence with the auxiliary in CAPITALS.

1. We've been waiting half an hour!
   We HAVE been waiting half an hour.
2. I like Mary a lot!
   ....
3. You promised!
   ....
4. I won't come!
   ....
5. It's been raining a lot!
   ....
6. I love the sun!
   ....
7. We rang three times!
   ....
8. We warned you!
   ....

Notice how important all these patterns are in everyday spoken English .

Grammar Summary

Short forms	Full forms
Normal speech *(I'm sorry)*	Stress in speech *(I **am** sorry)*
Informal writing (letters to friends)	At the end of a sentence. *(Yes, I am.)*
	In questions. *(Are you going?)*
	Most writing.

The verb (be)

I'm	you're	he's	I am	you are	he is
I'm not	you're not/	he isn't	I am not	you are not	he is not
	you aren't				

The verb (have)

we've	she's	they'd	we have	she has	they had
we haven't	he hadn't	she hasn't	we have not	he had not	she has not

The verb (do)

she doesn't	she does not
they don't	they do not
we didn't	we did not

Will

I'll	I will
I won't	I will not

Would

they'd	they would
they wouldn't	they would not

The short forms:

's	can be **is** or **has**	It's raining. He's remembered.	She's waiting. Jack's taken it.
'd	can be **had** or **would**	He'd already gone. I'd like to go.	Who'd you told? They'd never believe you.

In normal speech the short, unstressed, forms are used.

Grammar Comment

1. In most written English the full form is used. In a letter to a friend you can use short forms.

2. In spoken English short forms are normal. In statements the full form gives special emphasis. There is an important difference in meaning:

   I**'m** sorry.   —   for something small and unimportant
   I **am** sorry.   —   for something serious

3. It is important in speech to listen carefully for short forms. You must hear the difference between **It's come** and **It's coming.** Both contain **'s**, but the first means **has** and in the second, **is.**
   In most situations, you must hear, understand and use short forms. Remember that short forms are the most common forms in spoken English.

UNIT 3

Practice 3.1

The sentences on the left have short verb forms. The ones on the right have full forms. Fill in the missing ones.

1. I'm coming.   ..I am coming..........................

2. ..You're right..................   You are right.

3. We aren't very pleased.   ....

4. ....   She is married.

5. It isn't very expensive.   ....

6. ....   We have been here before.

7. They haven't done it yet.   ....

8. ....   He has changed his job.

9. She hasn't changed a bit.   ....

10. ....   We had met them before.

11. It doesn't matter.   ....

12. ....   I do not care.

13. She didn't write back.   ....

14. ....   They will not be there..

15. I'll speak to her.   ....

16. ....   I would like to leave.

When you have finished, circle all the short forms and underline the full forms.

Practice 3.2

Remember that 's can be the short form of **is** or **has**.

      It's hot   = **is**
      It's arrived = **has**

Is it **is** or **has** in the following?

1. He's leaving.   ....   6. It's been raining.   ....

2. He's left.   ....   7. Where's the key?   ....

3. She's in.   ....   8. What's he been doing? ....

4. She's been in.   ....   9. Who's come?   ....

5. It's raining.   ....   10. Who's coming?   ....

UNIT 3

Practice 3.3

In the following dialogues B always disagrees. Complete the second line, using the full form of the auxiliary.

1. A John's coming to the party.

   B I don't think he .is..................

2. A I'm sure I know that guy over there.

   B I don't think you ....

3. A Mary's already left.

   B I don't think she ....

4. A There's going to be a Firework Display.

   B ....

5. A He knew where he was going.

   B ....

6. A I'd love to go to South Africa.

   B ....

7. A I think it'll rain.

   B ....

8. A You and I agree, don't we?

   B ....

9. A We've seen that film before, haven't we?

   B ....

10. A Would you like another?

    B ....

11. A Wasn't it built about 1945?

    B ....

12. A The whole idea came from the States.

    B ....

Practice 3.4

Look at the clues opposite and fill in the full forms of the auxiliaries in the shape.

UNIT 3

Here are the clues for the shape opposite.

Across
I'm going to invite you.
What're you going to do about it?
What's the matter?
You are coming, aren't you?
Who'd have believed it?

Down
What've you done?
Who's been sitting in my chair?
Isn't that John over there?
I'd better leave now.
Won't it be too expensive?

Practice 3.5

Which do you say?

1. When you touch someone accidentally:
    a. I'm sorry.
    b. I **am** sorry.

2. When your friend tells you that his mother is in hospital:
    a. I'm sorry.
    b. I **am** sorry.

3. When you like strawberries very very much:
    a. I like strawberries.
    b. I **do** like strawberries.

4. When your friend tells you that the train leaves at 5 past and you thought it was 5 to.
    a. You're right.
    b. You **are** right.

5. When you are very surprised that your friend is right — because he is usually wrong!
    a. You're right.
    b. You **are** right.

6. When a friend asks you round on Saturday:
    a. I'm going away this weekend.
    b. I **am** going away this weekend.

7. Your friend thinks you are joking. He doesn't believe you:
    a. I'm going away this weekend.
    b. I **am** going away this weekend.

8. A student asks you about pop singers:
    a. I like David Bowie.
    b. I **do** like David Bowie.

9. You are a member of the David Bowie Fan Club. You think he is terrific.
    a. I like David Bowie.
    b. I **do** like David Bowie.

10. You agreed to meet a friend at 7. You arrive 2 minutes late. Your friend says:
    a. I've been waiting for 2 minutes.
    b. I **have** been waiting for 2 minutes.

11. You agreed to meet a friend at 7. You are half an hour late. Your friend says:
    a. I've been waiting half an hour.
    b. I **have** been waiting half an hour.

12. You are on a train. You are sure the lady who just passed is your old teacher. Your friend doesn't agree. You whisper:
    a. It's Miss Spencer. I saw it on her luggage.
    b. It **is** Miss Spencer. I saw it on her luggage.

21

Grammar Summary

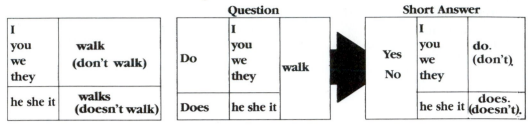

I you we they	walk (don't walk)
he she it	walks (doesn't walk)

Question

Do	I you we they	walk
Does	he she it	

Short Answer

	I you we they	do. (don't)
Yes No		
	he she it	does. (doesn't).

I usually **get up** about seven.

Does Tony **drive** to work?
▷ No, he **cycles.**

The football season usually **starts** in August.

Regular actions or events

I **like** tea but I **don't like** milk in it!

What **does** this **mean** please?

The River **Danube flows** through Vienna.

Facts

Next Monday **is** a national holiday.

Classes **begin** next week.

Facts known about the future

I **don't want** to go out this evening.

I'm sorry I **don't understand.**

I **feel** sick.

Thoughts and feelings at the time of speaking

Grammar Comment

The present simple is one of the commonest tenses in English. Although it is called the present simple, it is used for many different times:

all time	—	Water **boils** at 100°C.
present time	—	I **think** so.
future time	—	We **leave** tomorrow.
regular time	—	I **play** on Tuesdays.

When you use the present simple, the question 'when?' seems unnecessary or ridiculous:

      I **come** from Liverpool. (The question when is silly!)

      I **declare** the conference open. (When? Now, of course!)

      The Tiber **flows** through Rome. (When? Always! What a silly question!)

All other forms of the verb (the present continuous, the present perfect, etc) add **extra** meaning to the basic meaning of the verb. Whenever none of these extra meanings is needed, the present simple is used. This shows you that this is a very common and a very important tense.

It is called 'simple' because it does not divide the action in any way. It is used to give what the speaker thinks are the simple facts.

UNIT 4

Practice 4.1

Complete the questions with these words:

Auxiliaries: **does, is , are, do**
Full verbs: **flows, sleep, live, eats, take, boil, come, mean, lie**

1. What temperature .... water .... at?
2. Which river .... through Paris?
3. What animal .... in China and .... bamboo?
4. Where .... the Pope ....?
5. .... light travel faster than sound?
6. Where .... kangaroos .... from?
7. Which islands .... in the middle of the Atlantic?
8. How long .... it .... to fly from London to New York in Concorde?
9. What .... 'likely' .... ?
10. .... horses .... standing up?

Now match up the questions with these answers:

a. Yes, it does.   **b.** Australia.   **c.** Possible   **d.** The Seine.   **e.** 100°C   **f.** The Giant Panda.
g. Yes, they do. **h.** The Canaries.   **i.** The Vatican   **j.** About three hours.

Practice 4.2

Fill in the spaces in this conversation with these verbs:

get up, jog, do, play, cycle, have, be, stay, watch, go, like, swim, feel, believe

John What do you usually do on Saturdays?

Steve Well, I usually .... early, about 6.30; then I .... around the park before breakfast.

John What! I don't .... you. What do you .... next?

Steve Well, the football season starts in August, so I usually .... football with my team, or I .... with my brother in the country. We both .... new bikes, so we .... at least 30 kms. What .... you ....?

John Well, I certainly .... football. You see, I .... lazy. I .... at home and .... TV.

Steve And what about Sundays? .... you .... out then?

John No, I .... quite late. Sometimes I .... to the beach when the weather is good, but I .... swimming.

Steve I .... understand you. My family .... in the sea every weekend in the summer, and we all .... at least 10 kms in the winter. We are all very fit.

John Oh, not me. I .... understand you either. I .... much happier with **my** weekends.

23

UNIT 4

Practice 4.3

Use some of the words in the box, but **no other words.** Make 10 sentences. There are a lot more. How many can you make in total?

1. ....
2. ....
3. ....
4. ....
5. ....
6. ....
7. ....
8. ....
9. ....
10. ....

My total is .... sentences.

```
like          you
         it
that     know
              do
   one
              to
   n't
does          they
```

Practice 4.4

Here are four descriptions of the present simple; which is the best description of these sentences? Write **A, B, C, or D,** beside each.

A	For regular actions or events	**C**	For facts known about the future
B	For facts	**D**	For thoughts and feelings at the time of speaking

1. I always take sugar in my coffee. ....

2. Oh, I love these cakes. ....

3. Conakry is the capital of Guinea. ....

4. Where is Guinea? ....

5. The shops open at 9 am. ....

6. The bus takes 10 minutes. ....

7. The bus arrives at 10.15 tomorrow morning. ....

8. They never get home late. ....

9. He wants to earn more money. ....

10. The school holidays finish next week. ....

11. I feel a bit tired. ....

12. How do you feel? ....

24

UNIT 4

Practice 4.5

Here are 10 'riddles' — strange problems. Match the questions and answers; then try them out on your family and friends.

1. What flies, but is never hungry?   **a.** a key
2. What flies and sometimes buzzes?   **b.** a cat
3. What swims in water and sometimes walks on dry land?   **c.** a crocodile
4. What plays, but cannot run?   **d.** a plane
5. What likes fish, but never goes fishing?   **e.** a kangaroo
6. What opens the door, but never says, 'Hello'.   **f.** a bee
7. What gives you a shock, but cannot be seen?   **g.** a record
8. What tells you where you are, but cannot speak?   **h.** electricity
9. What flies, but has no wings?   **i.** a map
10. What takes its babies everywhere, but never in a pram?   **j.** time

Now make a list of all the verbs in the present simple in the riddles:

....

....

....

Practice 4.6

What do they do?

Read the information about John, Mick, and Diana. One is a musician; one is a teacher; and the other is a gardener. Who does what?

John works hard from 9 am to 4 pm most of the year.
Mick often finishes work at 2 am.
Diana usually starts work at 6 am.
John and Diana work very near their home but Mick doesn't.
John and Mick always work inside, but Diana doesn't.
Mick earns a lot of money, but John and Diana don't.
Diana often works in the cold and wet.
John sees children every day, but the others don't.
Diana likes music. Mick plays his guitar every day.

John is a ....

Mick is a ....

Diana is a....................................

UNIT 4

Practice 4.7

The present simple is very often used in proverbs. Here are 4 of the commonest English proverbs. Match up the two halves, then write them in full.

1. Many hands		**a.**	has a silver lining
2. Too many cooks		**b.**	saves nine
3. A stitch in time		**c.**	spoil the broth
4. Every cloud		**d.**	make light work

1. ....

2. ....

3. ....

4. ....

Write the proverb number beside the correct explanation:

(i) Things which seem to be bad often have a good side. ....

(ii) It is best to solve problems as soon as possible — before they become much bigger problems. ....

(iii) Jobs are finished quicker if more people help. ....

(iv) If too many people help, a job becomes impossible. ....

Practice 4.8

Make ten 2-word sentences by matching up the following:

1. Birds		**a.**	flows
2. Fish		**b.**	destroys
3. People		**c.**	fly
4. Flowers		**d.**	kills
5. Dogs		**e.**	fall
6. Leaves		**f.**	swim
7. Water		**g.**	burns
8. Wood		**h.**	forget
9. Fire		**i.**	bark
10. Speed		**j.**	smell

1	2	3	4	5	6	7	8	9	10

UNIT 4

Practice 4.9

Fill in this table with information which is true for you.

	I	My parents	My best friend	Most people I know
like (a thing)				
like (a person)				
hate				
live				
never				
sometimes				

If you have filled in each box, you can now write 24 true sentences:

1. ....
2. ....
3. ....
4. ....
5. ....
6. ....
7. ....
8. ....
9. ....
10. ....
11. ....
12. ....
13. ....
14. ....
15. ....
16. ....
17. ....
18. ....
19. ....
20. ....
21. ....
22. ....
23. ....
24. ....

Grammar Summary

				Question				Short Answer	
I	'm (not) am(not)		Am	I				I	am. ('m not).
he she it	is(n't) 's (not)	coming	Is	he she it	coming	Yes No		he she it	is(n't).
we you they	're (not) are(n't)		Are	we you they				we you they	are(n't).

're not is used more than **aren't.**

Look, Mary**'s getting** into that car.	At the time of speaking
I**'m not looking forward to** the interview.	
Excuse me, **is** anyone **sitting** here, please?	
Who**'s** Katy **talking** to?	
They**'re building** a block of flats over there.	True at the moment, but not always
We**'re looking for** a new house.	
Is your baby **sleeping** all night yet?	
▷ No she **isn't**, not yet.	
Karim**'s working** on night shift next week.	Present plans for the future
When **are** they **flying** to India?	
Are you **coming** to the party on Saturday?	
▷ No, I**'m not** as a matter of fact.	

Grammar Comment

There are two parts to the meaning of the present continuous:

    a. It describes a **limited period** — a period with a beginning and an end.

    b. The period described is **around now.** It may be a short period at the moment of speaking or a longer period in which the moment of speaking is a small part.

You can see both parts of the explanation are true for the examples in the Grammar Summary:

    Look, Mary**'s getting** into that car.
    (A short period at the time of speaking)

    We**'re looking** for a new house.
    (Not at this very moment, but true for a limited period until we find one)

    Karim**'s working** on night shift next week.
    (The arrangement covers the limited period from when the arrangement was made in the past until a fixed point in the future.)

Do not use the present continuous for situations that are long-term or permanent; then you usually need the present simple.

UNIT 5

Practice 5.1

Write short answers to these questions.

1.	Are you getting tired?	Yes, ..I am...........
2.	Are you feeling all right?	No, ...
3.	Am I doing it correctly?	Yes, ...
4.	Am I coming too?	No, ...
5.	Is your mother getting better?	Yes, ...
6.	Is your father helping?	No, ...
7.	Is it finishing soon?	Yes, ...
8.	Are we paying for ourselves?	Yes, ...
9.	Are you and Bill paying for us?	No, ...
10.	Are they flying to India?	Yes, ...

Practice 5.2

Complete these dialogues with auxiliaries and, where necessary, **-ing.**

1. **A** .... thinking of leaving.

   B Are you? It's rather early.

2. **A** .... you look .... for the way out?

   B Yes, I am actually. Do you know where it is?

3. **A** Mary' .... try .... to learn to play the piano.

   B Oh, no!

4. **A** ....your father still work ....?

   B Yes. He works late every Friday.

5. **A** You're wet! Don't tell me .... rain .... again!

   B I'm afraid it is!

6. **A** We'........... go........... to New York next week!

   B Lucky you!

7. **A** .... you and your sister gett........... the same train?

   B I think we are.

8. **A** Our teachers .... plann........... a party.

   B .... you jok...........!

A Present Continuous Joke

Excuse me, why are you jumping up and down?
— I've taken my medicine, but I forgot to shake the bottle!

UNIT 5

Practice 5.3

Match up the two parts of each sentence.

1. Are you going to the party
2. I'm taking the train
3. Oh no, look!
4. Is the new baby sleeping
5. Hello,

a. am I speaking to John Williams?
b. all night yet?
c. on Saturday?
d. this week because the buses are on strike.
e. Peter's getting on the wrong bus.

1	2	3	4	5

Practice 5.4

Here are 3 descriptions of the present continuous:

A: At the moment of speaking
B: For things which are true at the moment, but not always
C: Present plans for the future

Mark the following sentences A, B, or C.

1. When is she coming to London? ☐
2. Alex is phoning home. ☐
3. We are saving our money for a new car. ☐
4. She is walking to work this week. ☐
5. Are you leaving early tomorrow morning? ☐
6. Call the police! Some men with guns are going into the bank! ☐
7. Where is John going now? ☐
8. Zoe is studying for her exams. ☐
9. The Minister is visiting the school next week. ☐
10. On Tuesday the office is closing early. ☐

Practice 5.5

How many sentences can you make from the two boxes below? Each sentence should make sense!

1.	I'm dreaming of
2.	I'm thinking about
3.	I'm worrying about
4.	I'm expecting

a.	a surprise.
b.	a white Christmas.
c.	my teacher.
d.	buying some new clothes.
e.	going away for a few days.
f.	not having enough money.
g.	eating too much.
h.	some good news.

I made .... different sentences.

UNIT 5

Practice 5.6

Fill in this dialogue with verbs in the present continuous.

A .Are. you. playing........ tennis this afternoon? (play)

B I'm afraid not. I .... this afternoon. (work)

A Again! And .... at the weekend? (work)

B I'm afraid so. I .... much tennis this year. (not play)

A I .... to get that idea! (begin)

B I want to, but I'm too busy. I .... for my exams. (study)

A You .... yourself with all this work! (kill)

B But I .... my exams in three weeks and they're important. (take)

A Why are they so important?

B Well, I .... to get into university in the autumn. But before that I .... playing tennis when my exams are finished. (try, look forward to)

Can you find one example of each use of the present continuous (see Practice 5.4)? Write them here:

A ....

B ....

C ....

Practice 5.7

Fill in the verbs in the spaces. Use the present continuous.

1. Sh..sh..sh. Please be quiet. I .... (think).

2. I wish you'd turn that music down. I .... to make a phone call. (try)

3. I was sure it was you in that car! So — you haven't told anyone that you .... to drive. (learn)

4. I just don't understand the people next door. Whenever I call in, they .... the television. (watch)

5. Jill's visa has arrived at last! She .... for the States tomorrow. (leave)

6. Would someone answer the door. In case you are all deaf, the bell ....! (ring)

7. It's far too warm in here! I .... to sleep! (go)

8. Why .... Jim .... a coat? .... he .... rain? (wear, expect)

9. **A** What do you think you ....! That's my car you .... to get in to! (do, try)

   B Oh, I'm so sorry. It's the same colour as mine.

10. Isn't that Marie over there with another new boyfriend? .... you .... what I ....? (think, think)

UNIT 5

Practice 5.8

Can you complete these sentences with ideas that are true for you.

AT THE MOMENT

I'm thinking of ....

I'm dreaming about ....

I'm worrying about ....

I'm looking forward to ....

Next weekend I'm ....

NEXT YEAR

I'm thinking of ....

I'm planning to ....

Practice 5.9

Sheila is speaking to a friend, Joyce. Joyce is surprised because she saw Sheila driving. Fill in the verbs using the present continuous.

Sheila You know I .... (learn) to drive, don't you.

Joyce You know, I thought I saw you in a car the other day. I said to myself, "Sheila .... (learn) to drive, and she hasn't told anyone!"

Sheila Yes, I .... (keep) it a secret. You see, this is between you and me, but I .... (think) of changing my job.

Joyce Oh, I see. What .... (think) of doing?

Sheila I .... (apply) for a job at the airport.

Joyce I hope you get it. So, who .... (teach) you?

Sheila I .... (have) lessons with the ABC school, but my brother .... (take) me out, too. In fact, Richard .... (come) to pick me up after work.

Joyce How ....Richard .... (get on)?

Sheila He's much better now. After that operation, he was very weak, but he .... (get) stronger every day now. I think he .... (start) work again in a fortnight.

Joyce And that will be the end of your lessons?

Sheila Yes, that's why I .... (have) a lesson every day at the moment. As soon as he starts work, he won't be able to take me out.

32

UNIT 5

Practice 5.10

Complete each of these examples using the present continuous.

1. Mick (buy) a flat near his new job.

   ....

2. He (sell) his old car because he (plan) to walk to work.

   ....

3. (Get) you tired?

   ....

4. Why (not watch) the TV? The football's on!

   ....

5. (Go) Zoe on holiday to Italy next year?

   ....

6. No, I think she (stay) at home.

   ....

There are 3 uses for the present continuous:

a. for something happening at the time of speaking.
b. for something true at the moment but not always.
c. for talking about present plans for the future.

Look at the examples above, are they use **a**, **b**, or **c**?
Fill in this table with the example numbers.

Use a	
b	
c	

Practice 5.11

Write present continuous sentences to complete this dialogue, then complete the box to say whether the examples are use **a**, **b**, or **c**.

Mick   Hallo, can I speak to John please?

Alex   I'm sorry John is not here, he (**1.** work) in Portugal now. Who (**2.** speak)?

Mick   It's Mick. Is Sue there?

Alex   Not now. She (**3.** play) tennis until 4 o'clock. But what (**4.** you do) these days?

Mick   Well I (**5.** look) for a job. I'm not going back to Africa but I (**6.** hope) to get a job near here for a year at least.

Alex   Sue and I (**7.** go) out later. Would you like to join us?

Mick   Sorry I can't, my parents (**8.** come) for dinner. But let's meet next week.

Alex   That's fine. I'll give you a call on Tuesday. See you next week.

Use a	
b	
c	

Grammar Comment

The difference between the present simple and the present continuous is not as easy as many people think. It depends on the point of view of the speaker or writer. Many ideas in the present simple can also be expressed in the continuous form.

1a. I **live** in Berlin.
  b. I'm **living** in Berlin.

2a. What **do** you **think?**
  b. What **are** you **thinking?**

3a. We **leave** tomorrow.
  b. We're **leaving** tomorrow.

4a. I **don't eat** much.
  b. I'm **not eating** much.

From these examples you can see that sometimes the difference in meaning is very small and sometimes very large.
We could re-write these sentences in the following way:

1a. I see Berlin as my permanent home.
  b. I am in Berlin for a limited time, for example as a student.

2a. Summarise your opinion.
  b. What is in your mind at the moment?

3a. I see our departure as a fact; perhaps it is a holiday with a fixed departure time.
  b. We have a plan; probably arranged by us, not decided by, for example, the airline or the tour company.

4a. Usually.
  b. At present I am not very well so I don't want much to eat.

You can see the difference between the present simple and the present continuous very clearly in the following situations:

> I usually **drive** to work, but this week I'm **taking** the bus.

> We always **play** squash on Wednesdays after work, but the sports centre is closed on Wednesdays this month, so we're **playing** on Thursdays instead.

The present simple looks objectively at facts, actions, or events. It takes an **overview** of a situation. For example:

> Sheila always **catches** the 8.30 train.
> Mary never **takes** the bus.
> Bill sometimes **comes** with me.

The reason I can make these statements about the three people is because I have an overview of their habits. The present simple is the natural verb form to make general statements like these.
By using the present continuous, the speaker draws special attention to the **limited period** of a particular fact, action, or event.

> Sheila **is catching** the 8.45 this morning.

The present continuous adds extra meaning — the idea of an event which is **limited in time.**

UNIT 6

Practice 6.1

Present simple or present continuous?

In the following pairs, only one sentence is possible. Mark the impossible sentences with X. Check your answers in the key; then draw a line through the impossible ones.

1. **a.** I like tea.
    b. I'm liking tea.

2. **a.** What does this word mean?
    b. What is this word meaning?

3. **a.** I don't want to go to a film.
    b. I'm not wanting to go to a film.

4. **a.** We look for a new house.
    b. We're looking for a new house.

5. **a.** I come from Leeds and my sister was born there too.
    b. I'm coming from Leeds and my sister was born there too.

6. **a.** I believe you're telling the truth.
    b. I'm believing you're telling the truth.

7. **a.** The children love hamburgers and coke.
    b. The kids are loving hamburgers and coke.

8. **a.** Who is that man over there that Katy talks to?
    b. Who is that man over there that Katy's talking to?

Practice 6.2

Write the correct questions.

1. Ask me where I live.

    ....

2. You meet me on holiday in Majorca. Ask me about my hotel.

    Where ....

3. Ask me my job.

    ....

4. I am busy with some unusual activity. Ask me about it.

    ....

A present tense joke

1st sheep *Baa baa baa*
2nd sheep *Moo moo moo*
1st sheep *Why don't you say baa?*
2nd sheep *I'm learning a foreign language.*

UNIT 6

Practice 6.3

Here are 7 descriptions of 7 sentences. Can you match them up?

1. A plan for the future.

2. A fact that is always true.

3. A regular action.

4. Something happening at the moment of speaking.

5. A fact about the future.

6. Something true, but not always.

7. A feeling at the moment of speaking.

a. John usually forgets his watch.

b. They're knocking down the old theatre.

c. We're going to China next summer.

d. The sun rises in the East.

e. School starts on the 7th September.

f. Watch out, the dog's running across the road!

g. I feel really dizzy.

1	2	3	4	5	6	7

Practice 6.4

Write complete sentences from the following ideas:

1. We/usually/go/to France/every summer/but/this summer/we/go/to Tunisia.

   ....

   ....

2. I/usually/get/the bus/but/today/I/walk to work.

   ....

   ....

3. I/play tennis/on Tuesdays/but/this month/I/play/on Wednesdays instead.

   ....

   ....

4. Karim/usually/work/on the night shift/but/this winter/she/work/on the morning shift.

   ....

   ....

36

UNIT 6

Practice 6.5

Complete these sentences. You will need the present simple for one and the present continuous for the other.

1. go

I .... crazy.

I .... to Spain every summer.

2. see

I .... John off at the airport this evening.

I .... what you mean.

3. think

I .... I'll go home now.

I .... of having an early lunch. What about you?

4. start

I .... crosswords but never finish them.

I .... to forget people's names. It's old age, I suppose.

5. have

I usually .... supper about 10.

I .... a party this Saturday. Are you free?

6. do

I always .... my homework as soon as I get home.

Today I .... my homework before I go home.

7. speak

I .... German well, but no French at all.

I .... Could you wait till I've finished, please!

8. get

I think I .... a cold.

I .... colds every winter.

9. catch

I .... the 8.55 bus every day.

I .... the sleeper to Glasgow this evening.

10. enjoy

This is a great disco. I .... myself, aren't you?

I only .... discos when the music is extra-loud!

Can you see why you need to choose the continuous in some cases, and the simple in others? It always helps to look at the *other* words in the sentence, and, above all, to think about what the sentences *mean*.

Grammar Summary

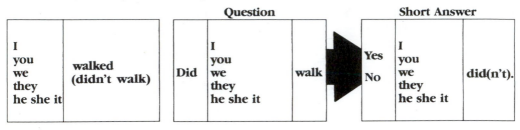

Stefan **wanted** to catch the early train but he **missed** it.

I **told** you it **started** at 7 o'clock. I **knew** it did.

Where **did** you **go** last night?
▷ We **went** to the pub for a drink.

Did you **lock** the door?
▷ Yes, I **did,** don't worry.

Single actions, thoughts or feelings finished before the time of speaking

They **told** me I **needed** to wear glasses.

Why **didn't** you **tell** him?
▷ He **said** he **knew** about it already.

Reporting what someone said (after verbs like *said, told, asked*)

Grammar Comment

We use the simple past to talk about events which we see as completed in the past:
> The French **invaded** Britain in 1066.
> I **went** to France yesterday. (which means I am home again.)
> I **lived** in Paris for 5 years.
> We **knew** you were at home.
> He **said** he knew you.

Each sentence refers to something in the past which the speaker sees as complete. It does not matter how long ago or how recently it took place; or whether it was a state or an action.

The tense is accurately described as the 'simple past'. It is 'past' because it is completed or finished. It is 'simple' because the speaker does not want to emphasise that it was a period of time or a series of repeated actions.

You can say:
> We **lived** in Paris for 5 years. (a period)
> We **lived** in Paris from 1972 till last year. (a period)
> We **left** Paris on May 10th. (a point)

The past simple describes the action as a whole. Other tense forms describe different aspects of an action, for example:
> The past continuous looks at the action as a period.
> — I **was getting** worried about you. (See Unit 9)
> The present perfect looks back at the action from now.
> — I've **known** him for years. (See Unit 14)

The past simple often occurs with time expressions like these:
> **yesterday, last week, in 1985, from 1965 to 1983,**
> **a few days ago, in those days, in the sixteenth century**

UNIT 7

Practice 7.1

Put the verb (in brackets) into the past simple.

1. I'm sorry I'm late, I .... the bus. (miss)

2. I .... to Peter on the phone yesterday. (talk)

3. Steve .... to the office last Friday. (cycle)

4. John .... some money and .... it to the police. (find, take)

5. Zoe .... to do her homework yesterday. (forget)

6. Sarah .... her some flowers for her birthday. (buy)

7. The doctor .... me to take the medicine every day. (tell)

8. He .... me to work late at the office every day last week. (ask)

9. I .... anyone come into the bank. (not see)

10. Where .... you .... last weekend? (go)

11. What .... you .... to the party? (take)

12. .... you .... Jack at the party? (see)

13. .... you .... all night? (dance)

14. And what about you? .... you .... this exercise? (enjoy)

Practice 7.2

Jack has just been on holiday. He is telling Carol about it and she wants to know more. Make more questions like Carol's first question.

Jack	We went to Rome. We saw the Coliseum.
Carol	*Where else did you go?* ....
Jack	We went to Florence.
Carol	Really? Where ....
Jack	We bought some lovely leather things.
Carol	Really? What ....
Jack	We visited the old Roman Forum.
Carol	Really? Where ....
Jack	We met a lot of American tourists.
Carol	Really? Who ....
Jack	We ate dozens of pizzas.
Carol	Really? What ....
Jack	We enjoyed every minute of it?
Carol	Really? What (most) ....

UNIT 7

Practice 7.3

Here are some short news items from the paper. Fill in the verbs in the past simple. Choose from these verbs.

go   flood   spend   hope   collide   last   die(2)

win   beat   fall   cause   come   explode   find

become   live   celebrate

1. One man .... and another 6 were badly injured when a bomb .... in a Belfast pub last night.

2. Two trains .... in central France yesterday afternoon, killing 5 people and injuring many more. Both drivers .... in the accident.

3. A man is helping police with their enquiries after two children playing in a field .... the body of a woman. The woman, identified as Mrs Joan Smith .... in the area.

4. The pound .... yesterday to its lowest level for 12 months. The Prime Minister, in a speech in Manchester, said she .... interest rates would fall still further.

5. Mrs Ellen Norrish .... the oldest woman in Britain yesterday when she .... her 112th birthday. She .... the day as usual at her home surrounded by her 6 daughters, 18 grandchildren, and 35 great grandchildren.

6. A freak storm .... havoc in Suffolk yesterday morning when torrential rain .... many villages in the Ipswich area.

7. Workers on London Underground .... on strike for two hours early yesterday evening. Buses were also affected and traffic in central London .... to a complete standstill.

8. Jimmy Connors .... the French Open yesterday in Paris. He .... Ivan Lendl in a match that .... 2 hours 40 minutes.

Practice 7.4

There are 8 verbs in the past simple in each box (2nd form). Can you circle them? The words can be across, up, down or diagonally.

```
B R O K E M
E Y A T E S
C O S T Z T
A B H A M O
M T O R E O
E A T O L D
```

```
E D I H A G
K E P T R O
M D E O P R
D E S A T G
I E I E A O
D N E P S T
```

40

UNIT 7

Practice 7.5

Match the questions and responses so that each pair makes a joke.

1. Why did the man cross the road?
2. Why did the elephant cross the road?
3. Did I hear that you buried your cat last week?
4. What did one eye say to the other eye?
5. What did the baby porcupine say to the cactus?
6. What did one wall say to the other wall?

a. Is that you, Dad?
b. To pick up the squashed chicken.
c. There's something between us that smells.
d. I'll meet you at the corner.
e. To get to the other side.
f. We had to. She died.

1	2	3	4	5	6

Did you notice that the questions were all past simple questions?

Practice 7.6

Here are the beginnings of 10 past tenses. Each dash (—) is one letter. What are the complete words?

1. r e g r e — — — —
2. h e s i — — — — —
3. b o r r — — — —
4. b e l i — — — —

5. f i n — — — — —
6. h a p p — — — —
7. a n s w — — — —
8. o p — — — —

Here are the endings of 10 past tenses. Each dash (—) is one letter. What are the complete words.

9. — — — — — b e r e d
10. — — l k e d
11. — — k e d
12. — — — — e d

13. — — — k e d
14. — — — — — t e d
15. — — — n e d
16. — — — — g e d

Practice 7.7

What were the questions?

1. What ....? We went to the cinema.
2. How ....? We all went in Steve's car.
3. Did ....? Yes too fast! We were very frightened!
4. Why ....? We were late.
5. What ....? That new horror film.
6. Did ....? No we didn't, we stayed in the cafe till late.

41

past continuous

Grammar Summary

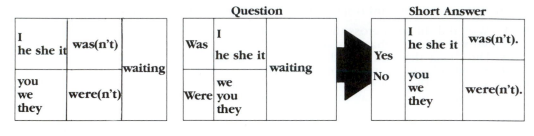

	Question			Short Answer	
I he she it **was(n't)** waiting	Was I he she it waiting		Yes	I he she it **was(n't).**	
you we they **were(n't)**	Were we you they		No	you we they	**were(n't).**

I **was watching** the News when you rang.

What **were** you **doing** when you heard the crash?
▷ I **was getting** dressed.

I **was** just **thinking** of ringing him when he walked in.

We got married while we **were living** in York.

Were they **waiting** when you got there?
▷ No, they **weren't.**

An event, finished before the moment of speaking, which went on for a period.

Often the *longer* of two actions is in the past continuous and the *shorter* in the past simple.

Grammar Comment

When we talk about a past event as a simple fact, we use the past simple. If we are more interested in the **process** of the activity or the **period** of the activity, we use the past continuous. Look at these questions:

Why **were** you **waiting** outside the station last night?
What **were** you **doing** at 8.30?
Were you **expecting** me to ring you?
What **were** you actually **thinking** about?

The emphasis is on the continuing process of waiting, doing, expecting, or thinking.

Very often the past continuous describes a 'background' action while something else happened, for example:

I **was washing** my face when my nose started to bleed.

The present continuous can be used for a present plan *(I'm meeting him tomorrow)*. In the same way, the past continuous can be used for a plan or arrangement in the past:

We **were meeting** him at 9.
They **were having** a party at the weekend.

The past simple is much more common than the past continuous. There is a full discussion of the difference between them in Unit 9.

UNIT 8

Practice 8.1

Complete these dialogues, with short answers, and verbs in the past continuous.

1. Was he waiting for you?

   No, ... He .... still ....! (work)

2. Were you driving when the lorry hit you?

   No, thank goodness, ... Rob .... I ....

   .... at the map. (drive, look at)

3. Were the children sleeping when the snow started?

   Yes, ..., but they soon woke up!

4. I'm sorry. Were we making a terrible noise?

   I'm sorry to say .... It .... everyone (annoy).

5. Were you trying to ring me?

   Yes, ...

   And I .... to ring you! (try)

6. Was your father working in India when you were born?

   Yes, ...

7. Was it still raining when you came in?

   Yes, ... It .... very heavily. (rain)

8. Was I snoring?

   Yes, ... !

Practice 8.2

John/find a pound/walk down King Street
John found a pound while he was walking down King Street.

Make sentences in the same way.

1. Tom - lose his wallet - visit London.

   ....

2. Liz - meet a friend - wait for the train.

   ....

3. The aeroplane - crash - take off.

   ....

4. Peter - run out of petrol - drive to London.

   ....

UNIT 8

Practice 8.3

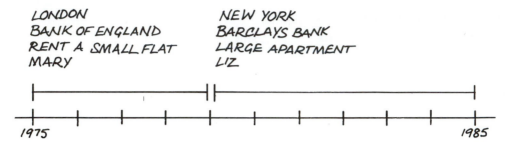

LONDON
BANK OF ENGLAND
RENT A SMALL FLAT
MARY

NEW YORK
BARCLAYS BANK
LARGE APARTMENT
LIZ

1975   1985

Use the information above to ask and answer questions about Robert. You will find the past continuous the most natural form for the questions. Sometimes you will only need to give a few words in the answers.

1. Where/live/1976?

    A Where were you living in 1976?

    B In London.

2. Who/go out with/1977?

    A

    B

3. Where/work/1978?

    A

    B

4. Where/work/1982?

    A

    B

5. Live/small flat/1983?

    A

    B

6. Who/go out with/1984?

    A

    B

7. Work/Barclays/before/go to America?

    A

    B

8. Live with friends/work in New York?

    A

    B

44

UNIT 8

Practice 8.4

Why did you say it?

Here are eight questions. Why did you ask them? Match up the questions with the reasons.

Q1 Were you standing on the corner of Church Road last night?

Q2 Were you driving a Mercedes yesterday morning?

Q3 Were you expecting a letter?

Q4 Was John visiting someone in hospital today?

Q5 Was it freezing in Iceland?

Q6 Who was speaking to you just now?

Q7 Where were you living in 1985?

Q8 Were you sleeping?

Reasons:

R1 I know you've just come back from a business trip.

R2 You took a long time to answer the phone.

R3 I'm sure it was you I saw waiting.

R4 I thought you had always lived there.

R 5 I saw you speaking to the postman.

R6 I think you passed me on the motorway.

R7 I saw him outside the hospital with a huge bunch of flowers.

R8 I heard the sound of voices.

Now use the questions and reasons to make dialogues like this:

Q1	Q2	Q3	Q4	Q5	Q6	Q7	Q8

   A Question
   B Why do you ask?
   A Reason

UNIT 9 — *past simple or continuous*

Grammar Comment

We can say:

> I **watched** the film on TV.
> I **was watching** the film on TV.

Both are possible sentences. Each is correct in a different situation.

The first gives us the simple facts. It gives an overview of 'what happened'.

The second gives us the same facts, but with an extra focus on the continuing or extended process of 'watching'. This is clear in the following situations:

A   I didn't see you at the meeting last night.
B   No, I **stayed** at home and **watched** the film on TV instead.

A   I tried to ring you last night.
B   Oh, I'm sorry. I **was watching** a film on TV. I didn't hear the phone.

In the first situation, B is **only** giving the facts.

In the second situation, B has to give a reason for not hearing the phone. He was involved with another extended activity, so in his excuse he stresses that activity. It helps to think of a picture — with something going on in the background and in the foreground. The past continuous is used for the 'background' action and the past simple is used for the 'foreground' action.

When we look at two different actions, we see the difference between the past simple and the past continuous.

> What **were** you **doing** when the phone rang?
> — I **was having** a bath.

> What **did** you **do** when the phone rang?
> — I **got** out of the bath and **answered** it.

In the second situation we are only interested in the actions as complete wholes; not the process, just the actions themselves. In the first situation we are more interested in the process of the action.

Use the past simple for simple facts about the past:

> The war **started** in 1939.
> The earthquake **killed** over 5000 people.

Use the past continuous when you have a reason to be specially interested in the process or extension of the activity:

> I **was boiling** some water when I burnt myself.

> Who **were** you **talking** to when I came in?

> I hear you've just come back from China. What **were** you **doing** there?

> I wish I **was lying** on a beach somewhere hot.

UNIT 9

Practice 9.1

Complete these situations. Usually you will need one past simple and one past continuous in each.

1. I .... my favourite TV programme when you .... (watch, ring)
2. We .... the carpet when we .... the diamond. (clean, find)
3. My mother .... my room when she .... your letter. (tidy, see)
4. We .... along the beach when we .... we saw a body in the sea. (walk, think)
5. How many people .... behind you when the tickets .... out? (queue, run)
6. Where .... when I .... you yesterday evening? (go, pass)
7. What .... I .... before you .... me? (do, interrupt)
8. I .... and I .... into the man who reads the news on TV. (shop, bump)
9. .... your friends .... for you when you ....? (wait, arrive)
10. I .... of writing to you when I .... that you were coming in today. (think, hear)
11. I .... my goldfish when one .... out of the tank. (feed, jump)
12. I .... my friend in Australia when my dad .... in and .... me who I .... to!!! You can imagine how angry he was when he .... that I .... an international phone call. (phone, come, ask, speak, discover, make)

Practice 9.2

Here are 5 beginnings and 8 endings. Can you match them up. There are lots of possible answers. Make a list of all the possibilities.

Beginnings
1. The phone rang . . .
2. The Queen arrived . . .
3. We got lost . . .
4. It started to rain . . .
5. I lost my wallet . . .

1	
2	
3	
4	
5	

Endings
a. . . . while we were walking home.
b. . . . while I was shopping yesterday.
c. . . . while we were looking for your house.
d. . . . while I was having a bath.
e. . . . while the Prime Minister was having a bath.
f. . . . while we were having an argument.
g. . . . while we were making dinner.
h. . . . while I was waiting for you.

Can you make a really funny sentence using two of these halves? Write it:

....

UNIT 9

Practice 9.3

Last night one of the most important banks in town was robbed. The robbers got away with over £5 million in used banknotes. The police know that the crime took place between 11.30 and 12. A fair-haired young man was seen driving away from the bank in a silver Ford Fiesta at 5 minutes past midnight. Here is his story.

"I spent yesterday evening on my own. I got home from work at about 6.30. I then had a shower and changed clothes. I watched television most of the evening. About 9.30 I decided to go over to see if my girlfriend was at home - her telephone seemed to be dead. I got there in about 20 minutes. She was at home, writing letters so we had a cup of tea and watched television till about 11.30. I then left and went down to start my car. It wouldn't start, so I spent about 20 minutes trying to fix it. I suppose that was about 10 to 12. So, before I left, I went upstairs to my girlfriend's flat to wash my hands. She had already gone to sleep, and she didn't hear me knocking on the door. I decided to drive home with dirty hands. I got home about a quarter past 12"

The police are interviewing the young man. Complete the questions and answers.

1. What were you doing at 8.30 yesterday evening?

   — I .... television.

2. Did you watch television all evening?

   — No, I .... I .... to go and visit my girlfriend.

3. Was it late when you .... to see her?

   — I .... home about 9.30.

4. What .... she .... when you got there?

   — She .... letters.

5. And how long .... you ....?

   — Till about 11.30.

6. And when .... you .... home?

   — About a quarter past 12.

7. But it only .... you 20 minutes to get there. Why .... it .... you twice as long to get back? What .... you .... between 11.30 and a quarter past midnight?

   — I .... to get my car to start.

8. And how long .... it .... you to get it started?

   — About 20 minutes, I think.

9. .... you .... straight home?

   — No, I .... upstairs to my girlfriend's flat to wash my hands.

10. What .... she .... when you went back?

    — Well, I never .... in - you see, she .... so she .... me knocking at the door, so I .... straight home.

11. .... anybody .... you working on your car?

    — No, I don't think so.

12. And your girlfriend .... you either?

    — No, she ....

13. Well, young man, you are in deep trouble. Somebody .... your car
    outside the bank in Victoria Road at 11.43pm. You ....
    inside reading a newspaper. At 12.05 you .... out and opened the
    boot. At the same time, two men armed with guns .... out of the
    bank. The three of you .... off at high speed. While you ....
    .... outside in the car, they .... the bank!

    — How do you know it was me?

14. Very easy, young man! Somebody .... your car parked outside the
    bank - registration D453 RGB. We .... to your girlfriend. We know
    that you .... her yesterday evening, but you ....
    .... at 11.30. You .... at 11.20. And she .... not
    .... at 11.50. She .... some more letters. You
    are under arrest.

Practice 9.4

Fill in the verbs using either the past simple or the past continuous.

When I was in Turkey last year, I .... (have) my first experience of an
earthquake. It .... (be) about 11 o'clock at night. I .... (be)
in my hotel room and .... (take) off my clothes when I ....(think)
I .... (hear) someone banging in the room below. Suddenly the whole
room .... (begin) to shake. It wasn't the person underneath! The hotel
.... (shake) because of an earthquake!

My first thought was to get out, but I .... (stay) on the third floor! So
I .... (run) out of the room and .... (start) to go down the
stairs. Suddenly all the lights .... (go) out. While I .... (go)
down the stairs, I .... (meet) someone who .... (shout) "Get
down to the bottom of the stairs as fast as you can, and hide underneath." I
.... (do) as he .... (say). When I .... (get) there, there
were several other people. They .... (tell) me to stay under the stairs
and we .... (not come) out until we .... (think) the earthquake
was over.

They told me afterwards that the stairs are the strongest part of a house. Now you know
what to do during an earthquake!

Practice 9.5

Fill in the verb in either the past simple or the past continuous.

1. Guess what! I .... Alan at the station yesterday. (see)

2. Really? What .... he .... there? (do)

3. He .... he .... a friend from Portugal. Later I .... I .... Diana when I was in the market. (say, meet, think, see)

4. I am surprised! What .... she .... there? (do)

5. Well, you know she's become a vegetarian - she .... lots of vegetables. And just as we .... each other, I suddenly .... Steve! (buy, see, catch sight of)

6. What a coincidence! What .... he .... there? His wife does all their shopping. (do)

7. Well, I don't know. He .... past too fast, I don't think he .... us. (drive, notice)

Practice 9.6

Only one sentence in each of these pairs seems really natural and sensible. Which one? You will need to think about the meaning of the sentences carefully.

1a. We queued at the box office when the tickets ran out.
 b. We were queueing at the box office when the tickets ran out.

2a. He stole money from the firm when he lost his job.
 b. He was stealing money from the firm when he lost his job.

3a. He smoked very heavily when he died.
 b. He was smoking very heavily when he died.

4a. I began to think you had forgotten my birthday when your present arrived.
 b. I was beginning to think you had forgotten my birthday when your present arrived.

5a. I tried to ring him when he walked in!
 b. I was trying to ring him when he walked in.

6a. He worked out in the gym when he had a heart attack.
 b. He was working out in the gym when he had a heart attack.

7a. I looked for my pen when I realised I had left it at home.
 b. I was looking for my pen when I realised I had left it at home.

8a. The car stopped when the lights changed.
 b. The car was stopping when the lights changed.

Both sentences in the last pair are possible. Which one tells you the lights went:

   i) from red to green? ....
   ii) from green to red? ....

UNIT 9

Practice 9.7

Complete these examples with the past simple or the past continuous.

1. I (think) of going out when you (call).

   ....

2. We (met) while we (studying) in Liverpool.

   ....

3. When she (travel) on the underground, someone (steal) her bag.

   ....

4. The thief (take) the money when the staff (have) lunch.

   ....

5. Steve (drive) to London when he (remember) to phone Alex.

   ....

Practice 9.8

Either fill in the gaps using the past simple or the past continuous, or look at the table at the end of the story.

A sad story.

In September 1988, Mr and Mrs Smith (1)............................. in the top floor flat of a high building. One day Mrs Smith was at home. It was a beautiful day, the sun (2) .... and in the town below, people (3) .... the good weather. While Mrs Smith (4) .... out of the window she (5) .... her husband walk in to the building. As he got out of the lift, she (6) .... the door, very surprised to see him home so early from the office. He (7) .... his wife that he (8) .... her.

Of course Mrs Smith was shocked and upset. While he (9) .... his clothes into a suitcase, Mrs Smith (10) ....

As he (11) .... out of the door she was still crying. Mrs Smith listened while the lift went down. When it (12) .... at the ground floor, she walked to the window, opened it and (13) .... At that exact moment, Mr Smith walked out of the building.

He wasn't thinking of his wife, he (14) .... of his new life, when suddenly Mrs Smith (15) .... on top of him. He was killed instantly but Mrs Smith was completely unhurt. People said she (16) .... when she recovered from the shock but I'm not sure if that is true.

Match the numbers in the blanks to the right verb. Some are done for you.

15	landed		stopped
	was thinking		was putting
	was looking		was leaving
1	were living		jumped
	opened		were enjoying
	was smiling		told
	was crying		walked
	was shining		saw

irregular verbs

Grammar Summary

There are about 180 irregular verbs. Some are very unusual. Here are the most useful.

First form	Second form	Third form	First form	Second form	Third form
All forms the same			**Second and third forms the same**		
cost	cost	cost	bend	bent	bent
cut	cut	cut	build	built	built
hit	hit	hit	feel	felt	felt
hurt	hurt	hurt	keep	kept	kept
let	let	let	leave	left	left
put	put	put	light	lit	lit
set	set	set	lend	lent	lent
shut	shut	shut	mean	meant	meant
split	split	split	meet	met	met
			send	sent	sent
Similar sound groups			shoot	shot	shot
beat	beat	beaten	sleep	slept	slept
bite	bit	bitten	spend	spent	spent
eat	ate	eaten	spoil	spoilt	spoilt
fall	fell	fallen	get	got	got
forget	forgot	forgotten	lose	lost	lost
forgive	forgave	forgiven	sit	sat	sat
give	gave	given			
hide	hid	hidden	bring	brought	brought
shake	shook	shaken	buy	bought	bought
take	took	taken	fight	fought	fought
tear	tore	torn	think	thought	thought
wear	wore	worn	catch	caught	caught
			teach	taught	taught
blow	blew	blown	feed	fed	fed
fly	flew	flown	find	found	found
know	knew	known	have	had	had
throw	threw	thrown	hear	heard	heard
grow	grew	grown	hold	held	held
draw	drew	drawn	make	made	made
			pay	paid	paid
begin	began	begun	read	read	read
drink	drank	drunk	say	said	said
ring	rang	rung	sell	sold	sold
sing	sang	sung	stand	stood	stood
shrink	shrank	shrunk	understand	understood	understood
			tell	told	told
freeze	froze	frozen	stick	stuck	stuck
speak	spoke	spoken	win	won	won
steal	stole	stolen	shine	shone	shone
break	broke	broken	**All forms different**		
wake	woke	woken	be	was/were	been
choose	chose	chosen	become	became	become
drive	drove	driven	come	came	come
write	wrote	written	do	did	done
ride	rode	ridden	go	went	gone
			run	ran	run
			see	saw	seen
			show	showed	shown

Grammar Comment

If a new verb comes into English, it is always regular, for example:

> We **computerised** our accounts last year.
> My wife **video-ed** the programme for me.

Everyone knows that **video-ed** is regular and they know its pronunciation. No one is quite sure yet about the spelling!

UNIT 10

Practice 10.1

There are 27 irregular verb forms hidden in this box. Most go across or down, but for two you must read upwards! Can you circle them?

```
A  D  G  I  V  E  N  D  A  H
C  C  A  U  G  H  T  P  F  R
O  O  V  Y  O  C  O  M  E  S
S  L  E  P  T  H  R  D  L  O
T  R  U  H  H  O  N  R  T  L
U  N  D  E  R  S  T  O  O  D
C  E  T  A  O  E  O  V  S  R
K  P  E  R  W  F  L  E  W  A
I  O  S  D  N  I  D  U  O  N
F  O  R  G  O  T  T  E  N  K
```

Practice 10.2

What are the other irregular past tenses which rhyme with the following? The number you need is given for each one.

1. **caught**   (5) ...taught...

2. **blew**   (5) ...flew..

3. **spoke**   (2) ....

4. Now write **six** verbs which have all three forms the same. ....
   ....

Practice 10.3

Fill in the correct forms of the verbs in the following:

begin   catch   bite   choose   come   bring   cost   break   buy

1. As soon as I went outside, it .... to rain.

2. When I was in India last year, I was .... by a snake.

3. I'm very sorry — I've .... your pen.

4. Have you .... me my book back?

5. I think I .... this cold at church last week.

6. She said she .... that colour because she liked it!

7. Which .... first — the chicken or the egg?

8. When I .... this car, it .... a fortune, and it still does!

53

UNIT 10

Practice 10.4

Fill in the correct form of the verbs in the following.

freeze   find   drive   eat   forgive   forget   fall   drink   give

1. I don't feel very well. I think I've .... too much coffee.
2. John .... to Scotland, but he said it was the last time.
3. I think I've .... something which didn't agree with me.
4. Be careful getting on and off buses in London. I .... off one!
5. Yes, officer, I .... the wallet on the corner of Smith Street.
6. I have .... you, but I have not ....
7. My room was so cold I ....!
8. Dad .... me two pounds. That wasn't very much, was it?

Practice 10.5

Fill in the correct form of the verbs in the following.

hide   keep   lend   lose   grow   hear   get   know   leave

1. That plant just .... and .... It got too big for the house!
2. Have you .... the latest? There's going to be an election.
3. My brother and I .... in the garden until Aunt Mary had left.
4. Now I'm going to tell you all about it. I've .... it a secret until now.
5. I .... Margaret when we were children.
6. I once .... a good friend £10 and never .... it back. Never again!
7. Have you .... college yet?
8. I'm sure I .... my keys in the bank.

Practice 10.6

There are 11 irregular second and third forms of the verb hidden in this box. Can you circle them? They can go across or down.

I	S	A	T	O	S	E	E
L	U	S	A	W	T	I	S
G	P	S	K	G	O	T	H
H	S	T	E	A	L	G	I
T	O	O	K	S	E	E	N
S	E	L	L	O	N	T	E
I	N	E	S	H	O	N	E
T	A	U	G	H	T	O	N
H	S	O	L	D	L	I	T

UNIT 10

Practice 10.7

Fill in the correct form of the verbs in the following.

shine   sell   mean   see   see   pay   meet   set   run   ring   send   buy

1. When I said I wasn't going to come, I .... it.

2. Oh hello, we .... on the bus, didn't we?

3. Who ....? I must give them my share.

4. Jill .... Ring her back, will you.

5. We ...., but we still missed the connection.

6. I'm sure I've .... you somewhere. Wait a minute. Yes, I ....

   you at the meeting last Monday.

7. I .... my old bike and .... a new one.

8. I think we .... 60 Christmas cards last year.

9. Have you .... the video to record the tennis?

10. The sun .... every day we were in Portugal!

Practice 10.8

Fill in the correct form of the verbs in the following.

spend   come   stand   take   lose   go   think   wake   write
shoot   show   tear   tell   understand   sleep   steal   stick   freeze   teach

1. The men who .... the seals have been put in prison.

2. I'm sure that film has never been .... on British TV before.

3. I'm sorry to say I .... very badly last night.

4. Isn't it time you .... to Sandy in America?

5. He told me he'd .... £1000 on holiday!

6. We .... for an hour waiting for a bus which never ....

7. I'm sure I haven't .... my wallet. I'm sure it has been ....

8. The lock's totally .... I think it must be .... solid.

9. Sue .... her umbrella and we wished we had!

10. Our teachers .... a lot, but I'm not sure how much we learned.

11. Don't turn round! I think you've .... your new dress.

12. I .... you it was a stupid idea, and now you see just how stupid!

13. I always .... you .... French, but I can see I was wrong!

14. I'm sorry I'm late. I .... up, then I .... back to sleep again.

Grammar Summary

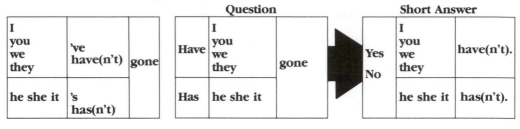

				Question				Short Answer	
I you we they	've have(n't)	gone	Have	I you we they	gone	Yes No	I you we they	have(n't).
he she it	's has(n't)		Has	he she it			he she it	has(n't).

We haven't seen Tom for a long time.

Has Paula **taken** her driving test yet?
▷ No, she **hasn't.**

Have you ever **been** to the Tower of London?
▷ Yes, but I **haven't been** there for twenty years!

I've never **heard** that before.

The speaker is looking back from the present to the past.

Grammar Comment

The present perfect is a present tense. It is always based at 'Now', the present moment, the moment of speaking. We use it to **look back** from the present to the past. It is the present tense which is strongly connected with the past:

> I'm afraid I**'ve broken** your pen. (I tell you **now** about what happened **then**)
> It**'s** just **started** to rain. (I see the rain **now**)
> Have you read today's paper? (Yet, before **now**)

These examples look back on the recent past, but we can also use it to look back on the more distant past:

> I**'ve** always **taken** sugar in my coffee.
> I**'ve visited** the Far East — but that was when I was much younger.
> We**'ve lived** here for six months. (and still do)

It is common to look back on things close to us. This is why the present perfect is often used with 'just':

> We**'ve** just **got** engaged.
> It**'s** just **started** to rain.

It is less common to look back on the more distant past, but in both cases we use the present perfect. It does not matter whether the action is complete or not. The main reason we choose the present perfect is because it 'looks back' from the moment of speaking:

> Mary**'s had** a little boy. (complete)
> We**'ve lived** here for six months. (and still do)

It is a **present** tense, about something **now,** but it always **looks back** to **before now.**

UNIT 11

Practice 11.1

Bill, Sue, Dave, Ellen, and Andy are talking about where they have been on holiday. Fill in the spaces using the information below.

	France	Japan	USA	Spain	Austria
Bill	YES	NO	NO	YES	NO
Sue	YES	NO	YES	YES	NO
Dave	NO	NO	YES	NO	NO
Ellen	YES	NO	YES	YES	NO
Andy	NO	YES	NO	YES	NO

1. Bill .... been to France, but Dave ....

2. Andy is the only person who .... visited Japan.

3. Three people .... been to the United States.

4. Only one person .... been to Spain.

5. Ellen and Andy .... been to Spain, but Andy .... been to France.

6. Dave is the only one who .... visited only one foreign country.

7. Nobody .... been to Austria.

8. Two people .... been to three countries.

9. Sue and Dave .... both been to the United States, but neither .... been to Japan.

10. .... and .... been to the same countries.

Now write about yourself, and people you know:

11. I .... been to ...., but I .... never visited ....

12. I have a friend who .... been to ...., but I .... been there myself.

Practice 11.2

Match up these comments and responses to make three jokes.

1. Doctor, doctor, I've eaten a pencil. What should I do?

2. Doctor, doctor, I've just swallowed a sheep.

3. Doctor, doctor, I've swallowed a roll of film.

a. Don't worry, let's see if it develops.

b. Use a pen, instead!

c. Are you feeling baaaaaaaad?

1. ....   2. ....   3. ....

UNIT 11

Practice 11.3

Look at the pictures and decide what the people in each picture **have just** done.

1. _She's just had a baby_ ....

2. ....

3. ....

4. ....

5. ....

6. ....

7. ....

8. ....

UNIT 11

Practice 11.4

Complete these two-line dialogues.

1. Just/see/the latest Jaguar
   A I've just seen the latest Jaguar!
   B Have you? So have I

2. Already/buy/my ticket
   A ....
   B ....

3. Spend/all my money
   A ....
   B ....

4. Meet/your brother's new girlfriend
   A ....
   B ....

5. Get very wet
   A ....
   B ....

6. Buy a CD player
   A ....
   B ....

Practice 11.5

Rewrite the following sentences putting the word (in brackets) in the most natural place.

1. Have you been to Sri Lanka? (ever)

   ....

2. He's had some very good news. (just)

   ....

3. I've wanted to be rich. (never)

   ....

4. Haven't you finished? (yet)

   ....

5. We've been very good friends. (always)

   ....

6. People have mistaken me for John Wayne. (often)

   ....

7. Don't worry. I've locked the door. (already)

   ....

8. It hasn't rained very much. (lately)

   ....

UNIT 11

Practice 11.6

It is time for the general election. The Prime Minister is making a list of all the things the Government has done in the past 4 years. What are they?

1. build more houses than the previous Government
   We've built more houses than the previous Government.

2. create more jobs than any other party
   ....

3. bring down unemployment to 1974 levels
   ....

4. reduce inflation by half
   ....

5. give extra money to the Arts
   ....

6. modernise the army
   ....

7. employ more police
   ....

8. make industry more efficient
   ....

9. help the north of England
   ....

But the Opposition do not agree. They want to attack the Government's record. What do they say?

10. make the rich even richer
    ....

11. destroy the education system
    ....

12. forget Scotland and Wales
    ....

13. damage British industry
    ....

14. shake confidence in Britain's economy
    ....

15. cut money for hospitals
    ....

16. forget pensioners
    ....

17. not take an interest in young people
    ....

18. leave the country in a mess
    ....

UNIT 11

Practice 11.7

The present perfect is about **looking back from 'Now'**, the moment of speaking, to earlier time. In each of these examples A says something 'Now', which makes B **look back to 'before Now'**. Make a natural answer; in each case you will need the present perfect.

1. **A** Why are you looking so happy?

   B ..I've just passed my exam................................... (exam)

2. **A** What's the matter with you?

   B .... (break leg)

3. **A** Why don't you ring Angela?

   B .... (twice, must be out)

4. **A** Would you like to go and see the new Superman film this evening?

   B ....(I'm afraid, already)

5. **A** Why on earth do you want to see the Tower of London?

   B ....(never, before)

6. **A** Shall we have a snack at that little restaurant there?

   B .... (sandwiches with me)

7. **A** Why have you still got 'L' plates on your car?

   B .... (test, not yet)

8. **A** Why are you limping?

   B .... (hurt)

9. **A** Where's your old bike? Don't you use it any more?

   B .... (sell, new)

10. **A** That's a very nice ring. . . does it mean good news?

    B .... (Yes, just engaged)

Notice that in each case the two people are **talking about 'Now'**; the viewpoint of the conversation is the present moment, but in each case B wants to **look back** to something **before now** which **connects with 'Now'**.

A common word

Hello Harry. Have you had a holiday yet?
— Have I had a holiday? Yes, Hilary and I have just had a hitch-hiking holiday in the Highlands but we haven't had much rest. Hilary has had flu. I have had a bad cough. We have had my parents visiting so we have hardly had any free time. I certainly haven't had a chance to catch up with all the work I hadn't done earlier.

As you can see **have** is very common in English, as an auxiliary and as a full verb.

Grammar Summary

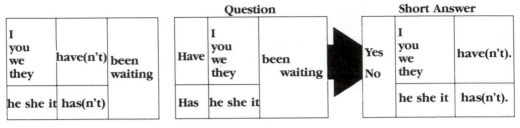

I you we they	have(n't)	been waiting
he she it	has(n't)	

Question

Have	I you we they	been waiting
Has	he she it	

Short Answer

Yes No	I you we they	have(n't).
	he she it	has(n't).

Have you **been waiting** long?

How long **have** you **been learning** English?

I**'ve been thinking** of changing my job.

Carmen **hasn't been feeling** too well recently.

Why are you crying?
▷ I**'ve been chopping** onions.

You don't look surprised.
▷ I'm not. I**'ve been expecting** this to happen.

The speaker is looking back from the present to a period in the past. The period is continuing at the moment of speaking or has stopped.

Grammar Comment

The present perfect continuous is very similar in meaning to the present perfect simple. It **looks back** from the present to an action or activity in the past.
The continuous form — like all continuous forms — places more emphasis on the period or process of the activity:

> I**'ve been waiting** for you for over an hour!

When we look back from the present it is usually to the recent past. This is especially true of the present perfect continuous.

These examples all show the reason, immediate at the moment of speaking, for the choice of the present perfect continuous:

> You look very hot. **Have** you **been running**?
> I can smell alcohol. **Have** you **been drinking**?
> Your eyes are very red. **Have** you **been crying**?

In each of these situations, the continuous form must be used because there is a strong link between the moment of speaking and the previous action — thus creating two points in time = a period.

One of the best ways to understand the choice of the present perfect continuous is to look at more examples and decide why the speaker emphasises the activity:

> I**'ve been worrying** about you. Why are you so late?
> I**'ve been trying** to ring you all morning, but your phone's been engaged.

UNIT 12

Practice 12.1

Complete the following sentences. You will have to use:

haven't   4 times
hasn't   once
've   4 times
's   once

1. I'.................... been thinking about you.

2. I'm sorry, I .... been paying enough attention.

3. You'.................... been living there for a while, haven't you?

4. You .... been eating enough. You're getting too thin.

5. He'.................... been feeling ill all day, doctor.

6. It .... been working for 2 years! Can you mend it?

7. We'.................... been waiting for you. Where were you?

8. We .... been working very hard, have we?

9. They'.................... been living on very little money.

10. They .... been behaving themselves at all!

Practice 12.2

John, Bill, Mary, Pete, Liz, Ralph, Betty and Sheila haven't seen each other since they left school ten years ago. Here is a list of their jobs and where they live. What do they say to each other when they meet?

1. John   Leeds   Furniture factory
2. Bill   Australia   Farm
3. Mary   Dublin   Travel agents
4. Pete   Home   No job
5. Liz   Aberdeen   Hospital
6. Ralph   London   Theatre
7. Betty   Cornwall   Hotel
8. Sheila   Paris   An international bank

1. I've been living in Leeds. I've been working in a furniture factory.

2. ....

3. ....

4. ....

5. ....

6. ....

7. ....

8. ....

UNIT 12

Practice 12.3

What **have** the people in these pictures **been doing?** You will need the present perfect continuous.

1. ....

2. ....

3. ....

4. ....

5. ....

6. ....

7. ....

8. ....

Practice 12.4

Every child grows up learning the story of Goldilocks and the Three Bears. Do you remember that the three bears came back to their house and discovered that somebody had been there. They asked three questions. They used the present perfect continuous! What were the questions?

1. sit on my chair

   ....

2. eat my porridge

   ....

3. sleep in my bed

   ....

They used the present perfect continuous because they were **looking back** on a period. There was a reason 'Now' (no food in Nr. 2!) to look back to 'before Now'.

Practice 12.5

Your job is to try to interview someone for a job. Before the interview you are thinking about all the questions you could ask about the person's present job. What are the questions? They will sound most natural if you use the present perfect continuous.

1. How long/work/there?

   ....

2. What exactly/do/there?

   ....

3. How much/earn?

   ....

4. How many hours a week/work?

   ....

5. Enjoy your work?

   ....

In the following the present perfect simple will seem more natural. Can you see why? If not, look at Unit 13.

6. Why/decide to leave your old job?

   ....

7. Why/apply for this job?

   ....

UNIT 13 present perfect or pres perf continuous

Grammar Comment

1. The difference between the present perfect and the present perfect continuous is sometimes very clear:

    > He's **lost** his hair since his operation.
    > He's **been losing** his hair since his operation.

    In the first example, he has no hair left. He is totally bald. His hair-loss is seen **as a whole.** In the second example, he may still have some hair, but it is getting thinner and thinner. His loss of hair is seen as **a process,** taking place over time.

    > He's **fixed** the TV.
    > He's **been fixing** the TV.

    In the first example, the TV is now working. The repair is seen **as a whole.** It is completed and finished.
    The second sentence could be a response to the question, "Why is there a screwdriver on top of the TV?". The fixing may or may not be finished. Again, the fixing is seen as **a process,** extended in time.
    In each of the above, there is a clear difference of meaning. We use the present perfect to look back on an action **as a whole.** We use the present perfect continuous to look back on **the process or period** of an action.

2. Sometimes the difference is small and is only a matter of emphasis:

    > I've **lived** here for 4 years.
    > I've **been living** here for 4 years.

    > I've **thought** about it a lot. (and have, perhaps, decided)
    > I've **been thinking** about it a lot. (and, perhaps, need more time.)

    > He's **worked** there since he was a boy.
    > He's **been working** there since he was a boy.

    The first examples give facts; the second examples give more emphasis to the extended period, and the on-going process of living, thinking, and working.

3. In some situations only one form is possible:

    > *You've **cried,** haven't you?*
    > You've **been crying,** haven't you?

    The tears in the other person's eyes force the speaker to ask about the present cause of the crying. Crying is a period and, therefore, we need the continuous form.

    > **Have** you ever **visited** Fiji?
    > ***Have** you ever **been visiting** Fiji?*

    The use of **ever** suggests that the speaker is only interested in knowing the fact. The speaker is looking back over **all** time before now, **as a whole,** so the simple form is the only one which is possible.

4. If you make a mistake by using one form rather than the other, you will seldom be misunderstood, but if you want to use English accurately, you will have to study this difficult difference. Take your time to consider lots of examples.

UNIT 13

Practice 13.1

Only one of each of these pairs of sentences is possible. Which one? Can you see why the other sentences are impossible? An explanation is given in the Grammar Comment.

1. I've just been swimming./I've just swum.

2. Have you been hearing your results yet?/Have you heard your results yet?

3. Have you been buying a new car yet?/Have you bought a new car yet?

4. You've grown since I last saw you!/You've been growing since I last saw you!

5. Great news — I've passed my exam!/Great news — I've been passing my exam!

6. I've lost my new pen./I've been losing my new pen.

7. I've started to learn to drive./I've been starting to learn to drive.

8. I think I've broken my arm!/I think I've been breaking my arm!

Practice 13.2

In the following situations, one sentence is more natural than the other. Which is it?

1. I'm really tired.
   a. I've been driving for 12 hours non-stop.
   b. I've driven now for 12 hours non-stop.

2. Where on earth have you been?
   a. I've been waiting here in the rain for an hour.
   b. I've waited here in the rain for an hour.

3. Why are there tears in your eyes?
   a. I've chopped onions.
   b. I've been chopping onions.

4. Why are you so sweaty and hot?
   a. I've run.
   b. I've been running.

5. Robert! I haven't seen you for ages!
   a. What have you been doing since we last met?
   b. What have you done since we last met?

6. I can smell alcohol!
   a.
   b.

Notice that in each situation, the only possibility is the one with the present perfect continuous. This is because the speaker is **looking back** to an event 'before Now' which is **extended in time** — it is naturally a **period** of time.

Practice 13.3

Sometimes both the present perfect and the present perfect continuous are possible with very similar meanings, eg:

> **I've waited for 10 minutes.**
> **I've been waiting for 10 minutes.**

Sometimes, one is almost impossible or **very unlikely**.
Which of the following are **very unlikely?**

1. a. I've known Andy for years.
   b. I've been knowing Andy for years.
2. a. I've crashed the car.
   b. I've been crashing the car.
3. a. Have you spent all your money yet?
   b. Have you been spending all your money yet?
4. a. I've never visited anyone in hospital.
   b. I've never been visiting anyone in hospital.

UNIT 13

Practice 13.4

We use the present perfect continuous to look back on a period. If we want to look back on a single action or the action as a whole we use the present perfect simple. For example:

I've been smoking since I was a boy.
I've given up at last.

Make similar sentences with these ideas.

1. They/save up for a holiday/for months
— go to China

....

....

2. He/go out with Jane/for 5 years
— ask her to marry him
— she/refuse!

....

....

....

3. They/dig for gold in these hills/for years
— find it at last

....

....

4. I/try to learn Esperanto/for six months
— give up!
— decide/to learn to play golf instead!

....

....

....

5. We/plan to have a big party
— decide to have it on the 16th
— invite 50 people
— not invite/anyone from the office!

....

....

....

....

6. I/look for my pen
— somebody/steal

....

....

UNIT 13

Practice 13.5

Study these pairs of sentences. After each pair there are two interpretations which comment on the meaning. Match up the sentences with the interpretations.

1. She hasn't visited me.
2. She hasn't been visiting me.
   a. perhaps she did a long time ago, but stopped.
   b. never.

1	
2	

3. I haven't got The Times.
4. I haven't been getting The Times.
   a. perhaps I forgot to buy one today.
   b. I used to buy it, but no longer do.

3	
4	

5. I've had a lot of pain.
6. I've been having a lot of pain.
   a. with my injured leg.
   b. recently, and at the moment.

5	
6	

7. I've forgotten to put sugar in your coffee.
8. I've been forgetting to put sugar in your coffee.
   a. my memory is getting worse and worse.
   b. I usually remember, but today I forgot.

7	
8	

9. She's had her hair done.
10. She's been having her hair done.
    a. specially for today.
    b. that is why she's so late.

9	
10	

11. What has gone wrong?
12. What has been going wrong?
    a. on this occasion.
    b. over a period.

11	
12	

13. Have you seen Liz?
14. Have you been seeing Liz?
    a. regularly, on different occasions.
    b. perhaps, this morning.

13	
14	

15. The dog has died.
16. The dog has been dying.
    a. may not be dead yet.
    b. is dead.

15	
16	

17. I have learned English.
18. I've been learning English.
    a. I have started.
    b. I have nothing more to learn.

17	
18	

If you were in doubt about any of the sentences, you could not be in doubt about the last one! Notice if a single action, or an action or event **as a whole** is referred to, the simple is used. If something **extended in time** is referred to, the continuous is used.

UNIT 14 present perfect or past simple

Grammar Comment

The basic difference between the past simple and the present perfect is:

> The **past simple** is a **past** tense.
> The **present perfect** is a **present** tense.

We use these two tenses to talk about the past, but from two different points of view. Look at these examples:

> I first **met** John in 1985.
> I **have known** John for four years.

Each sentence is looking at the same information, but from two different perspectives. The past simple mentions the fact of first meeting in 1985. The present perfect **looks back** from the present to 1985. The difference in a nutshell is as follows:

> Use the past simple to describe a past activity in a simple factual way.
> Use the present perfect to look back from the present on a past activity.

Look at the following examples with those ideas in mind:

> I **ate** too much at the party.
> I've **had** too much to eat over the past few days.

> I first **came** here on holiday in 1963.
> I've **been coming** here on holiday since 1963.

> I **started** learning English when I was 12.
> I've **been learning** English for 5 years.

The difference between the two is clear when we look at some of the other words in a sentence:

ago
— They **lived** there 5 years **ago.**
— She **died** 3 months **ago.**
— **ago** marks the end of a period in the past. It cannot be connected with the present, so it is impossible to use **ago** with the present perfect

since
— It **hasn't changed since** the war.
— We've never **been** back **since** we were children.
— **since** tells us of a period starting some time in the past. It is common to use the present perfect with **since**.

ever
— **Have** you **ever been** to Hawaii?
— **Has** she **ever written** to you?
— **ever** is very rare with the past simple.

yet
— **Have** you **been** to the bank **yet**?
— **Has** he **paid** you the money back **yet**?
— **yet** means 'up to now', so the present perfect is the natural tense to use with **yet**.

The past simple always talks about **then,** and definitely **excludes now.** The present perfect always **includes** the present. These examples show the difference in a nutshell:

> **Did** you **see** Peter this morning?
> (This can only be said in the afternoon or evening.)
> **Have** you **seen** Peter this morning?
> (This must be said before the end of the morning.)

Note: American English can use **just** and **yet** with the past simple, but this is not true for British English.

UNIT 14

Practice 14.1

Write short answers to these questions:

1. Did you meet your aunt yesterday?   Yes, I *did*..........................
2. Have you ever met your uncle?   No, I ....
3. Have you ever missed the train?   Yes, I ....
4. Did you miss it this morning?   Yes, I ....
5. Did you enjoy dinner?   Yes, I ....
6. Have you ever eaten rabbit before?   No, I ....
7. Have you ever forgotten to lock the door?   Yes, I ....
8. Did you lock it this morning?   Yes, I ....
9. Has Paula taken her driving test yet?   Yes, she ....
10. Did she pass?   No, she ....

Notice the present perfect examples **look back** from 'Now'; the past simple examples refer to a specific event in the past.

Practice 14.2

Match up the two sentences with the phrases in the list. Then write out the complete sentences below.

We haven't seen Tom . . .

We saw Tom . . .

a. at Christmas.
b. on the 26th.
c. yet.
d. since last weekend.

e. for ages.
f. yesterday.
g. last week.
h. for 20 years.

1. ....
2. ....
3. ....
4. ....
5. ....
6. ....
7. ....
8. ....

Notice with the past simple the phrases answer the question *When?* With the present perfect they define a **period** between 'Now' and another time in the past.

UNIT 14

Practice 14.3

Dead or alive?

Look at these two sentences:

1. My parents lived in Yorkshire all their lives.
2. My parents have lived in Yorkshire all their lives.

The difference between them is the difference between the past simple and the present perfect. The first sentence suggests the "pure" past, and so **"and now they are dead"**. The second sentence suggests looking back from 'Now', and so **"and they still live there."**

Match up the following pairs of sentences with their "meanings".

1. I worked for the BBC for years.   a. and I still work there.
2. I've worked for the BBC for years.   b. but now I do not work there.

3. We were married for 27 years.   a. but my wife died last year.
4. We've been married for 27 years.   b. and we are still married.

5. I believed in God for many years.   a. and I still do.
6. I've believed in God for many years.   b. but now I don't.

7. I was a friend of Pete's for years.   a. but we are not friends now.
8. I've been a friend of Pete's for years.   b. and we are still good friends.

9. I thought about moving abroad.   a. and I think I might.
10. I've thought about moving abroad.   b. but I gave up the idea.

Practice 14.4

The past simple has no link with the present. The present perfect is always linked to the present, it is used to **look back** from 'Now' to 'before Now'.

For example: I **met** Stefan 3 years ago.
                I**'ve known** Stefan for 3 years.

In the first sentence you are only interested in the meeting 3 years ago, but in the second sentence you are looking back from 'Now'.

Write sentences from the words given.

1.   I/start to read *Death on the Nile* on holiday.

     I/only read the first two chapters so far.

     ....

     ....

2.   I/buy 10 peaches this morning.
     I/eat 9 already.

     ....

     ....

3. Bill/win £5000 in a lottery.
He/spend most of it already!

....

....

4. Jill/do French at school.
She/forget most of it by now.

....

....

5. Pete/leave home last Tuesday.
He/hitch-hike over 200 miles in the last three days.

....

....

6. Some friends of mine/buy an old car for £50.
They/travel all over Europe in it in the past year.

....

....

7. I/start my homework after dinner.
It's almost bedtime and I/do hardly anything yet!

....

....

8. I/buy a new pad of paper yesterday.
I/almost used it all up already!

....

....

In each second sentence there is a word or phrase which clearly shows the link to 'Now'.
Write those words or phrases here:

1. ......So far...............................   **5.** ....

2. ....   **6.** ....

3. ....   **7.** ....

4. ....   **8.** ....

UNIT 14

Practice 14.5

Fill in the correct verbs in the dialogues.

1. (be, have, break)

.... you ever .... involved in a bad accident?

— Yes, I .... actually. I .... a very bad accident on my motorbike about a year ago. I .... both legs.

2. (be, be, go)

...........................you ever .... to the top of a very high building?

— Yes, I .... — only last month. When I .... in Paris. I .... to the very top of The Eiffel Tower.

3. (win)

.... you ever .... a lot of money?

— No, I ...., but once I .... £10 in a lottery.

4. (find, take, hear)

.... you ever .... anything valuable?

— Yes, I once .... a diamond ring. I .... it outside the station and I .... it to the police. I .... never .... anything more about it.

5. (lose, take, go)

.... you ever .... anything of any value?

— Yes, I .... my watch off at the swimming pool, and when I ....back for it, it wasn't there.

6. (feel, be, go, come)

.... you ever .... really ill?

— Twice in my life, and both times on a boat. The first time .... when we .... to France last summer, and the second time .... when we .... back!

7. (have, argue)

.... you ever .... a fight with anyone?

— Yes, I .... a fight with one of my best friends last week. We .... about something really silly and unimportant.

8. (do, wear, carry, ask, say, think)

.... you ever .... something really crazy?

— I .... something really silly last summer. On one of the hottest days, I .... a winter coat and .... an umbrella. Everyone .... me why. I .... I ....it was going to rain.

74

UNIT 14

Practice 14.6

Now answer truthfully about yourself.

1. Have you ever been involved in a bad accident?

    ....

2. Have you ever been to the top of a very high building?

    ....

3. Have you ever won a lot of money?

    ....

4. Have you ever found anything valuable?

    ....

5. Have you ever lost anything of any value?

    ....

6. Have you ever done something really crazy?

    ....

Practice 14.7

Match up parts 1, 2 and 3 to make 10 sentences. Each sentence will have a past simple and a present perfect verb!

Part 1
1. Edwin Herbert Land
2. Alexander Graham Bell
3. John Logie Baird
4. Wilhelm Röntgen
5. Thomas Edison
6. Galileo
7. Alfred Nobel
8. Sir Frank Whittle
9. Sir Alexander Fleming
10. George Eastman

Part 2
a. invented the modern camera
b. discovered X-rays
c. invented the jet engine
d. invented television
e. discovered penicillin
f. invented the telephone
g. invented the thermometer
h. invented the electric light bulb
i. invented dynamite
j. invented the polaroid camera

Part 3
k. which has opened up international communication.
l. which has made candles things of the past.
m. which has allowed us to take instant pictures.
n. which has brought Dallas into our sitting-rooms.
o. which has revolutionised air travel.
p. which has saved thousands of lives.
q. which have saved many broken legs.
r. which has allowed us all to take pictures.
s. which has allowed us to measure temperature.
t. which has killed millions of people.

1	2	3	4	5	6	7	8	9	10

Notice the simple past tells us about an event finished in the past and 'away' from 'Now'. The present perfect connects 'Now' with the past — dynamite **has killed** a lot of people between 'Now' and when Nobel invented it.

Grammar Summary

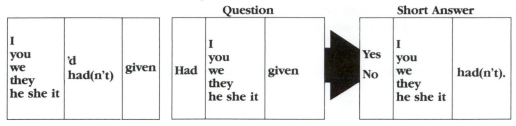

I **hadn't met** him until the meeting last week.

He got the job because he**'d learned** to type.

I**'d** never **seen** snow until I came to England.

We**'d finished** by twelve o'clock.

The speaker is looking back from the past on the earlier past.

Grammar Comment

1. The past perfect talks about what happened **before** a point in the past. Very often we mention that point, for example:

> By last May I **had** only **saved** £500.
> I **had** always **been** afraid of the dark until I went on that course.
> I checked before I left the office and the letter still **hadn't arrived.**
> Before 1988, no one **had** ever **heard** of George Bush.

2. The past perfect is used when we report what someone said:

> He told me that he **had** never **met** anyone as selfish or self-centred. That's why they argued so much.

> The President announced that he **had decided** not to stand for re-election.

3. The past perfect **looks back** from a point in the past to a point **further** in the past. This is similar to the way the present perfect **looks back** at the past from the present.

UNIT 15

Practice 15.1

Underline all the 3rd forms of the verb in the following passage.

> The old man looked at the broken tree. There was sadness in his eyes. There had been a very bad storm during the night. The wind had almost blown the tree down. Branches lay around; the white wood like open wounds without the blood. He thought back to the day when he had planted it . . . many years ago. The tree had grown taller year by year until it had reached almost as high as the roof. He remembered the day his son had climbed up and hidden in the branches — and wouldn't come down. He remembered how the war had come and taken his wife and son from him. The house had burnt down. But the tree had survived. It had reminded him of all those other things. Until last night. What could an old man do now?

Now write the words you have underlined:

1.	5.	9. ....
2.	6.	10. ....
3.	7.	11. ....
4.	8.	12. ....

Practice 15.2

Complete these situations. Number 1 is done for you.

1. I was nervous as I sat in the car waiting for my driving instructor. (drive)

   I had never driven before...

2. I was terrified as we waited for the plane. (fly)

   ....

3. My knees were knocking as I stood up at the wedding. (give a speech)

   ....

4. When I reached the top of the ski lift, I wanted to die. (ski)

   ....

5. As I changed into my tennis things, I wished I'd never agreed to be Martina's partner. (play tennis)

   ....

6. If only I had refused to go to the choir practice! (sing in public)

   ....

Practice 15.3

Last year Peter, who is Danish, met Maria, who is Mexican. They fell in love immediately. There have been many changes in Peter's life. He said, *"I'd never known what love was until I met Maria".*
What else did he say?

1. Mexican food — taste

   I'd never tasted Mexican food until I met Maria.

2. Spanish — speak

   ....

3. Spanish music — listen

   ....

4. Mexico City — visit

   ....

5. The Atlantic — cross

   ....

6. Fall in love

   ....

7. Enjoy life so much

   ....

8. Live abroad

   ....

UNIT 15

Practice 15.4

We often use the past perfect when we write or say what someone said.

> John: *"I went on the bus."*
> **John said he'd gone on the bus.**

Report these statements using the past perfect:

1. Mary: *"I went on my own."*

   Mary said .... on her own.

2. Bill: *"I enjoyed the film a lot."*

   Bill said ....

3. Pete: *"I walked home."*

   Pete said..

4. Diane: *"John gave me a lift."*

   Diane said ....

5. James: *"It cost £50".*

   ....

6. Jean: *"I expected to be on time".*

   ....

7. Brian: *"I thought I was right".*

   ....

8. Liz: *"Mike spoke to me about the problem".*

   ....

9. Mr Black: *"I waited until the shop closed."*

   ....

10. The Policewoman: *"I didn't see exactly who did what."*

    ....

UNIT 16   the future (1)

Grammar Summary

There is no special verb form to talk about the future in English.

We	're going to leave 'll leave 're leaving leave	at seven o'clock tomorrow morning.

All these are correct. They give the same facts. The choice depends on the *reason* the speaker sees for the future event.

(be) going to

					Question				Short Answer	

I	'm (not)		Am	I			I	am. ('m not).
you we they	're (not) are(n't)	going to come	Are	you we they	going to come	Yes No	you we they	are(n't).
he she it	's (not) is(n't)		Is	he she it			he she it	is(n't).

Oh dear, I**'m going to sneeze.**

Look at those clouds – it**'s going to rain.**

She**'s going to change** her job.

There is evidence (*a tickle, clouds*) now for the future event.

What **are** you **going to do** this evening?
▷ I**'m going to watch** the film on TV.

There is a long-term *decision* about the future.

Grammar Comment

English has no one future 'tense'. In Units 16 and 17 you can study 4 different ways to talk about the future:

> **(be) going to**
> **will**
> **present continuous**
> **present simple**

The differences between them are sometimes very small. If you choose the wrong form, people will probably understand what you are trying to say. The best way to understand the differences is to look at, and listen for, lots of examples.

(be) going to is very common in spoken English.

It is the future form which is strongly connected with the moment of speaking. It **looks forward** from that moment. For example:

> Blue sky at last: It**'s going to be** a lovely day.
> Watch out! That parcel**'s going to fall!**
> I've got the flu!
> — Oh no! That means we**'re** all **going to get** it!

In each of these situations, there is a clear reason **now** for talking about the future.

In the following situations the reason is a decision which has already been made before now, and to which attention is now called:

> Jane**'s going to hand** in her resignation at the end of the week.
> We**'re going to fly.** We went by train last year, but it took too long.
> Well, I**'m going to have** a cup of tea. What about you?

UNIT 16

Practice 16.1

Match up the two halves of these sentences:

1. Look at those clouds;
2. Watch out,
3. Be careful of that dog,
4. Oh, Oh, Oh,
5. What a lovely morning,
6. John's eating too much,
7. I'm freezing,
8. Anna isn't very happy,

a. I'm going to sneeze!
b. he's going to get fat.
c. I'm sure she's going to resign.
d. your bag's going to fall!
e. I think it's going to snow.
f. it's going to bite.
g. it's going to be a nice day.
h. it's going to rain.

1	2	3	4	5	6	7	8

Notice, in each case the speakers are thinking of **evidence now** which makes them think of the future events.

Practice 16.2

On January 1st many people in Britain make a New Year Resolution — they promise themselves that they are **going to do** one new thing in the new year — to be a better person. For example, they might say:

I'm going to stop losing my temper.

Look at the pictures and decide what you think these people are going to do. You will need some of these words:

sweets   harder   jogging   give up   haircut   help

1. He's going to give up smoking.   2. ....

3. ....   4. ....

5. ....   6. ....

UNIT 16

Practice 16.3

Richard has been very ill. His doctor has told him he must go abroad for the winter — for at least 6 months — and he must go somewhere warm.

He is taking the following things with him. What is he **going to do?**

1.   A guitar and a "Teach Yourself Guitar' book

   He's going to teach himself to play the guitar.

2.   Lots of writing paper and envelopes

   ....

3.   10 novels by Charles Dickens and 1 by Tolstoy

   ....

4.   A tennis racket

   ....

5.   His swimming trunks

   ....

6.   A map of the area he is going to and a compass

   ....

7.   A cassette recorder and his favourite cassettes

   ....

8.   An alarm clock

   ....

9.   A computerised chess board

   ....

10. A 'Teach Yourself Chinese' course

   ....

Practice 16.4

Use **going to** to write a natural sentence which you might say in each of these situations. Here are some of the words you will need, but you will need other words too.

   late   **run out of**   **have**   **get**   **go to sleep**   **clear up**   **spill**

1.   You are very tired. You need a day off work.

   ....

2.   You're at home, and a bit hungry. You want a sandwich.

   ....

3.   There isn't a garage for 20 kilometres. Your petrol gauge shows 'Empty'.

   ....

4. A friend plans to meet you from the train at 5 o'clock. It is a quarter to 5. You know the journey is certain to take at least another half-hour.

   ....

5. Someone has filled his cup of coffee very full.

   ....

6. Someone is climbing through the window of the house opposite. The people who live there are on holiday.

   ....

7. It's grey, and it's raining, but the clouds are getting higher, and brighter.

   ....

8. It is a warm afternoon at work. You are tired and bored.

   ....

Practice 16.5

Look at these pairs of sentences. In each case one sentence is very common in everyday conversation and the other is very unusual. Cross out the unusual ones. Can you see a pattern in your choices? An explanation is given in the answers.

1. Leave that, I'll carry it for you.
   Leave that, I'm going to carry it for you.

2. I'll see you tomorrow.
   I'm going to see you tomorrow.

3. I've read the report and it seems important so I'll ask the boss about it.
   I've read the report and it seems important so I'm going to ask the boss about it.

4. I'm so far behind with my work that I'll work next Saturday.
   I'm so far behind with my work that I'm going to work next Saturday.

5. This is the third time this has broken. I'll complain.
   This is the third time this has broken. I'm going to complain.

6. I thought I heard the phone but don't worry, I'll answer it.
   I thought I heard the phone but don't worry, I'm going to answer it.

7. I'll post those letters for you if you like.
   I'm going to post those letters for you if you like.

8. I'm so tired I'll go to bed.
   I'm so tired I'm going to go to bed.

Remember **'ll** is usually used for an **immediate decision**, at the moment of speaking, **(be) going to** for a **more definite, longer-term plan or decision.**

Grammar Summary

will, 'll, won't

On the fast train they**'ll arrive** at 8 o'clock.

It looks as if it**'ll be** a nice weekend.

There **won't be** a Christmas party this year.

Something the speaker thinks is certain to happen.

I'm tired. I think I**'ll go** to bed.

Will Maria **be** back soon?
▷ No, she **won't be** back today, but she**'ll be** here all day tomorrow.

What **will** you do?

When **will** you **get** your results?
▷ I **won't know** before the end of August.

The speaker's opinion, or decision or feeling formed at the moment of speaking.

Present continuous

What time **are** you **leaving** tomorrow?
▷ We**'re getting** the 6.50 train.

I**'m working** late every evening next week.

They**'re going** out this evening.

The speaker *knows* because of something which has already happened, usually an arrangement with another person.

Present simple

My birthday **is** on a Wednesday this year.

Christmas Day **falls** on a Sunday this year.

Ramadan **ends** in two weeks time.

Events fixed by the calendar or an official timetable. A fact you can look up.

Grammar Comment

1. **'ll** is very common when making an immediate response to something:

   (The phone rings.)   — I**'ll answer** it.
   (You have a letter to post.)   — I**'ll post** it for you.
   (You need a lift.)   — I**'ll take** you in my car.

2. The present continuous is usual to talk about arrangements for the future; fixed **before** the moment of speaking, but which happen **after** the moment of speaking:

   I**'m leaving** in a few minutes.
   I**'m seeing** the doctor next week.

   Sometimes the difference between this future and **(be) going to** is very small:

   I**'m taking** the car. I**'m going to take** the car.

   This is because there is very little difference in some situations between a decision and an arrangement.

3. The present simple is a less common future form. It is best described as the 'look it up' or the 'objective' future. It is used when the information is factual, and can usually be found in a chart or timetable when anyone can look it up.

UNIT 17

Practice 17.1

Liz and Tom are having an argument. Fill in **will**, **'ll**, or **won't** in their dialogue.

Liz   Why .... you speak to me?

Tom   I just ....!

Liz   I .... tell you why I'm angry if you .... tell me why you're angry.

Tom   Well, I .... tell YOU anything.

Liz   But why .... you?

Tom   Why .... I? You want me to tell you why I .... speak to you!   I .... tell you something, I .... never speak to you again! And that is final!

Liz   I think you ....!

Tom   No, I ....!

Liz   You just have!

Practice 17.2

Fill in the spaces using these verbs with **will**, **'ll** or **won't**.

close   see   give   boil   take   get   open   speak   marry   start   be

1. Maria, I love you. .... me?
   Yes, Steve, I ....

2. Oh, I've never felt as ill in my life!
   Sit down, and I .... the doctor.

3. The lock .... It's completely frozen.
   I .... some water to melt the ice, then.

4. I must be leaving.
   Goodbye, I .... you tomorrow then.

5. Which bus should I get?
   Well, if you get the 8 o'clock, you .... home by 10.

6. When do you think you .... your results?
   I think they .... in the post tomorrow.

7. Bill's not working hard enough.
   OK, I .... to him firmly.

8. Brrr . . . it's cold in here, isn't it?
   Oh, I'm sorry. I .... the window.

9. Why .... you .... me a lift?
   Oh, I'm sorry. Don't you know? My car ....

10. I think there's something wrong with my bike.
    I .... a look at it for you, if you like.

Practice 17.3

Fill in these verbs in this dialogue. The most natural form is the present continuous.

have	hire	play	wait	go	plan	sleep	leave	stay	start

Sheila I thought you started your holiday today.

Rachel No, it's a week today. I'm pretty busy until then. I ....
against Liz in the tennis competition tomorrow morning, then I ....
to the disco tomorrow evening. I .... at my parents
tomorrow night because it finishes after the last bus.

On Sunday I .... for lunch with my parents. We
.... some relatives round for the day.

Sheila What a bore!

Rachel I .... to escape about 4 in the afternoon!
And then I .... my summer holiday on Wednesday. I
.... for the north of Scotland by sleeper that night. I
.... a car when I get there — for a tour of old Scottish
castles.

Sheila I hope the ghosts .... for you!

Look again at the examples — can you see who the 'arrangement' is with in each case?
In every case you can see **why** Rachel knows about the future event.

Practice 17.4

How old must you be to go on holiday with your friends — not your parents? Richard
is 14 years old and wants to go on holiday with a couple of friends from school. His mother
is very worried and has lots of questions to ask him. What are they? The present continuous
is most suitable to ask about Richard's arrangements.

1. Who/you/go with?

   ....

2. Where/you/go?

   ....

3. Why/you/go there?

   ....

4. How/you/get there?

   ....

5. Where/you/stay?

   ....

6. Why/you/not/come with us?

   ....

UNIT 17

Practice 17.5

An itinerary is the detailed plan for a long journey. Here is the itinerary for a trip to Europe by a group of American tourists. They are at the airport and have just met their hostess, Trudy. Fill in the verbs in the present simple in her speech. You will need these verbs:

come   arrive   stay   have   fly   take   leave   spend   touch   go

Sat 3/6:	**Leave Chicago for Paris** **A couple of days sightseeing in Paris**
Tue 6/6:	**Fly to Rome** **2 nights in Rome**
Thu 8/6:	**9 am train to Venice** **2 nights in Venice**
Sat 10/6:	**10 pm flight to Athens** **2 nights in Athens (Hilton)**
Mon 12/6:	**Fly to Vienna late afternoon** **3 nights in Vienna**
Thu 15/6:	**7.30 am flight to London** **3 nights in London**
Sun 18/6:	**11 am flight to Chicago via New York**

Good morning everybody, My name is Trudy and I shall be your hostess for your trip. I just want to give you a few details of our itinerary. Our flight today will take about nine hours and we .... in Paris about 3pm local time. We .... in Paris for 3 nights. Then on Tuesday we .... to Rome on an Air France flight. It .... quite early on Tuesday morning, but I'll give you more details later. Then we .... 2 nights at the Hotel Excelsior in Rome. It's a very comfortable hotel and I'm sure you will enjoy it.

On Thursday we .... the train to Venice. We'll be travelling First Class of course. After Venice we .... to Athens on Alitalia's morning flight. We're staying at the Athens Hilton, by the way. Then we .... the weekend in Athens. I hope you'll all want to join me on Sunday morning when we .... for an early morning walk up to the Acropolis. Then late on Monday afternoon we .... the Olympic Airways flight to Vienna where we .... for 3 nights. I know you'll just love Vienna.

I'm afraid it's an early start on Thursday morning. We .... at 7.30 for London where we .... till the Sunday, and then back home. Today we .... direct to Paris, but when we .... back from London, the plane .... down in New York. I'm sure it's going to be the holiday of your lives, so let's all enjoy ourselves.

Look through and see if you can find other verbs which refer to the future. Why are these **not** also present simple? Look again at the rules.

UNIT 17

Practice 17.6

Answer these questions. You may have to look some of them up.

1. Which day of the week does Christmas Day fall on this year?

   ....

2. On which day of the week is your birthday next year?

   ....

3. When is the next Public Holiday in your country?

   ....

4. How many days does February have next year?

   ....

5. How many days does February have in the year 2000?

   ....

6. When is the next Leap Year?

   ....

Practice 17.7

Here are six sentences and six explanations. Match the explanations with the sentences they best describe. If you find this difficult, look back at the explanations already given.

1. There is evidence now for the future event.

2. There is a long-term decision about the future.

3. Something the speaker thinks is certain to happen.

4. The speaker's opinion, or decision or feeling formed at the moment of speaking.

5. The speaker knows because of something which has already happened, eg a decision.

6 Events fixed by a calendar or an official timetable.

a. I'm sure there **will be** a party at the end of the course.

b. **I'm going to visit** my mother at the weekend.

c. No, I invited YOU. **I'll pay.**

d. Look at the temperature! It**'s going to be** another really hot day.

e. The London train **leaves** in exactly 7 minutes.

f. We**'re moving** house next weekend.

88

Practice 17.8

Choose the correct future verb form to complete the following situations. Use:

> will, 'll, won't
> present continuous (be + -ing)
> present simple

1. A Surprise Letter (**do, find, find, ring**)

   Man Look at this letter. It says we have to move out of the house. They're going to build an office block.

   Wife But what .... ? We have nowhere to go. Where .... somewhere else to live?

   Man Don't worry. We .... somewhere. I .... the landlord tomorrow morning. There must be a mistake.

2. Plans for Saturday evening (**go, have, ring, do**)

   Boy Would you like to come out with me on Saturday evening?

   Girl Saturday? That's a bit of a problem. I .... shopping with a friend all afternoon, and she .... a party that evening. She wants me to go to it. I .... you later and tell you what I .... If I'm free I'd love to go out with you.

3. Ringing the Station (**go, get, have to, arrive, arrive, have to**)

   Man Could you help me? I .... to Exeter tomorrow. Can you tell me when the 11 o'clock .... in?

   Girl Let me see. You .... change on the 11 o'clock. It .... at 1.35.

   Man And the 2 o'clock, when ....?

   Girl Oh, don't get that one. You .... change twice!

4. Love Scene from Film (**meet, play, be**)

   Man I'm leaving you. You don't love me any more.

   Woman How can you think such a thing?

   Man I know you .... that man tonight.

   Woman Tonight I .... cards with my friends.

   Man I heard you on the phone. You are lying. By midnight you .... on the night train to Paris in a First Class Compartment with another man.

   Woman So, the truth is out . . . at last I shall be free . . .

Two future jokes

Will you love me when I'm old and ugly?
— Of course I do!

We're having my Grandmother for Christmas lunch.
— Really, we're having chicken.

Grammar Summary

There is no special form of the verb for the imperative in English.

Mix the flour and the sugar.	Instructions
Take two tablets every four hours.	
Take the second turning on the left.	
Come in, **make** yourselves at home.	Invitations
Please **start, don't wait** for me.	
Open your books, **turn** to page 5 and **look at** the first picture.	Telling someone what to do (instructions or orders)
Hurry up! It's twenty past seven.	
Don't forget to post that letter!	
Don't be late!	
Push.	Signs and notices
Insert 2 × 50p.	
Keep off the grass.	

Note

To suggest doing something together use *Let's*. **Let's** go now or we'll be late.
  Let's take the car.

Two negatives are possible: **Let's not** tell Jenny, she'll only worry.
  Don't let's tell Jenny, she'll only worry.

Grammar Comment

1. There is no special imperative form in English. Where other languages have a special form, English uses the first form of the verb — the infinitive without **to.**

2. A very common use of this form in normal conversation is for friendly invitations:

> **Come** in and **take** your jacket off.
> **Have** another piece of cake.
> Please **don't wait** for me.
> **Enjoy** yourselves.

3. Another common use is to give friendly informal advice:

> **Get** the early train. It's much faster.
> **Speak** to Mary. She'll be able to help.
> **Don't go** alone. It's not really safe.
> **Make** sure you're on time.

4. It is best to learn to use the imperative in situations or functions, rather than as a grammatical form. But remember it is not used, as some older books suggest, for 'giving orders etc.'. It is used for many different functions, most of them much more friendly than 'giving orders'!

UNIT 18

Practice 18.1

Here is a recipe for a simple omelette. Put the following verbs in the correct spaces:

break   make   turn   pour   heat   add   put   beat

.... 2 eggs and .... them in a bowl. .... them and .... salt and pepper to taste. .... a frying pan with a little butter or oil, then .... the egg in. .... sure the bottom of the omelette doesn't burn. .... it over when the bottom is cooked.

Practice 18.2

Have you ever had a puncture while riding your bicycle? If you haven't, here is the way to fix it when it does happen. Put the correct verbs in the spaces.

take   remove   put   be   replace   leave
mark   dry   stick   loosen   fill

.... the outer tyre off one side of the wheel, having of course removed the wheel from the bicycle! .... the valve and .... the inner tube. .... a large bowl full with water. .... the inner tube in the water until you see air bubbles. .... the hole and .... it with white chalk. .... the patch over the hole and .... it under a heavy weight until the repair has set. .... the inner tube on the wheel. .... careful not to make another hole while putting it back on. If you do, you will have to start all over again!

Practice 18.3

Fill in the verbs in the following dialogue.

turn   ask   go   cross
carry on   turn   go

— Excuse me, can you tell me how to get to Lawrence Road, please?

— Yes, certainly. .... straight up here to the traffic lights. .... over and .... up until you come to the roundabout. .... right then .... along as far as the next roundabout. .... left there then first right. Lawrence Road is the second street on the left. .... someone if you get lost, but it's really very easy to find.

— Thank you very much.

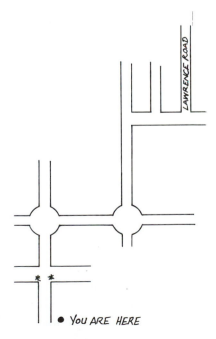

● You ARE HERE

UNIT 18

Practice 18.4

Fill in the verbs used to give invitations or suggestions in this dialogue.

Here are some of the verbs you will need. You will need some of them more than once.
Sometimes you need the negative with **don't**.

**use   come   relax   wait   keep   put   take   be   get
say   tell   make   sit   worry**

John   .... in, both of you. .... your coats off. Now,
.... into the sitting room and I'll get you something to drink. Mary's
just coming . . .

Mary   Hello, it's lovely to see you both. .... in, ... yourselves
at home. .... and .... near the fire, it's a cold evening.
John, ... Carol and Peter something to drink.

Peter   I had some trouble with the car — could I wash my hands, please?

Mary   Of course. The bathroom's upstairs . . . John, ... the light on for Peter
. . . . the green towel, Peter, it's clean.

Peter   Thank you. Now, Carol, ... until I get back before you tell them the
news.

Mary   What news? .... on Carol, ... us everything.

Peter   .... a word until I get back! .... them
guessing — I'll only be a moment . . .

Mary   .... any notice of him. ....
about him! I'm curious so .... us the news.

John   .... impatient. .... for Peter, and
.... until I've got everybody a drink. ...., Carol, you have
all evening to tell us your news.

Practice 18.5

How to make bread
Ingredients:
750g wholemeal flour   1 packet of instant yeast
1 teaspoon salt   1 teaspoon brown sugar
1.2 l. warm water

Complete the recipe, using these verbs:

allow   divide   leave   mix(2)   bake   put   add(2)   remove

The method:

1. .... the flour with the yeast, salt and sugar in a bowl.

2. .... the water. .... together, then .... a little more
    water if necessary.

3. .... the dough into 3 bread tins. .... them to rise.

4. When the dough has risen, ... the tins in a pre-heated oven.

5. .... for 30 minutes at 200°C. Then .... the tins.

6. .... the loaves to cool.

UNIT 18

Practice 18.6

Say all of these in a different way using **Let's not . . .**

1. I don't want Jim to know. (tell)

   ....

2. It doesn't matter how much it costs. (worry)

   ....

3. It's too cold to go swimming.

   ....

4. I can't afford more than £5. (spend)

   ....

In these examples you need **Let's not . . . Let's . . . instead.**

5. wait for the bus — walk.

   ....

6. go to France — go to Spain.

   ....

7. buy her a book — get some flowers.

   ....

8. waste time — get on with it.

   ....

Practice 18.7

The imperative is used for many different functions. Match these examples with the functions:

1. Come in and make yourself at home.
2. Open your books at page 43.
3. Get a number 5 bus; that's direct.
4. Mind the floor - it's wet!
5. Lend me a pound, will you?
6. Turn left at the traffic lights ...
7. Enjoy yourself!
8. Don't forget to post that letter!

a. Giving an instruction
b. Giving directions
c. Warning
d. Making a friendly remark
e. Inviting
f. Making a suggestion
g. Asking for something
h. Reminding

1	2	3	4	5	6	7	8

Grammar Summary

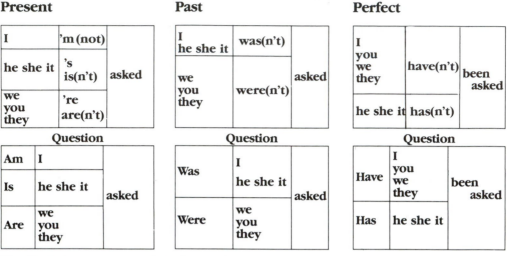

Present

I	'm (not)	
he she it	's is(n't)	asked
we you they	're are(n't)	

Past

I he she it	was(n't)	
we you they	were(n't)	asked

Perfect

I you we they	have(n't)	been asked
he she it	has(n't)	

Question

Am	I	
Is	he she it	asked
Are	we you they	

Question

Was	I he she it	
Were	we you they	asked

Question

Have	I you we they	been asked
Has	he she it	

The **Short Answers** are made in the usual way:
Were they **made** in India?   ▷ **Yes, they were.**
Have you **been offered** the job?   ▷ **No, I haven't**

The passive is usual if *who* did the action is not known, or is not as important as *what* happened. It is also used if "a general group" of people did the action.

These shoes **were made** in Brazil.   It **was opened** by the Queen last year.
Football **is played** all over the world.   The packet **was sent** more than a week ago.
Have you **been invited** to the wedding?   **Has** it **been damaged?**
Has Jill **been told** yet?

Grammar Comment

1. The passive is sometimes presented as an alternative to the active. This is not helpful. We use the passive when it allows us to express our meaning best. The starting-point of a sentence — sometimes called the topic — partly tells us what structure to use. If I talk about my pet dog, I am more likely to start with his name than I am with the car which killed him:

> Rover **was killed** by a car this morning.
> A car killed Rover this morning.

The second sentence is unlikely. When the first word comes into our mind, we have little choice about the structure to follow.
Notice how the passive example in the following pair is more natural:

(A printed sign on a door)   This door **must be kept** locked at all times.
                              You must keep this door locked at all times.

2. Sometimes the passive is the best way to express an idea, for example:

when we do not know who did something:
> He **was killed** in the earthquake.

when the topic of the sentence is less important than what we want to say about it:
> Our teacher **was chased** by a man-eating tiger.

UNIT 19

Practice 19.1

We use the passive in order to bring the topic we are interested in to the beginning of the sentence. In the following pairs, which is the more natural sentence?

1. a. Smoking is not allowed until you are inside the terminal building.
    b. You are not allowed to smoke until you are inside the terminal building.

2. a. The fish served in this restaurant are caught locally.
    b. We catch the fish we serve in this restaurant locally.

3. a. Some things are best left unsaid.
    b. You shouldn't say some things.

4. a. Cameras must be left at the cloakroom.
    b. You must leave your camera at the cloakroom.

5. a. My car is being repaired today.
    b. The garage is repairing my car today.

In each of these pairs, the passive sentence was more natural. Why? Because then the topic of the sentence ('What the sentence is about') comes first, which is an important feature of English.

Practice 19.2

Sometimes you can choose what comes first in a sentence:

Peter paid the bill.

The bill was paid by Peter.

If you want to talk about **Peter** , you will choose the first sentence. If you are talking about **the bill**, then you will choose the second.

Re-write each of these sentences and use a passive.

1. Mrs Jones killed her husband in a fit of anger.
    Mr Jones .... by his .... in a fit of anger.
2. The guerillas killed over 50 people.
    Over 50 people .... the guerillas.
3. The bomb destroyed most of the top floor.
    Most of the top floor .... the bomb.
4. How much did they pay you?
    How much .... you ....?
5. They began the rebuilding in 1975.
    The rebuilding .... in 1975.
6. The police arrested 20 demonstrators.
    ....
7. We finished the job by 10 o'clock.
    ....
8. The police have closed the road to through-traffic.
    The road has ....

UNIT 19

Practice 19.3

Add the verb to the following questions. Add the auxiliary in the short answer.

find   tell   teach   complete   misunderstand

1. Was the building .... in time?

   No, it ....

2. Has Jill been .... about it yet?

   Yes, she ....

3. Were you .... well when you were at school?

   No, I ....

4. Are you often .... when you speak English?

   I'm afraid I ....

5. Has your car been .... yet?

   Yes, thank goodness, it ....

Answer these questions about your own country.

teach   build   give   spoil

6. Are girls .... the same opportunities as boys?

   ....

7. Are foreign languages .... to most students?

   ....

8. Has the countryside been .... by pollution?

   ....

9. Have many motorways ....?

, ...

Practice 19.4

Complete the sentences with these verbs:

build   make   invite   give   send   thank
fix   write   pull down   open

In the later examples you must add an auxiliary too.

1. It was .... in 1937.
2. Were these shoes .... in India?
3. Have you been .... to the wedding?
4. Why haven't you been .... the job?
5. The tickets were .... to you over a week ago.
6. Have you .... for your present yet?
7. Has the TV .... yet?
8. This song .... long before I was born!
9. Our old house .... so that they could build a motorway.
10. Our school .... by the Queen last year.

UNIT 19

Practice 19.5

A volcano has erupted in southern Italy. It had lain dormant for over 200 years until yesterday. Here is the report from last night's 9 o'clock news. Underline all the examples of the passive, then using the report complete the sentences.

> "Here I am standing on top of a pile of rubble. Yesterday it was a school. It seems that over 2000 people have been found so far. Many hundreds more have still to be traced. The volcano erupted just as everyone in this sleepy little town was having breakfast. Some were killed by the blast and the heat. Some were killed when their houses collapsed — they were buried alive in the rubble. Children were killed as they were being driven to school by their parents. Most of the people who died had been born here, and had lived all their lives in this village. The blast was felt 50 miles away. As we look out from this scene of chaos to the beautiful hills and mountains around, it is difficult to believe what has happened. Lives which were happy have been ruined; families which were happy have been split up; a whole community has been destroyed. This is Michael Buck for the 9 o'clock news at the scene of the disaster."

1. Many people have not yet been ....
2. Because so many buildings fell down, lots of people were .... alive.
3. Many of the children were in cars which were being .... by their parents.
4. The effects of the eruption were .... by people living many miles from the scene.
5. The school has been ....
6. Most of the dead were people who had been .... in the area.
7. Because so many families have been .... up, the community has been ....
8. It may be weeks before we know how many people have been ....

Practice 19.6

Sometimes the best way to say what we want to say is to use the active:
> I didn't lose my watch.

And sometimes the best way to say what we mean is to use the passive:
> **It was stolen** by someone at the party.

Write a passive sentence in each of the following examples.

1. Her husband didn't die. (murder)

   ....

2. I didn't jump. (push)

   ....

3. Everyone thinks I resigned, but I didn't. (sack)

   ....

4. I didn't leave, you know. (ask to leave)

   ....

5. People think I taught myself to play the guitar. (teach/by John Williams)

   ....

Practice 19.7

Look at these news items. There are 10 examples of the passive. Underline the passives. Have you found all the examples?

Fire engine crash

A fire engine rushing to a blaze collided with a car in Shepherds Bush Road, Hammersmith, yesterday. One bystander was treated for shock. Another fire crew was sent to tackle the fire.

Birthday bag

An Italian from Santa Cruz, Bolivia, who will be 81 tomorrow, was arrested at Amsterdam airport when customs officers found 6lb of cocaine in a suitcase he was carrying.

Soldier shot

A 23-year-old soldier was shot last night while patrolling the Rosemount area of Londonderry. He was later said to be very seriously ill in hospital. A large force of troops and police moved into the area after the shooting.

£15m relief fund

The Comic Relief concert in February raised £15,816,555 for charity. Eighty per cent went to Africa, half through Oxfam and half through the Save the Children Fund. The rest was spent on other charity projects.

Thief snowballed

Mrs Kathy Weibel, 60, used a snowball to force one of two robbers from escaping on a motorcycle after they raided her village shop, near Lucerne, Switzerland, the Blick newspaper said yesterday. A man was arrested as he tried to escape on foot. — AP

Police magazine tells the story of a recent incident in Llanelli, when PC Dick Williams refused orders from his control room to report to the scene of a hit and run incident. "What do you mean, no?" asked control. Williams replied: "It's me that's been knocked down."

Meat thief eaten

A man who sneaked into a wild animal park near Harare, Zimbabwe, to steal meat was eaten by lions, the Herald newspaper of Harare said yesterday. — AP

Tractor crushes girl in sack

A three-year-old girl who hid in a sack while her mother was picking potatoes was run over by a tractor at a farm near Ramsgate, Kent.

UNIT 19

Practice 19.8

Mrs Smith went out for a while. When she came back she soon realised someone had been in the room. What *has been changed*? Look for eight things which *have been done*. You will need the passive to describe the changes.

1. ....
2. ....
3. ....
4. ....

5. ....
6. ....
7. ....
8. ....

Grammar Summary

Present

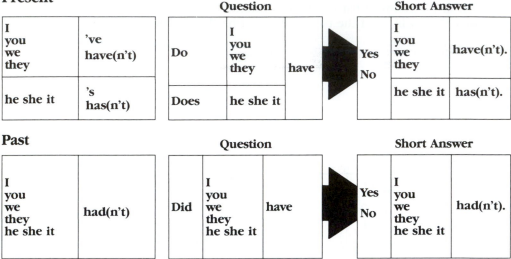

Past

When **(have)** is used as a full verb it makes questions and negatives like all other full verbs.

Did you **have** a good weekend?	Pass time, experience
Have a good trip!	
Are you **having** trouble with that?	
What **do** you usually **have** for breakfast?	Meals, food, drink
Do you **have** lunch at work?	
What shall we **have** for dinner?	
Have you **had** something to drink?	
I'm going to **have** a shower.	With *bath, shower*

Grammar Comment

You can use **have** as a full verb. In this case **(do)** is used to make questions and negatives:

> **Do** you **have** any brothers or sisters?
> We **don't have** enough money.
> I **had** a very bad cold last week.
> — That's funny. So **did** I.

But you can also use **have** as an auxiliary:

> **Have** you seen Mary?

> **Have** you any change?
> — No, I **haven't** I'm afraid.
> — Neither **has** John.

For possession you can say:

> We **have** a cottage in the country.
> We**'ve got** a cottage in the country.

British English uses both, but prefers the second.

100

UNIT 20

Practice 20.1

Put a √ in the right hand column to show how (have) is used in each sentence.

	AUXILIARY	FULL VERB
1. I've got to rush. I'm late already.		
2. Have you got your ticket?		
3. Are you having a holiday this year?		
4. Have you ever been to Paris?		
5. Have you got a new car?		
6. He's having a lot of trouble at work.		
7. I've got an appointment now.		
8. The phone rang while I was having a bath.		
9. You haven't met Zoe, have you?		
10. Have you had something to eat?		

A have joke
What has 6 legs, 4 ears, and a tail.
— A man on a horse.

Practice 20.2

Put part of **(have)** in each of these sentences. Then underline the **group of words** which gives a special expression containing **(have)**. Make sure you know what all the expressions mean.

1. I .... nothing to say. I don't want to discuss it.
2. Let me buy you a drink. What will you ....?
3. Shall we .... something to drink with our lunch?
4. Jack isn't at work today. He rang to say he .... a heavy cold.
5. It's a lovely afternoon. I'm going to .... a walk.
6. I'm sorry he can't come to the phone just now. He .... a bath.
7. We .... a meeting tomorrow evening. I hope you will be there.
8. We .... a party next Saturday. Would you like to come?
9. I .... enough! Stop that noise at once!
10. What's the use of .... money if you don't spend it?
11. I .... the impression he was a bit upset about it.
12. You .... no alternative; you'll have to see the doctor.
13. I .... a friend who I think will be able to help you.
14. I don't want to .... much to eat. I'll just .... a sandwich.
15. Do you .... a single room with bath for two nights, please?
16. I can't come this week. I .... so much to do before I go on holiday.
17. We .... some friends for lunch on Sunday.
18. I .... a lot of trouble with my leg but then I .... an operation and that did the trick.

Notice that **(have)** can be used in many different expressions. It is **not** usually used in British English for "possession". Then, we usually prefer **(have) got.** But if you know the simple rules for **(have)** and you learn the special uses in this practice you will have lots of useful expressions to help your English.

Grammar Summary

Present

I	'm (not)
you we they	're (not) are(n't)
he she it	's is(n't)

Question

Am	I
Are	you we they
Is	he she it

Short Answer

Yes No	I	am. ('m not).
	you we they	are(n't).
	he she it	is(n't).

Past

I he she it	was(n't)
you we they	were(n't)

Question

Was	I he she it
Were	you we they

Short Answer

Yes No	I he she it	was(n't).
	you we they	were(n't).

John **is** four now.
Omar **was** a builder in Iran.

(be) as a full verb

Are you **coming** with us?
He **was doing** 75 when the police stopped him.
Have you **been waiting** long?

(be) as an auxiliary to make continuous verb forms

The bridge **was opened** by the Queen last year.
My car **has been stolen.**

(be) as an auxiliary to make passive verb forms

Grammar Comment

1. Look at these pairs of sentences:

    We**'re not** going.   She**'s not** French.
    We **aren't** going.   She **isn't** French.

    Both forms are possible and correct. The unstressed forms with **isn't** and **aren't** are neutral. By giving **not** its full form, there is a little more stress on it.

2. This difference is also clear in the question forms:

    Are you **not** going?
    Aren't you going?

    The question with the full form of **not**, which would also be stressed, suggests the speaker is surprised that you might **not** be going.

3. Remember how important it is to listen for auxiliaries. In particular, it is important when you hear **'s** to know whether it means **is** or **has**, for example:

    It**'s** arrived. (has)   It**'s** arriving. (is)

4. **(be)** as a full verb can be followed by many different kinds of words:

    He **is** a doctor. (noun)
    She **is** asleep. (adjective)
    There **were** four of us. (number)

    Don't be surprised when you find **(be)** in many different constructions. It is one of the most common verbs in English.

UNIT 21

Practice 21.1

Underline all forms of the verb **to be**:

Teach your baby to read!

This headline has been seen in the newspapers this week. Every parent wants their baby to be a super-baby. It has been suggested that babies are faster and quicker learners than adults believe they are. Babies were usually kept very quiet and some parents used to think that a good baby was a quiet baby. But now parents are told to speak and read a lot to very young children. Now teachers are saying that these children are learning faster than some of their classmates even when the children are as young as three or four years old. So if there is a young baby in your house, start today, and maybe in a few months time the baby will be reading this to you.

How many forms did you find? ....

Practice 21.2

Fill in part of **(be)** in each of the spaces:

What do you want to .... when you grow up? What a silly question to ask a child! But it .... one if the commonest questions adults ask. The child doesn't know what .... possible. He cannot imagine all the different jobs that .... available to him in the modern world — thousands more than .... available to the silly adult asking the question. And how many more different kinds of jobs will there .... by the time the child .... an adult?

The child .... growing up in a world where we can never .... sure what .... round the next corner. And we expect him to .... sure about his or her future. No wonder many children answer, 'lorry driver'!

Practice 21.3

Use **(be)** + one of the words below to complete the sentences. Remember to write the short form of **(be)** where possible.

upset	long	hungry	afraid	funny	thirsty
careful	sleepy	early	exhausted	old	late

1. I'm going to have a sandwich. I'm hungry ....
2. I'm going to bed. I ....
3. I'm sorry I .... The traffic was very bad.
4. Slow down! We .... It doesn't start for another 25 minutes.
5. I .... I think I'll have a coke.
6. Why .... you ....? It isn't dangerous.
7. It's not very difficult. You can do it if you ....
8. He makes me laugh. He .... very ....
9. Last week I .... very .... I heard some very bad news.
10. When we got to the top of the mountain we .... completely ....
11. How .... when you left school?
12. How .... the journey from beginning to end?

Grammar Summary

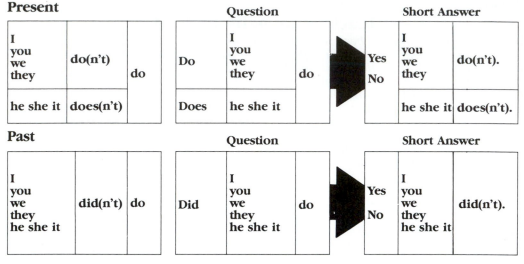

Present

Question

Short Answer

Past

Question

Short Answer

(**do**) is used both as an auxiliary and as a full verb.
The full verb uses are marked in these examples.

Do you **do** your own cooking?
Who is going to **do** the washing?
Paul **did** his homework but Ann didn't **do** hers.
Did you **do** anything exciting at the weekend?

Did you **do** those letters?
▷ I'm afraid I haven't **done** them yet.

What do you **do?**
▷ I'm a nurse.

Grammar Comment

Although (**do**) is used as a full verb, its use as an auxiliary is central to English structure. (**do**) is the one word which makes English structures completely regular. In many basic structures the first auxiliary is very important. The first auxiliary is used:

      to make question forms
      to make negatives
      to make tags
      to add stress
      to give short answers (Yes, it is.)
      to agree (So do I)

Without (**do**) the rules for making these structures would contain many exceptions. By using (**do**), **all** these structures become **totally regular.** This depends on the most powerful rule in English grammar:
      If a structure needs an auxiliary and none is present, use part of (**do**), as a
      so-called "dummy auxiliary."
Understanding how (**do**) works is one of the keys to using English correctly.

UNIT 22

Practice 22.1

Mark ✓ in the column to show when part of the verb **(do)** is used as a full verb or an auxiliary verb.

	AUXILIARY	FULL VERB
1. I do like your new paintings.		
2. Did you finish the washing up?		
3. Did you see the President?		
4. I didn't listen to the radio.		
5. She does the cooking for all the family.		
6. Did you miss the plane?		
7. Why did you send all the letters today?		
8. What did he say to you?		
9. What did you do then?		
10. Have you done anything interesting today?		
11. I didn't like him, did you?		
12. Don't do that!		

Practice 22.2

Most people eat butter, but some **don't.**
Some people hate milk, but most **don't.**

Use one of those patterns to make sentences with these ideas:

1. know how to read and write

   ....

2. like small children

   ....

3. speak another language fluently

   ....

4. read a paper every day

   ....

5. own a television set

   ....

6. enjoy travelling

   ....

7. believe the earth is flat

   ....

8. used to believe the earth was flat

   ....

Practice 22.3

Look at these eight sentences. Change the other sentences in the same way:

a. **I play tennis.**

b. I don't play tennis.

c. Do you play tennis?

d. My brother plays tennis.

e. My sister doesn't play tennis.

f. Does your brother play tennis?

g. We didn't play tennis yesterday.

h. Did you play tennis yesterday.

1. a. I speak German.

b. ....

c. ....

d. ....

e. ....

f. ....

g. ....

h. ....

2. a. I take the train.

b. ....

c. ....

d. ....

e. ....

f. ....

g. ....

h. ....

3. a. I visit her.

b. ....

c. ....

d. ....

e. ....

f. ....

g. ....

h. ....

Practice 22.4

Use part of (**do**) in each of these examples.

1. I've got a lot to .... at work today. We're very busy at the moment.

2. I'm quite good at the theory but I can't .... anything practical at all.

3. If you .... the cooking, I promise I'll .... the washing-up.

4. I'd like to give you a little present. It's the least I can .... after all the help you've given me.

5. I don't know why Jack comes to work — he just sits there all day .... nothing.

6. His mother's a dentist, but I don't know what his father ....

7. The Government .... a lot for the elderly in the last few years.

8. Did you .... French at school?

9. I .... everything I can think of; I have no idea what else I can .... But I don't think anybody could .... more than I ....

10. What on earth .... here! I thought you were in Australia.

Now underline the special expressions which contain part of (**do**).

UNIT 22

Practice 22.5

The do's and don'ts of snakes.
Everyone is afraid of being bitten by a snake.

Here are the 8 **Do's** and **Don'ts** — to avoid being bitten. Which are the **Do's** and which are the **Don'ts**?
Write **Do** or **Don't** in the spaces.

1. .... watch where you step — especially in the forest. Many people are bitten when they stand on a snake by accident.

2. .... leave food and drink lying around your camp site. A hungry snake is an angry snake!

3. .... be particularly careful at night.

4. .... try to play with a snake or try to touch it.

5. .... try to touch a baby animal. Parents become very dangerous if someone tries to take their young away.

6. .... stay calm if you see a snake. Snakes sense when you are frightened.

7. .... make a loud noise or move suddenly. That will make a snake very aggressive.

8. .... treat snakes and all other animals with respect.

Practice 22.6

Here is a short text about the importance of **(do)** in English grammar. Fill in parts of **(do)** in the spaces.

Quite simply, 'do' is the most important word in English. This is very interesting because on its own it .... mean very much. Although it .... have much meaning, it .... play an important part in English grammar. Without .... you can't ask your friend if he plays tennis. Without .... you can't ask him if he played yesterday. And without .... you can't ask him if his friend plays. In short, asking questions becomes impossible without a part of 'do'.

When you want to talk about what you .... , or what you .... yesterday, this little word is important again. Of course, 'don't' and .... mean exactly the same thing — the only difference is that .... is used with he, she, and it. And in the past 'did' and '.............................' are used without changing.

You can agree with something by saying, 'So .... I' in the present, or 'So .... I' in the past. If someone says to you, 'I love China', you can respond to them, '............................. you!' to show you're surprised.

We could go on discussing all the uses of 'do' for a very long time. The lesson is clear: if you .... know how to use 'do' in English, you can't begin to speak. But .... worry if you make mistakes. It's most important to speak without worrying about making mistakes.

Practice 22.7

Complete the following with part of (do):

1. .... ask Philip to .... the cooking. He burns everything!

2. I'm a mechanic. What .... you ....?

3. So you went to London on Saturday! .... you .... anything nice?

4. Are you going to have time .... the shopping before the shops close?

5. I .... my homework but no one else in the class had .... theirs.

6. You can watch TV when you .... your homework.

7. .... well at school doesn't mean you'll get a good job.

8. Philip lives at No. 13. I'm sure he ....

Practice 22.8

Fill in part of (do) in the following jokes.

1. .... you hear about the man who jumped off a bridge in Paris?

   —He went insane.

   (insane-mad; in the Seine)

2. Why .... birds fly south in winter?

   — It's too far to walk.

3. **Man** Doctor, I think I'm a cat.

   Doctor When .... this feeling start?

   Man When I was a kitten.

4. I'm glad I wasn't born in France.

   — Why .... you think that?

   I .... speak French!

5. **Boy** I went to the dentist yesterday.

   Teacher .... your tooth still hurt?

   Boy I .... know. The dentist kept it.

6. **Girl** What's your dog's name?

   Boy I .... know. He won't tell me.

7. Yesterday my sister threw pepper in my face.

   — What .... you ....?

   I sneezed!

8. .... you hear about the man who was so mean he kept a fork in the sugar bowl?

9. Excuse me, ... you know the quickest way to the station?

— Yes, run!

10. Why .... Henry put a frog in his sister's bed?

— Because he couldn't catch a mouse!

11. How .... you stop yourself dying?

— Stay in the living room!

12. **Policeman**   Why .... you drive up that one-way street?

   Driver   I only went one way.

   Policeman   Why .... you see the arrows?

   Driver   Arrows? I .... even see any Indians!

13. How .... a vet look in a lion's mouth?

— Very carefully!

14. **Mum**   Why .... you go to Pete's party?

   Son   The invitation said 7-10 and I'm 11.

15. .... your digital watch tell the time?

— No, I have to look at it!

16. Waiter, waiter! There's a fly in my soup!

   .... worry, Sir. The spider on your bread will get it!

17. Waiter, waiter! .... you have frogs' legs?

   No, sir. I've always walked like this.

18. **Mum**   What is the difference between a cow and a letter box?

   Son   I .... know.

   Mum   Well, if you .... know, I'm not going to ask you to post this letter.

19. **Boy**   My cat sleeps with me at night.

   Girl   Ooh, that's not healthy.

   Boy   I know, but it .... mind.

20. What .... one ghost say to the other ghost?

   — .... you believe in people?

Grammar Summary

1. Modals are never about facts.

2. They are about the speaker's or listener's opinion *at the moment of speaking*.

> *David has long hair* is about David. It is a fact.
> *David must get his hair cut* is about David. It is also about the *speaker's opinion*.

> Questions with a modal are about the *listener's opinion:*
> *What should I do?* (= What do *you* think is the best thing to do?)

3. They can refer to past time or future time.

I **could ride** a bike when I was five.	Past time
I **could come** tomorrow.	Future time
You **must speak** French. (I know you took lessons).	Past time
If you're going to live in France you **must speak** French.	Future time
(You'll have to learn).	

Grammar Comment

1. The modal auxiliaries never use (**do**) to make questions or negatives: for example, *don't can* *doesn't must* are impossible.
Making questions and negatives with the modals is very simple.

Questions: Change the order of the subject and the first auxiliary.
He can come at 6 o'clock.
— **Can he** come at 6 o'clock?

Negatives: Add **n't** or **not** after the first auxiliary.
We should arrive before them.
— **We shouldn't** arrive before them.

2. Each modal has its own special meaning. They all have one idea in common. They do not express pure facts. Instead, they express the **speaker's** attitude, opinion, or judgement. Study the differences in the following pairs:

Helen is French.	This is a fact.
Helen **must** be French.	I think she is.
We leave at 6.	This is a fact.
We **must** leave at 6.	I have decided this.
It's mine.	This is a fact.
It **might** be mine.	This is my opinion.
You've left it at home.	This is a fact.
You **may** have left it at home.	This is an opinion.

In questions they ask for the opinion or judgement of the **listener.**

UNIT 23

Practice 23.1

Here is a list of the modal auxiliaries:

can could may might shall should will would must

Often more than one will fit into a sentence, but with different meanings, of course. Sometimes a particular auxiliary seems the most natural or most frequent, even if others are possible. Which is most likely in these examples?

1. If your finger isn't getting better you .... go to see the doctor.

2. He's a very good worker. Nobody .... work harder than he does.

3. It's been lovely to see you again. You and your wife .... come and have dinner with us some time soon.

4. I .... come tomorrow but I think it .... be better to wait until next week.

5. I'm sure nobody .... mind if you don't come but I think it .... be a good idea to send a little note.

6. It .... rain but I think it .... be all right at least until six o'clock.

7. .... we have a cup of tea?
   — Good idea! But .... I make it because I know you want to finish that this evening.

8. .... you change a pound?
   — I don't think I've got any change but I .... have. Let's see.

9. Come on, we .... hurry. We .... get there in time but I don't think so.

Practice 23.2

Here is the list of modal auxiliaries again:

can could may might shall should will would must

See how many of them you can fit into each of these sentences to make natural, correct English. Don't be surprised if there is more than one possibility for each sentence.

1. .... I bring a friend with me tomorrow?
2. I wonder if the weather forecast is on after the news. I think it .... be.
3. Where do you think they were going when we saw them last night?
   — I don't know, but they .... have been going to the concert.
4. People are putting their umbrellas up — it .... be raining again.
5. That's the second person who has told me, so I suppose it .... be true.
6. Nobody .... say a word!
7. Everyone was so surprised that nobody .... say a word.
8. Why are there so many children around town.
   — It .... be the school holiday; I'm not sure.
9. .... you give me a ring tomorrow, please?

How many did you fit in each case? Write the numbers here:

1. ....   4. ....   7. ....
2. ....   5. ....   8. ....
3. ....   6. ....   9. ....

Grammar Summary

Can always refers to different kinds of possibility.

Can you **come** round on Friday evening? ▷I'm afraid I **can't** manage Friday.	Possibility
Can you **tell** me the way to the Post Office, please? ▷ I'm sorry I **can't**. I'm a stranger here.	
Can you **drive?** ▷ Yes, I **can**.	
You **can't** park on a double yellow line.	Possibility decided by law or rules
Can I leave work early today please?	
Can we bring the children with us?	
Can you pass the salt please?	Requests (*Is it possible for you to . . . ?*)
Can you give me a hand with this please?	
Can I get a ticket for you?	Offers (*Is it possible for me to . . . for you?*)
Can we give you a lift?	
You **can't** be hungry. You've just had a big lunch.	Deduction – logical possibility. Always with *can't* (negative)
Anna **can't** have gone home. Her bag's still here.	

Grammar Comment

1. At a deep level there is a single meaning for each modal auxiliary. All uses of **can** refer to different kinds of possibility. But, if you are learning English it is often best to learn particular uses of the auxiliary like those listed in the Grammar Summary. It will help you to remember them if you learn one or two memorable sentences by heart so you can use them as 'pegs' to help you notice and use other similar examples.

2. Talking about ability and permission are the two most common uses of **can**:

           Can you swim?   **Can** I come later?
           — No, I **can't**.   — Yes, of course, you **can**.

   Can is more common than **may** to ask for permission.

3. **Can't** and **cannot** are similar in meaning: **can't** is the normal form in spoken English.

4. The opposite of **can't** where it refers to what is logically possible is **must**:

           You **can't** be hungry. You've just had dinner.
           You **must** be hungry. You had no lunch.

UNIT 24

Practice 24.1

What can they do? Use these verbs:

swim   ski   ride a bike   windsurf   sing   cook   play tennis   fly   talk

1. ..He can fly..........   2. ....   3. ....

4. ....   5. ....   6. ....

7. ....   8. ....   9. ....

Practice 24.2

Add **can** or **can't** to the short answers to these questions:

1. Can you dive?   No, I .can't.......   5. Can you speak Russian? No, ...
2. Can he come?   Yes, he ....   6. Can they hear us?   Yes, ...
3. Can he play?   No, ...   7. Can you spell it?   No, ...
4. Can she make it?   Yes, ...   8. Can anyone spell it?   Yes, John ....

Now answer the following questions about yourself. Tell the truth. Use **Yes, I can** or **No, I can't.**

9. Can you remember when you were 3 years old?

....

10. Can you ride a bike?

....

11. Can you stand on your head?

....

12. Can you speak 3 languages?

....

13. Can you remember which shoe you put on first this morning?

....

14. Can you remember the names of all your cousins?

....

113

UNIT 24

Practice 24.3

What questions would you ask:

1.   if you want to pay by credit card.

   ....

2.   if it is possible to dial direct to (your country).

   ....

3.   if it is possible to use the same ticket on the buses and the underground.

   ....

4.   if it is possible to change your ticket to a later flight.

   ....

5.   if I know how to use a word-processor.

   ....

6.   if I need help (with a heavy suitcase).

   ....

7.   if I am willing to lend you a pound.

   ....

8.   if I know how to read German.

   ....

9.   if I am free to baby-sit for you.

   ....

Notice **can** is used:
   a.   for possibility
   b.   for requests
   c.   for offers

Which way is it used in each of the examples above? Fill in this table.

1	2	3	4	5	6	7	8	9

Practice 24.4

Look at this example:

   John's jacket is still here. He **can't have** left.

Using the words in the column, complete these sentences:

1.   You've just had a huge meal.   (hungry)

   You ....

2.   I think I heard him speaking German.   (French)

   He ....

114

3. You've done nothing all day.   (tired)

You ....

4. He's just had another accident!   (very careful)

He ....

5. Well, she still hasn't arrived.   (coming)

She ....

6. There's no reply when you ring them.   (at home)

They ....

Practice 24.5

Look at these sentences. Each one contains **can.** Is it possible to replace **can** with **could?** Sometimes you might need to change the other words in the sentence too.

1. I can play table tennis.

2. Can you pass the butter, please?

3. I can come tomorrow if you like.

4. Can I give you a hand with that? It looks very heavy.

5. Is that Stan over there? I don't think it can be, he's taller than that.

6. Can I come in with my dirty shoes on?

7. Can I arrive a bit late tomorrow, please?

8. You can't be tired. You haven't done anything all day!

9. Can I give you a lift to the station?

10. You can only post a parcel at the Post Office in England.

11. I don't know where my pen is. I can't find it anywhere. Can I have left it at home this morning?

12. Can you drive?

13. Can you drive us home? I don't feel very well.

14. Sorry, this can't be my bag — mine's brown.

See if you can decide which use of **can** occurs in each of the examples. You will probably be able to see why in a few cases you cannot replace **can** with **could,** but in most cases it is possible, although the meaning is usually a little different.

A terrible joke
What kind of cans are there in Mexico?
— MexiCANS!

Grammar Summary

Could, like *can,* is about possibility. *Could* is more *remote* than *can;* remote relationships (polite requests), remote in time, or more remote logical possibility.

Could I speak to Hilary, please?	Polite requests
Could I have six of those oranges, please?	

Gerda **could** read when she was four.	Possibility in the past
Could you get a seat on the train?	
▷ I'm afraid we **couldn't.** It was very crowded.	
We **couldn't** find anywhere to park.	
You **couldn't** change money without your passport.	

Is that Carol over there?	In these examples *could* is similar
▷ I'm not sure – it **could** be.	in meaning to *might.* Logical possibility;
Do you think Paul **could** have gone home already?	something *might* be true.
You **could** have left it on the bus.	
I'm sure you **couldn't** have left it on the bus.	
Take a sweater. It **could** turn cold later.	

Grammar Comment

It is not helpful to think of **could** as the past tense of **can.** Modal auxiliaries do not have tenses like full verbs. **Could** can refer to the past, the present, or the future:

The Past

I **could** read much faster when I was younger.
Nobody **could** come yesterday.
(could = was able)

The Present

Could you pass the butter, please?
Could I have another, please?
(polite requests)

It **could** be John's.
He **could** be seriously ill.
(could = remote possibility)

The Future

You **could** kill two birds with one stone.
He **could** make a lot of money if he sold the picture.
(could = would be able to)

The use of **could** in polite requests is, perhaps, the most important when you speak English.

UNIT 25

Practice 25.1

Fill in **could** or **couldn't** in this dialogue.

Pete Bob asked if he .... come to our party this Friday.

Dave But we didn't invite him!

Pete I know! But what .... I say? I .... say to him, 'We don't like you and that's why we haven't invited you!'

Dave No, I can see you .... say that!

Pete I had to say 'yes'. What else .... I do?

Dave You .... have said that you would have to speak to me first!

Pete I ....! He asked me in front of Jane. I had no choice. I just .... get out of it.

Dave I know. I just wish we .... do something about him. He is so rude!

Practice 25.2

Dave is one of those people who can't make up his mind. Other people always have to suggest what he does. Make suggestions in these situations.

1. Flying is much too expensive. (take the train)

    ....

2. But food on trains is usually awful. (take your own)

    ....

3. But I can't sleep on trains. (book a sleeper)

    ....

4. I'll get bored on such a long journey. (some good books)

    ....

5. I don't like travelling alone. (ask a friend)

    ....

6. I'm not looking forward to this holiday. (stay at home)

    ....

Practice 25.3

Look at these two sentences:

> Jim **could** play the piano when he was 4 years old. Mary **couldn't** read until she was 6.
> In the first, **could** means 'was able to'. In the second **couldn't** means 'wasn't able to'.

Here some facts about the lives of Jim and Mary. Fill in the spaces.

1. Jim started to speak when he was 18 months old.

    Jim .... when he was 2 years old.

2. Mary started to speak much later — when she was 3.

    Mary .... until she was 3.

3. Jim learned to play the piano very quickly.

    Jim .... when he was 4.

4. Mary was slow at learning to read.

    Mary .... until she was 8.

5. Mary didn't learn to swim until she was 23!

    Mary .... until she was 23!

Write something true about yourself:

I could .... when I was ...., but I

couldn't .... until I was ....

117

Grammar Summary

You **may** have dropped it in the supermarket.   Likely, but not certain. (1)

I'd take a coat – it **may** turn cold later.

I **may** not have time to phone you this evening.

Do you think it was John we saw earlier?
▷ It **may** have been, I'm not sure.

May I borrow your dictionary for a moment, please?   Asking for permission. (2)

May we have a few days to think about it?

Note
Mayn't is very unusual: *may not* is usually used.

Grammar Comment

When asking or giving permission **can** is more common than **may**:

       May I leave early? — Certainly, you **may**.
       Can I leave early? — Certainly, you **can**.

This use of **may** is now very formal and mostly used by elderly people.
When a British child asks his mother:

       Can I have some sweets?

It is an old-fashioned mother who replies:

       Of course you **can**, but you **may** not.
       (You are able to, but I am not allowing it.)

However, there is very little difference in meaning in the following:

       The umbrella **may** belong to Mario.
       The umbrella **might** belong to Mario.
       The umbrella **could** belong to Mario.

You could add **possibly**, or **perhaps** to all these sentences.

When you make them negative, **may not** and **might not** are again very similar, but **could not** means that the umbrella is definitely not Mario's.

UNIT 26

Practice 26.1

Decide whether to use **may, can,** or **can't** in these examples.

1.   You .... come, but you .... not want to.

2.   Let's talk now. I .... not have time to phone you this evening.

3.   Was that Alex?

     — It .... have been. I'm not sure.

4.   .... you show me the way out, please?

5.   You .... be hungry! Not after that huge meal!

6.   I'll have to go back to the shops. I think I .... have left my purse in

     the supermarket.

7.   Are there any jobs in your firm, Pete?

     — Mmmm . . . there .... be.

8.   If I were you, I'd take an umbrella. They said it .... rain later.

9.   .... you pass the sugar, please?

10. Very often you .... use 'can' and 'may' with very similar meanings.

     In fact, some people hardly ever use '.............................'. at all. When they ask for

     permission, they always use '.............................'. Of course, some parents are rather

     old-fashioned and they insist on children making a difference. So, if their child asks,

     'Can I have another cake?', the parent answers, 'Can! Of course you

     .... , but you .... not!'

Practice 26.2

Look at these sentences:

a.   You may have dropped it in the supermarket.
     (It is possible that . . . .)

b.   You may come in now.
     (Permission)

Which of the following sentences are like **a** and which like **b**?

a	b

1.   He may come with us if he asks first.

2.   I may not be able to ring you till later.

3.   May I open the window?

4.   It may have been the wind.

5.   May I borrow your grammar book?

6.   I think it may rain. Look at those clouds.

7.   He may still be waiting for you!

8.   You may have a week to think it over, but then I would like a
     decision.

119

Grammar Summary

I don't feel very well.
▷ It **might** be something you've eaten.

Where are you going for your holidays?
▷ I'm not sure; we **might** go to Scotland.

I'm surprised Chris isn't here yet. Do you think he **might** have forgotten?

I'm leaving early tomorrow so I **might** not see you.

Is this a 24 bus coming?
▷ It **might** be. I can't see the number yet.

Likely, but not certain.
Similar to *may*.

Note
Mightn't is unusual.

Grammar Comment

1. In spoken English **might** is more common than **may** to express uncertainty:
        Are you coming to the party.
        — I don't know. I **might.** I'll see.

        Are you going abroad again this summer?
        — We **might.** On the other hand, we **might** stay at home.

    Might is very common when the subject is **I** or **we.** When the subject is **he, she, it, they,** the uncertainty can be expressed by **might** or **could:**
        Is that Sandy over there?
        — I don't know. | It **could** be.
                         | It **might** be.

    The difference between **might** and **could** is clear from this situation:
        Will Mary be back in the office today?
        — She said she **might** be, but she wasn't sure.
        (There was a possibility of her finishing in time to return.)
        — She said she **could** be, if we ask her.
        (It was possible for her to change her arrangements.)

2. Study and compare the following ways of expressing **might + not.**
        I **might not** be back in time for dinner.
        I **don't think I'll** be back in time for dinner.
        I **probably won't** be back in time for dinner.
    The differences of meaning in these three sentences are very small.

UNIT 27

Practice 27.1

It **might** be John   means   **Perhaps it is John.**

It **might** have been John   means   **Perhaps it was John.**

Re-write these sentences using **might.**

1. Perhaps Pete is coming.

   ....

2. Perhaps it will rain.

   ....

3. Perhaps I'll be sick if we go by boat.

   ....

4. Perhaps she is right.

   ....

5. Perhaps that was the doorbell.

   ....

6. Perhaps we were wrong.

   ....

Practice 27.2

Complete the following using **might**, and other auxiliaries in each case.

1. Has the 7.25 arrived yet?

   — It .... Why don't you ask at the ticket office?

2. Is there a loo here?

   — There .... On the first floor, I think.

3. Have you got change for a five pound note.

   — I .... Let me see . . .

4. Are you going to university?

   — I .... It depends on my exam results.

5. Can you pick me up after work?

   — I .... But it depends when

   I finish.

6. Has it stopped raining?

   — It .... I'll go and check.

7. Do you know if there's a 12 o'clock bus on Saturdays.

   — There .... I know there is on Sundays.

8. Do I have to change trains?

   — I think you .... , but ask at the station.

Practice 27.3

Study these pairs of sentences. 3 of the pairs are very similar in meaning. 2 of the pairs have totally different meanings. Which are similar? Which are different?

1. John could have done it.
   John might have done it.

2. I couldn't buy it.
   I might not buy it.

3. Take a scarf. It could get cold later on.
   Take a scarf. It might get cold later.

4. I could have lost my wallet in the supermarket.
   I might have lost my wallet in the supermarket.

5. He could have gone to China with his company.
   He might have gone to China with his company.

Similar ....   **Different** ....

Grammar Summary

will + n't = won't

Will you sign the form, please?	Asking someone to do something
Will you phone me when you arrive?	*(Will you . . .?)*
I **will** if I have time.	Agreeing
I'**ll** give you a hand with that.	Offering to do something for someone
We'**ll** do the washing-up.	
She **won't** tell me where she's going tonight.	Refusing
I **won't** work on that machine. It's dangerous.	
Molly's car **won't** start.	
The baby **won't** stop crying.	
We **won't** see you next week. We'**ll** be on holiday.	Facts about the future
I'**ll** be back in a few minutes.	
Wait a minute! I'**ll** just get a sweater.	Immediate decisions at the moment of speaking
That's the doorbell – It'**ll** be John.	
I'**ll** have pizza and salad, please.	
You'**ll** catch the train if you leave now.	Likely conditions, see page 236.
You **won't** be happy if you don't buy it!	

Note
Will not is very strong. In speech the normal form is *won't*.

Grammar Comment

1. If you have learned that **will** is "the" Future in English, look again at units 16 and 17. **Will** is only **one** of several ways of talking about the future.

2. Remember that '**ll** and **won't** are the normal neutral forms in spoken English. **Will** or **won't** fully stressed sound very strong. Study the differences between:

   > I'll invite Jim.
   > I **will** invite Jim.

   The first is the normal form in friendly conversation. The second could be said in the middle of an argument.

   > We won't be coming.
   > We **won't** be coming.

   Again, the second is very strong; it could be said in an argument.

3. A key idea in understanding how **will** is used is that it often expresses a response to a situation or to what someone has said:

(I have too many bags.)	**Will** you carry this for me, please?
(I need your signature).	**Will** you sign this, please?
(A problem with the car.)	It **won't** start.
(A problem with the baby.)	She **won't** go to sleep.
(You are leaving.)	I'**ll** see you later.
(Going on holiday.)	'Bye. I'**ll** send you a card.

UNIT 28

Practice 28.1

Full or short form? Fill in **will** or **'ll** in the spaces.

1. Shall we go to the fair?

   — I .... if you ....

2. I .... get the shopping.

   — Do you think you

   .... have enough time?

3. Who .... be there?

   — I won't, but my brother ....

4. I .... ring if I can't come.

   — And so .... I.

5. You won't tell anyone, ... you.

   — I .... tell no one!

6. Hang on! I .... just go back for my jacket.

   — You .... miss the train if you do!

   — I .... catch a cold if I don't.

Practice 28.2

Sue has lots of problems. They won't go away! Match up the following half-sentences.

1. The children won't
2. The tap won't
3. The door won't
4. The dog won't
5. The baby won't
6. Sue's headache won't

a. close properly.
b. stop barking.
c. do what they're told.
d. go away.
e. go to sleep.
f. stop dripping.

Practice 28.3

If the speaker reacts to something at the moment of speaking the verb often contains **'ll**.
(The phone rings) ◆**I'll** answer it!
I don't feel well. ◆**I'll** get you a glass of water.

Write the reactions with **'ll** in these examples:

1. It's very warm in here, isn't it? (window)

   ....

2. Oh dear, I forgot to post these letters. (for you)

   ....

3. I've forgotten my dictionary. (lend)

   ....

4. I'm really thirsty. (make a cup of tea)

   ....

In the following, the speaker **sees** something, and reacts to it with a sentence containing **'ll.**

5. If you do that again, ... (scream)

6. Don't worry about getting home, ... (a lift)

7. Your hands are full. Don't worry .... (open)the door for you.

8. Well .... then, ... in a few days. (be off, be in touch)

Notice that when the speaker decides on something **at the exact moment of speaking**, as a reaction to something the speaker sees or hears, **'ll** is the most common verb form. Other forms used for future time are more associated with **earlier** planning or arrangements.

123

Grammar Summary

Shall we pick you up at the station?	Offering to do something
Shall I get a ticket for you?	
Shall we go for a walk after lunch?	Suggestions
Who **shall** we ask to the party?	
What **shall** we do about it?	

Note

Shall is unusual in modern English except in questions with *Shall I . . . ?* and *Shall we . . . ?*

Grammar Comment

Many old books gave the rule that **will** and **shall** are similar, and that you use **shall** with **I** and **we** and **will** with the other pronouns. It is true that **shall** is very often used with **I** and **we.**

These situations show that there is an important difference between **shall** and **will** and both can be used with all the pronouns (**I, he,** etc).

> When **will** I arrive?
> (You are booking a plane ticket. You are asking about a fact; *objective* information)
> When **shall** I arrive?
> (You are asking your host about a party. You are asking for an opinion, *subjective* information.)

We use **will** to talk about a simple, objective idea in the future. We use **shall** to express a personal, subjective view of the future event.

When a group of protesters sing the popular protest song *We shall overcome,* they are expressing their personal commitment: the world will change *because of us.* There would be no personal commitment if the words were *We will overcome.*

Think about the following pairs and how the speaker is more personally involved in the situations where **shall** is used.

> I'll give you a hand. (a normal offer of help)
> I **shall** give you a hand. (I insist)
>
> We'll see them tomorrow. (factual)
> We **shall** see them tomorrow. (I have decided.)

UNIT 29

Practice 29.1

Which is the natural sentence in each situation?

1. Making an offer:
a. Shall I help you?
b. Will I help you?

2. Making a suggestion:
a. Shall we get a taxi?
b. Will we get a taxi?

3. Asking for something:
a. Shall you open the window, please?
b. Will you open the window, please?

4. Reacting to something:
a. If that's the phone, I shall answer it.
b. If that's the phone, I'll answer it.

5. I don't feel very well.
a. — I shall get you a glass of water.
b. — I will get you a glass of water.
c. — I'll get you a glass of water.

We can see a simple rule from these examples:
Use **shall** to make **offers** and **suggestions.**
Use **will** to **ask** someone to do something.
Use **'ll** for **reactions** at the moment of speaking.

Practice 29.2

Find the correct question in the box for each of the situations below.

Shall	I	help you with your luggage? call the doctor for you? bring some sandwiches? open the window, please? get me a coffee, please? dance?
	we	
Will	you	have an ice-cream? give me a lift? get a ticket for you? leave before it gets busy?

1. ....
— Oh yes, let's. I hate crowds.

2. ....
— Good idea! It's very hot, isn't it?

3. ....
— I've been waiting for you to ask!

4. ....
— No, I think I'll be all right, thanks.

5. ....
— Certainly. Do you take sugar?

6. ....
— Yes please. Can I give you the money now?

7. ....
— Oh, please. This is so heavy.

8. ....
— Certainly. It's my turn.

9. ....
— No, it's all right. I'll bring some for you.

10. ....
— I'm sorry, but I haven't got my car.

Grammar Summary

Would you drop me at the station please?	Requests
Would you mind closing the window please?	
Would you mind if I came a few minutes late?	
Would you like a cup of tea?	Offers and invitations
Would you like to come with us?	
▷ That's very kind of you. I'd love to.	
Would you like some more cake?	
▷ No thank you, I'm fine but it's very nice.	
What **would** be the best thing to do?	Advice
What **would** you do?	
▷ If I were you I'd see the doctor.	
They **wouldn't** stop the noise even when I asked.	Refusing
My car **wouldn't** start this morning.	
I don't know what was wrong with the baby, but she **wouldn't** stop crying.	
You **wouldn't** enjoy the film, I don't think.	Talking about a hypothetical situation
Shall I bring my sleeping bag?	
▷ That **would** help.	

Grammar Comment

1. **Would** is a very important word in English conversation:

Would you like a coffee.	**Would** you mind?
Yes, **I'd** love one.	**Would** it matter?
Mmm, so **would** I.	**Would** she come?

2. **Would** is also important in written English, especially in business correspondence:

   We **would** be obliged if you would send us . . .
   We **would** appreciate your reaction.

3. In statements in spoken English **'d** is the normal form. Be careful not to mix up **would** and **had**:

   I'd love to. = **would**
   I'd met him. = **had**

   It is important in conversation to learn to listen so that you know when **'d** means **would** and when it means **had.** You must hear clearly before you can respond:

He**'d** like to come.	— Oh, **would** he?
He**'d** come.	— Oh, **had** he?

4. **Would** is often thought of as the conditional in English. This is not helpful. We often use it in sentences with 'if', but **would** is almost never used in the 'if — clause'. For example, *If it would rain* is impossible. See Unit 69.

UNIT 30

Practice 30.1

Match up the following questions containing **Would you like ....?** and answers.

1. Would you like a coffee?
2. Would you like some more?
3. Would you like to come with us?
4. Would you like me to pick you up?

a. — No, thank you. I've had enough.
b. — Thank you. I'd love one.
c. — Yes thank you. That's very kind of you.
d. — Yes thank you. I'd love to.

1	2	3	4

Practice 30.2

Match up the following requests, containing **Would you mind ....?** and responses.

1. Would you mind if I had a look at your paper?
2. Would you mind moving your bags, please?
3. Would you mind if I left early?
4. Would you mind holding this for me, please?

a. — Oh, certainly.
b. — Not at all, go ahead.
c. — Oh, sorry, I didn't realise.
d. — Well, actually, I'd rather you didn't. There's still a lot to do.

1	2	3	4

Practice 30.3

What would you do?
You are on the 25th floor of an office block. A fire has broken out on the 13th floor. Smoke is coming under your door. Everyone around you is shouting. Nobody knows what to do. Here are some possibilities. Write them using **I'd.**

1. close the door and wait to be rescued

....

2. go up to the top floor and wait for a helicopter

....

3. start going down the stairs

....

4. hang out of the window and scream

....

5. start praying and keep calm

....

What would **you** do?

....

What **wouldn't** you do?

....

UNIT 30

Practice 30.4

Look at these two sentences:

I'd prefer a cup of tea.　　　　　**I'd prefer** to leave now.
I'd rather have a cup of tea.　　　**I'd rather** leave now.

They are very similar in meaning and can be used in similar situations.
Notice when a verb follows **prefer** you need to use **to** .
Re-write the following.

1.　I'd prefer to get the earlier bus.

　　...

2.　I'd rather have a sandwich.

　　...

3.　We'd rather have a meal.

　　...

4.　I'd rather speak to the manager.

　　...

5.　Who'd prefer tea?

　　...

6.　I'd prefer to fly.

　　...

Practice 30.5

Answer each of the following remarks with **That would be ....** and an adjective.
Choose the adjective from this list:

lovely　surprising　awful　annoying　ridiculous

1.　Would you like a cup of tea?

　　...

2.　I'm not taking any money with me, I'm just going to use my credit cards.

　　...

3.　I've heard Jack's getting married, even though he's still only 17.

　　...

4.　I think we're too late. We're going to miss the train.

　　...

5.　If the Americans get control of the company, I'm sure I'll lose my job.

　　...

Practice 30.6

Use **would** and another verb to complete these sentences.
Here are the verbs you need:

drive   stop   take   read   go   object   get   be   please   help

1. We could take the car, then the journey .... about an hour.

2. Let's get her some flowers. I'm sure that .... her.

3. You could write to him but it .... quicker to phone.

4. I .... you to the station but I'm afraid I'm in an awful hurry.

5. I .... a ticket for you too, but I haven't enough money.

6. I'm sure nobody .... if you left a bit early.

7. I .... smoking but I get so nervous if I don't have a cigarette.

8. I'm sure they .... if I asked them but I think I can manage on my own.

9. I .... to Spain if I could speak Spanish, but I can't.

10. This letter's much too long — nobody .... such a long letter.

Practice 30.7

Re-arrange the words to make a correct sentence.

1. like coffee cup you of a would.

   ....

2. I you it like don't think would.

   ....

3. you my what in do position would.

   ....

4. an help aspirin perhaps would.

   ....

5. you I if mind came would.

   ....

6. they you let in why wouldn't

   ....

7. I I you that do were if would.

   ....

8. they know nobody would would.

   ....

Grammar Summary

You **should** tell the police about it.

I think you **should** go to the doctor.
▷ Perhaps I **should.**

If you don't feel better you **should** go to bed.

The train **should** be there by four o'clock.

Excuse me, I think it **should** be £2, not £3.

You **should** have told me that you don't eat meat.

Kurt **shouldn't** have left without paying.

The *speaker's* view of the correct situation, or thing to do.

Do you think I **should** tell Peter?

What do you think I **should** do?

Asking the *listener's* view of the correct thing to do.

Note
Questions with *Should I/we . . .?* are unusual; *Do you think I/we should . . . ?* is the usual form.

Grammar Comment

Should expresses what the speaker thinks is necessary:

> You **should** learn Russian.
> We **should** leave by 9 o'clock.
> You **should** send her a card.

Should is weaker and more personal than **must, have to,** or **ought to.** For this reason, it is very common in spoken English.
Should can be used to express:

An opinion	— They **should** close that road.
Advice	— You **should** stop seeing her.
Negative Advice	— You **shouldn't** go out without a coat.
Strong Moral Ideas	— We **should** help handicapped people.

Because **should** expresses a very personal opinion, it is often introduced by **I think** or **I don't think**:

> I think women **should** get equal pay.
> I think you **should** ask him to marry you.
> I don't think they **should** behave like that.

Should and **shouldn't** sound natural in tag questions:

> They **shouldn't** let it happen, **should they?**
> I **should** get my ticket early, **shouldn't I?**

UNIT 31

Practice 31.1

We very often use **should** and **shouldn't** to tell other people what to do — to give advice. What advice will you give in these situations:

1. My car's been stolen!

   (ring the police)

   ....

2. Peter still has my book.

   (ask for it back)

   ....

3. I bought this pen today and it doesn't work.

   (take it back)

   ....

4. I have a terrible cough.

   (smoke so much)

   ....

5. My eyes are very sore.

   (read so much)

   ....

6. My wife is annoyed with me.

   (work so late at night)

   ....

7. I'm getting fat.

   (eat so much)

   ....

8. I don't earn very much.

   (ask for a rise)

   ....

9. I feel tired and depressed.

   (have a holiday)

   ....

10. The video I bought two months ago won't work.

    (complain to the maker)

    ....

11. My children waste so much money!

    (give them so much)

    ....

12. My life is terrible!

    (complain so much)

    ....

Grammar Summary

I you we they he she it	ought (not) to	take

Question forms are very unusual (see below).

I **ought to** ring my mother.

You **ought to** phone your parents.

What do you think we **ought to** do about it?

People **ought not to** park here – it's dangerous.

Obligation (usually moral)

Note

Oughtn't is unusual; the usual form is *ought not*.

Questions like *Ought we to . . . . ?* are very unusual; the usual form is *Do you think we ought to . . . ?*

Grammar Comment

1. If you feel you **ought to** do something, you have a feeling of strong moral obligation:

    > I **ought to** write to Peter.
    > We **ought to** return that book.

    This means that when you tell someone what they **ought to** do, it can sound very strong:

    > You **ought to** wear a tie.
    > You **ought to** come on Saturday.

    You will sound friendlier if you introduce your suggestion:

    > I think you **ought to** . . .
    > I wonder if you **ought to** . . .

2. Because **oughtn't** is such a rare form, we use:

    > I **don't think you ought to** . . .

    or   You **shouldn't** . . .

3. To ask a question use:

    > What do you think we **ought to** do?
    > Who do you think we **ought to** tell?

    Alternatively, use **should:**

    > What **should** we do?

    Should is much more common that **ought to.**

UNIT 32

Practice 32.1

Here are five statements which most people would agree with. Add one word to each to make sense. You may need to use your dictionary.

fined   imprisoned   banned   punished   abolished

1. Terrorists ought to be severely ....
2. Countries which continue to kill whales ought to be heavily ....
3. Apartheid ought to be ....
4. Drug dealers ought to be .... for a long time.
5. People who drink and drive ought to be .... from driving.

Practice 32.2

Fill in **should** or **ought** in the following situations. Sometimes you might need a negative.

1. What .... we do about that window.
   — We .... to get someone to mend it!
2. I think we .... ask Mary round for tea.
   — I think we .... to, but I don't want to!
3. The Government .... to do something about unemployment.
   — I agree. Somebody .... to do something!
4. You really .... to go to the doctor, you know.
   — Yes, perhaps I ....
5. Who .... to be the next Prime Minister?
   — Well, I know who it .... to be, but I don't think he will win.
6. .... we ring Jim or can we just turn up?
   — Well, I suppose we .... to, but let's just turn up!
7. What do you think I .... do?
   — Well, I know what you .... to do, but I'm not sure if you'll agree!
8. You .... to complain to your boss.
   — Yes, I know I ...., but if I do, I think I'll lose my job.
   Then you .... be working there!

Practice 32.3

Arrange these words to make natural sentences.

1. he I to go ought think

   ....
2. you that to said have ought not

   ....
3. we you her to do tell think ought?

   ....
4. do do to it we you about what ought think?

   ....

Grammar Summary

I **must** remember to post this letter.	The speaker's view of what is necessary
You **must** read this book – it's really good.	
She **mustn't** go out until she's better.	
When **must** we be there?	Asking for the listener's view of what is necessary
Must you **make** so much noise?	
I don't know her age but she **must** be over 60.	Deduction, logically necessary
You **must** be tired after such a long journey.	
This **must** be the right road.	

Grammar Comment

Must always involves the speaker's opinion (in statements) or the listener's opinion (in questions).

Must expresses necessity. In statements the speaker feels that something is necessary. Questions ask for the listener's opinion about necessity.

> You **must** see The Tower of London.
> (I think it is necessary for visitors to see The Tower. It is a 'must' for any visitor to London.)
> She **must** be a foreigner.
> (She has a foreign accent so it is logically necessary for her to be a foreigner.)

Because **must** is a modal, its point of view is in the present:

> I **must** have my hair cut. (ie soon)
> I **must** be going. (ie immediately)

When we want to talk about necessity in the past, we use **had to**:

> I **had to** go on the later bus.
> We **had to** have coffee without sugar.

The basic meanings of **must** and **have to** are very similar. The main difference is the source of authority:

> **Must** = personal, subjective, opinion about what is necessary
> **Have to** = objective authority for what is necessary

For example:

> I **must** be there by 7 o'clock.
> (I don't want to keep them waiting.)
> I **have to** get the 8.30 train.
> (The 8.45 will be too late. I'll miss my plane.)

UNIT 33

Practice 33.1

Match up the sentences.

1. You must remember to brush your teeth.
2. You must be exhausted after the trip.
3. This must be the right road.
4. You must fill in this form first.
5. You mustn't go out until you're better.
6. Must you make so much noise?
7. I really must find something cheaper.
8. You mustn't disturb me.

a. This is too expensive.
b. If you don't, you'll have to go to the dentist.
c. I am very busy.
d. If you do, you might get worse.
e. Sit down and relax.
f. Try to be a bit quieter.
g. You can't do anything until it is completed.
h. There is no other way.

1	2	3	4	5	6	7	8

Practice 33.2

Look at this conversation:
> I'm sure I heard that lady speaking German.
> — Then she can't be French.

Notice that you can say She **must** be German.
or She **can't** be French.

It is **not** possible to say *She mustn't be French*.
Fill in **must** or **can't** in the following conversations.

1. I heard her talking about going to Zurich.
   — Then she .... be Swiss.
2. The ball was OUT, Mr McEnroe!
   — You .... be serious!
3. I'm thinking of emigrating to Australia.
   — You .... be joking!
4. That man went into the Director's office.
   — Then he .... have been the director!
5. Just look at the puddles.
   — Oh, it .... have been raining quite heavily.
6. Hello, my name's William Shakespeare.
   — You .... be. You died 300 years ago.
7. Sheila's putting her coat on.
   — Then she .... be leaving early.
8. They haven't sold many tickets for the concert.
   — Then it .... be worth going to.

Practice 33.3

Fill in **must** and **mustn't** in each of the following pairs:

1. a. You .... remember to ring when you get home.
   b. You .... forget to ring when you get home.
2. a. You .... go home without seeking Buckingham Palace.
   b. You .... visit Buckingham Palace while you're in London.
3. a. If we come, we really .... leave by 11 o'clock.
   b. If we come, we really .... stay later than 11 o'clock.
4. a. I .... let another day go by without writing to say thank you.
   b. I .... write to say thank you.

135

Grammar Summary

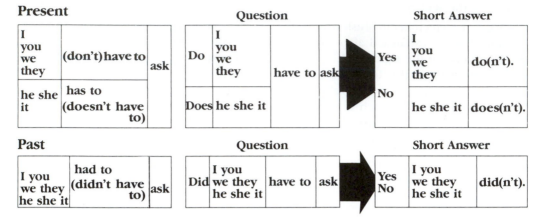

Present

I you we they	(don't) have to	ask
he she it	has to (doesn't have to)	

Question

Do	I you we they	have to	ask
Does	he she it		

Short Answer

Yes	I you we they	do(n't).
No	he she it	does(n't).

Past

I you we they he she it	had to (didn't have to)	ask

Question

Did	I you we they he she it	have to	ask

Short Answer

Yes No	I you we they he she it	did(n't).

Children over 14 **have to** pay full price.
The doctor says he **has to** stay in bed.
Did you **have to** wait long?
You **have to** be at the airport very early
because they **have to** search all the bags.

Necessity based on:
a rule
an authority
circumstances

'll have to

We'**ll have to** paint the house before we sell it.

We'**ll have to** go or we'll miss the last bus.

It's broken – you'**ll have to** buy a new one.

I'm afraid she'**ll have to** go into hospital.

The speaker's idea of
something necessary

Grammar Comment

The difference between **have to** and **'ll have to** is almost identical to the difference
between **have to** and **must**.
Have to expresses what is objectively necessary. **Must** and **'ll** involve the judgement
of the speaker, so there is very little difference in meaning between:

     I'**ll have to** go now.
     I **must** go now.

They are both used at the end of a meeting as a sign that you were on the point of
going. If you say:

     I **have to** go now.

the meaning is that there is a reason beyond your control which forces you to leave;
perhaps you have another meeting; your train is about to leave etc.

UNIT 34

Practice 34.1

Fay never reads notices. What will you say to her in these situations. You need **have to** in each situation.

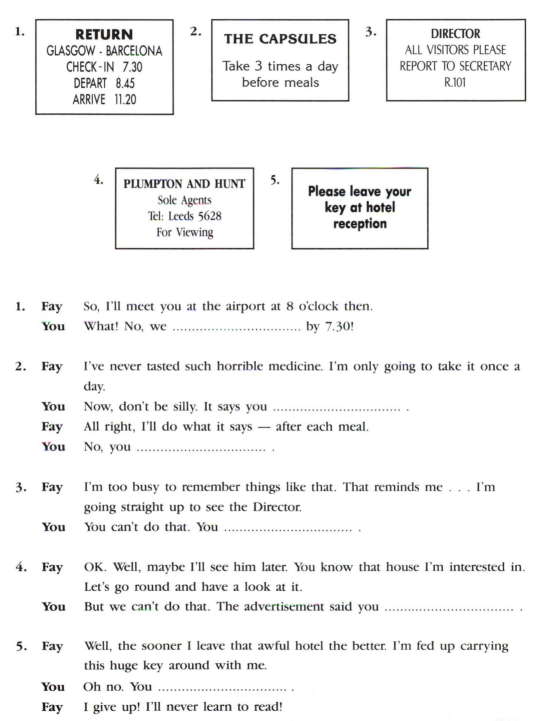

1.

RETURN
GLASGOW - BARCELONA
CHECK-IN 7.30
DEPART 8.45
ARRIVE 11.20

2.

THE CAPSULES
Take 3 times a day
before meals

3.

DIRECTOR
ALL VISITORS PLEASE
REPORT TO SECRETARY
R.101

4.

PLUMPTON AND HUNT
Sole Agents
Tel: Leeds 5628
For Viewing

5.

Please leave your key at hotel reception

1. **Fay** So, I'll meet you at the airport at 8 o'clock then.

   You What! No, we .... by 7.30!

2. **Fay** I've never tasted such horrible medicine. I'm only going to take it once a day.

   You Now, don't be silly. It says you ....

   Fay All right, I'll do what it says — after each meal.

   You No, you ....

3. **Fay** I'm too busy to remember things like that. That reminds me . . . I'm going straight up to see the Director.

   You You can't do that. You ....

4. **Fay** OK. Well, maybe I'll see him later. You know that house I'm interested in. Let's go round and have a look at it.

   You But we can't do that. The advertisement said you ....

5. **Fay** Well, the sooner I leave that awful hotel the better. I'm fed up carrying this huge key around with me.

   You Oh no. You ....

   Fay I give up! I'll never learn to read!

UNIT 34

Practice 34.2

Complete the following dialogues using **(have) to.**

1. .... you .... get a visa to go to Finland?
   — No, you don't, but you .... get one for Poland.

2. .... you .... fill in a form before you got your money back?
   — Yes, we ...., but at least we .... wait long before we got it.

3. How much .... you .... earn before you start paying tax in your country?
   — Everyone .... pay tax. It doesn't matter how little you earn!

4. When we flew to Rome last year, John .... pay full fare — and he's only 6.
   — Really, we only .... pay half fare for Rachel, but she was only 4 at the time.

5. What grades .... you .... get before you got into university?
   — They said I .... get two A's and a B, but they gave me a place with one A and two B's.

Practice 34.3

Must and **have to** are close in meaning. **Must** and **'ll have to** are even closer in meaning. The addition of **'ll** means that the speaker's judgement is involved. This is also true of **must**, but not true of **have to** on its own.

Re-write these sentences using **'ll have to.**

1. I must reply to that letter today.
   I'll have to reply to that letter today.

2. I must stop for petrol pretty soon.
   ....

3. You must give me your telephone number.
   ....

4. That boy must start behaving himself.
   ....

5. We must get her a present for her birthday.
   ....

6. You must work harder if you want to pass.
   ....

7. You're very tired. You must have a few days off.
   ....

8. I must buy myself a new watch — this is slow again!
   ....

Notice that it is necessary to use **'ll have to** in these sentences to keep the same meaning as **must**. If you use only **have to**, the meaning can be different. For example:

You must give me your telephone number.
You'll have to give me your telephone number.
= friendly ways to ask for someone's number.

You have to give me your telephone number.
= You are obliged to give me it. This sounds like a policeman.

UNIT 34

Practice 34.4

The difference between **must** and **have to** is very small; **have to** is used for **objective** necessity — perhaps what someone else, or some institution, thinks is necessary; **must** is used for what **the speaker** thinks is necessary.

We **have to** be there by 4.	Suggests that the doors are closed at 4 o'clock.
We **must** be there by 4.	Suggests that **I think** all the seats will be taken by 4 — so we'd better get there on time.

Link up these pairs of sentences with their possible meanings.

1. **a.** I must get my hair cut.
   b. I have to get my hair cut.

   x. I'm going for an interview and everyone tells me that I should look smart.
   y. I feel that my hair is too long.

2. **a.** We must start looking for a new house.
   b. We have to start looking for a new house.

   x. We are tired of our old house and feel we want a change.
   y. Our house is going to be demolished, because a new motorway is being built.

3. **a.** I must have a drink of water.
   b. I have to have a drink of water.

   x. I feel thirsty.
   y. The doctor has told me to drink more water.

4. **a.** I really must do something about the garden.
   b. I have to do something about the garden.

   x. The local authority have warned me to tidy my garden.
   y. I feel I should tidy up the garden.

5. **a.** We must do something about the dog.
   b. We have to do something about our dog.

   x. The police have warned us that if we don't control our dog better, they will take it away.
   y. We must look after our dog better.

6. **a.** We must do something about terrorism.
   b. We have to do something about terrorism.

   x. Unless we do something quickly, there will be a disaster. Every country in the world agrees about this.
   y. I feel strongly that something ought to be done.

7. **a.** It must be right.
   b. It has to be right.

   x. I think it is right from what I can see.
   y. We cannot finish it until it is totally clear that it is right.

8. **a.** You must wear a tie.
   b. You have to wear a tie.

   x. They won't let you in unless you wear a tie.
   y. I think you should wear a tie.

Grammar Comment

In Units 33 and 34 we have seen that the difference between **must** and **have to** can be very small:

> He **must** pay the bill.
> He **has to** pay the bill.

When we make these same sentences negative, by adding **n't** or **doesn't**, there is a great difference in meaning between **mustn't** and **doesn't have to**:

> He **mustn't** pay the bill.
> (It is **necessary** that he does **not** pay the bill.
> — under no circumstances should he pay the bill.)
> He **doesn't have to** pay the bill.
> (It is **not necessary** for him to pay the bill.
> — he can pay it if he likes, but if he does not pay it, that is fine.)
>
> **mustn't** = It is **necessary** to **not** do something.
> **don't have to** = It is **not necessary** to do something.

Here are some more examples:

> You **mustn't** drive without a licence. It's against the law.
> You **don't have to** drive; you could walk.
>
> You **mustn't** get the 10 o'clock train. It doesn't stop at the airport.
> You **don't have to** get the 9.45 train. You could get the 9.55 and still arrive in time.

With **mustn't** you have no choice. With **don't have to** you have a choice.

Can you choose the correct verb in these situations?

a. You are trying to park in a very busy street. You see a parking place, but your friend turns to you and says, "That's the doctor's house. You .... park there. Look, there's a sign telling you not to."

b. You have been invited to a Fancy Dress Party. Some people you know are going in fancy dress. Others are going in their normal clothes. You .... wear fancy dress.

c. You are visiting a famous church. There is a sign outside saying, "No photographs, please." You .... leave your camera outside the church, but you .... take any photographs inside.

You should have chosen **a. mustn't** (it is necessary to not park there) **b. don't have to** (it is not necessary) **c. don't have to, mustn't.**
If you did not choose correctly, read the comment carefully, again.

UNIT 35

Practice 35.1

Look carefully at the pictures. Complete the dialogues with **don't have to** or **mustn't.**


```
PARTY
at Steve's flat
come about 7.30
```

```
DANGER POISON
Do NOT drink
```

1. I don't want to be late for the party. I'm going to try to get there for 7.

— No, you .... be there till 7.30.

2. Mmmm...this looks interesting. I think I'll see what it tastes like.

— No, you ....!


```
FREE buses to town
WAIT HERE
```

```
DRY CLEAN ONLY
```

3. I haven't got any money. I can't get the bus into town.

— But you .... pay on this bus.

4. This jumper is filthy. I think I'll wash it.

— No, you .... wash it. It has to be dry cleaned.


```
DO NOT walk on
the grass
```

```
Walk in.
No appointment
necessary
```

5. This is a lovely part of the park. Let's have a game of football.

— No, we ....

6. I'd like to have a check-up. I think I'll ring the dentist.

— No, you ....

7. I'm fed up waiting for these lights to change. I think I'll just go.

— No, don't. You ....

8. Can Peter go to school today, doctor?

— No, Mrs Smith, he ....

UNIT 35

Practice 35.2

Here are a set of school rules. Fill in **mustn't** or **don't have to** in the sentences below.

> **Jeans are not allowed.**
> **Smoking is strictly prohibited.**
> **Pupils may wear either grey or white shirts.**
> **Shoes may be either black or brown.**
> **School ties are obligatory at all times.**
> **In summer pupils may choose tennis or swimming,**
> **and in winter, football or cross-country running.**
> **There is to be no running in corridors.**
> **No food may be taken into classrooms.**

1. You .... eat in class.
2. You .... play tennis in summer.
3. You .... wear jeans at any time.
4. You .... wear grey shirts.
5. You ....wear white or grey shoes, but you .... wear black. You may wear brown if you wish.
6. You .... be seen without a school tie at any time.
7. You .... smoke. Of course, this only applies to pupils!
8. You .... run in corridors.
9. In school rules 'you ....' is more common than 'you may' or 'you ....'!

Practice 35.3

Dick and Mary are getting ready for a visit to Dick's mother. They are going to be late if they don't hurry up.
Fill in **mustn't** and **don't have to** in this dialogue.

Mary   Hurry up! It's a quarter past! We really .... be late.

Dick   I know. You've already told me five times! You .... tell me again.

Mary   I'm sorry. Do we have to take a present?

Dick   We ...., but I think it would be nice. What about stopping for some chocolates on the way.

Mary   Oh no! We .... waste any more time. We're going to be late as it is.

Dick   Well, how about a bunch of flowers?

Mary   You mean, that bunch you gave me yesterday?

Dick   Yes, why not? If we give her your flowers, we........................ waste any money and we .... waste any time. How about it?

Mary   The answer is NO. They're my flowers. You bought them for me. We .... buy her a present. It's more important to arrive on time than to have a present. We .... be late, whatever we do!

UNIT 35

Practice 35.4

Link up the first part of these sentences with the second part:

1.	You don't have to be French	a.	to get your name in the paper.
2.	You don't have to be rich	b.	to understand Shakespeare.
3.	You don't have to be famous	c.	to appreciate Wimbledon.
4.	You don't have to be English	d.	to enjoy eating garlic.
5.	You don't have to play tennis	e.	to be able to tell jokes.
6.	You don't have to be a comedian	f.	to go abroad on holiday.
7.	You don't have to be Japanese	g.	to enjoy classical music.
8.	You don't have to play an instrument	h.	to be able to use chopsticks.

1	2	3	4	5	6	7	8

Practice 35.5

Pair up these remarks and responses. You will first of all have to complete the responses with either **mustn't** or **don't have to**.

1.	Shall I bring something to eat?	a.	Well, you .... let it worry you.
2.	I'm going to the hospital tomorrow.	b.	Well, they .... lend you anything.
3.	It's Mum's birthday on Tuesday.	c.	Well you .... have a credit card.
4.	I'm spending too much again.	d.	You can, but you ....
5.	I don't care whether I pass or not.	e.	You .... say things like that!
6.	My parents won't lend me enough.	f.	I know. I .... forget!

Now complete this sentence in a natural way:

7. You .... buy me a present but you .... forget to send me a card!

143

Grammar Summary

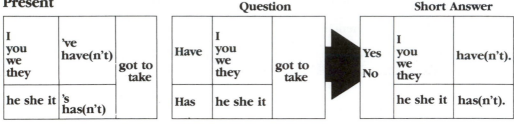

Present			**Question**				**Short Answer**		
I you we they	've have(n't)	got to take	Have	I you we they	got to take	→	Yes No	I you we they	have(n't).
he she it	's has(n't)		Has	he she it				he she it	has(n't).

He**'s got to** stay in bed for a few days.

You**'ve got to** put two 10 pence coins in to make it work.

I **haven't got to** get up early in the morning.

Sorry I can't stop – I**'ve got to** get to the bank before half past three.

Have we **got to** show our passports?

Note

(have) to and *(have) got to* are used with the same meaning.
had got to is unusual in the past; *had to* is normally used.

Grammar Comment

1. Study the following pairs:

   I **have to** go.   He **has to** pass the exam.
   I**'ve got to** go.   He**'s got to** pass the exam.

   Have got to is a common alternative to **have to** in spoken English. The question and negative forms are less common:

   Have they **got to** sell their house?
   They **haven't got to** do it.

   It is more common to say:

   Do they **have to** sell their house?
   They **don't have to** do it.

2. Questions with **you** are more common than questions with **he, she, it, we, they**:

   Have you **got to** work on Saturday?

3. In the past, **had to** is more common than **had got to**:

   We **had to** have a meeting yesterday.
   We**'d got to** have a meeting yesterday.

   Sentences with **had got to** stress the obligation and are used when you are not happy with what **'had got to'** happen. For example:

   We were told we**'d got to** be there by 7 in the morning!
   They said we**'d got to** pay an extra £30!

4. The negative **hadn't got to** is very rare. You can always use part of **(have) to** in situations where **(have) got to** is possible.

UNIT 36

Practice 36.1

Here are some sentences using **(have) got to**. The words are mixed up. Put them in the correct order.

1. believed/got/seen/it's/to be/to be

    ....

2. you've/you've/go/go/to/to/got/got/if

    ....

3. tonight/got/what/you/to do/have

    ....

4. to/bank/before/to get/got/the/they/I've/close

    ....

Practice 36.2

Look at this dialogue:

When have I got to be there by?
— You**'ve got to be** there by 6.

Answer the following questions with the words given.

1. When have we got to be at the station?
    You/before 7.30

    ....

2. When has John got to get up?
    He/by 8 o'clock

    ....

3. How long have I got to stay in bed?
    You/until the fever has gone

    ....

4. When has it got to be finished by?
    It/tomorrow afternoon

    ....

5. When have we got to buy the tickets?
    You/at least two weeks before departure

    ....

6. How many pills have you got to take?
    I/two in the morning and three at night

    ....

7. How long have we got to wait?
    You/for the Leeds train to arrive

    ....

Grammar Summary

(have) is not normally used to talk about possession; *(have) got* is normally used.
(have) got makes questions and negatives using *(have)* as auxiliary.
had got is unusual in the past; *had* is normally used.

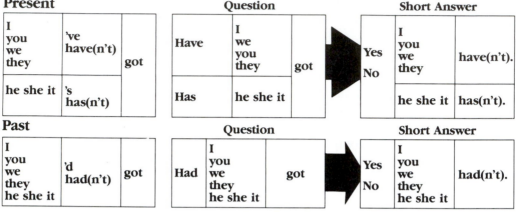

We **haven't got** a phone.   Possession
Anna**'s got** dark hair and blue eyes.
Have you **got** change for a pound please?
▷ I'm afraid I **haven't**.
They **hadn't got** any apples so I bought
some pears instead.

Have you **got** a free evening next week?   Certain expressions of time
Excuse me, **have** you **got** a minute please?
Have you **got** an appointment?

Grammar Comment

In British English all the following sentences are possible and natural:

We have a cottage in the country.   Do you have one?
We**'ve got** a cottage in the country.   **Have** you **got** one?

They don't have much money.   Don't you have any money?
They **haven't got** much money.   **Haven't** they **got** any money?

British English often prefers the forms with **have got** in spoken English.
In written English **have got** is rare.

American English prefers the forms with the verb (**have**).

In the past tense British English prefers (**have**):

We **had** a cat until last month.
We **had** a flat in the south of Spain until last year.
I knew I **didn't have** any idea where I was.
They **didn't have** anywhere to live.

The **had got** forms in the past are rare, because they usually express a strong idea or
contrast:

He **had got** Malaria at the time.
We **had got** a cat in those days.

UNIT 37

Practice 37.1

Use **(have) got** to complete these sentences:

1. Maria .... long dark hair.

2. I .... a car, but I .... a bike.

3. He .... 8 sisters and 4 brothers!

4. What's the matter? .... you
   .... a headache?

5. I'm afraid you can't see the Director
   unless you .... an appointment.

6. Excuse me, ... you
   .... change for the phone?

7. I .... a meeting this evening.

8. I wish I didn't have a meeting. I
   .... so much to do at home.

9. You .... a lovely car, but I'm sure
   you .... a big petrol bill, too!

10. We .... any children so we
    can go on holiday when we like.

11. .... you .... a phone?

12. A lot of people in the Third World
    .... enough to eat.

Practice 37.2

Answer these questions about yourself. Use **Yes, I have** or **No, I haven't**.

1. Have you got a phone? ....

2. Have you got a car? ....

3. Have you got a driving licence? ....

4. Have you got a video? ....

5. Have you got any English money? ....

6. Have you got fair hair? ....

7. Have you got green eyes? ....

8. Have you got lots of friends? ....

9. Have you got a British friend? ....

10. Have you got good taste? ....

11. Have you got a bad temper? ....

12. Have you got a good English accent? ....

A 'Have Got' Joke
My girlfriend is one of twins.
— How can you tell the difference?
Her brother's got a beard!

UNIT 37

Practice 37.3

Use **(have) got** with one of these expressions to say each of the examples in a natural way.
an appointment   the time   a minute to spare   a cold   my number

1.   Are you in a hurry?

   ....

2.   Is the dentist expecting you?

   ....

3.   Do you know how to phone me?

   ....

4.   Aren't you well?

   ....

5.   What time is it?

   ....

Practice 37.4

Complete the following dialogues using **(have) got.** Use short forms where possible.

1.   Why are you bending down? (stone in my shoe)

   ....

2.   Why aren't you coming out? (a cold)

   ....

3.   Why isn't Jane here? (flu)

   ....

4.   Have you finished your letters? (2 still to write)

   ....

5.   Does your sister have a family? (2 boys and a girl)

   ....

6.   What kind of car does he have? (a Mini and an Audi)

   ....

7.   These flowers look lovely. (a beautiful smell)

   ....

8.   What an enormous flat! (6 rooms)

   ....

9.   You look as if you have plenty of money! (enough)

   ....

10.   Most people don't know what to do with their money. (too much)

   ....

Practice 37.5

Here are two people. They are very different. One is very poor and the other is very rich. Complete the sentences below the pictures. Use **(have) got.**

1. She .... lots of money.

2. He .... lots of friends.

3. She .... a house in the country and a flat in town.

4. He .... nowhere to live.

5. She .... two children.

6. He .... a big family.

7. She .... plenty to eat.

8. He .... anything to eat.

9. Her country .... too much food.

10. His country .... too many people and not enough to feed them with.

11. Her children .... lots to look forward to.

12. His children .... much to look forward to.

13. She .... two television sets.

14. He .... enough water to stay alive.

UNIT 38   (be) used to, (get) used to

Grammar Summary

I'm **used to** getting up early.

He's **not used to** driving on the left.

We **aren't used to** very hot weather in England.

To talk about what is normal

How's your new job?
▷ Oh I'm **getting used to** it, thank you.

Have you **got used to** our winters yet?
▷ I'm **getting used to** them, slowly!

I **was** just **getting used to** my old job
when they moved me.

I don't like this new medicine.
▷ Don't worry. I'm sure you'**ll** soon **get used to** it.

To talk about the process of changing
to a new normal situation

Note
(be) used to and *(get) used to* use these patterns:

He	**isn't** **hasn't got**	**used to**	his new job yet. it. living in London.	(noun) (pronoun) (. . . *ing* form)

used to + first form, *I used to live in London,* has a different meaning; see page 154.

Grammar Comment

1. **(be) used to** tells us about a state:
   > We'**re used to** space travel.
   > I'**m used to** getting up quite early.

   (get) used to tells us about a process:
   > It took me a long time **to get used to** flying.
   > We **got used to** this place very quickly.

2. Do not confuse the three similar forms:
   > We **used to** live in Paris. (notice the verb form — **live**)
   > We'**re used to** living in Paris. (notice the verb form — **living**)
   > We **got used to** living in Paris.

   It helps to **think of** them in the following way:
   > We used to   —   live in Paris.
   > We're used to   —   living in Paris.
   > We got used to   —   living in Paris.

   The -ing form follows **(be) used to** and **(get) used to.**
   We're used to live in Paris is impossible.

3. Because **(get) used to** is about a process, something extended over a period of time, it is often used with a continuous form of the verb:
   I **was** just **getting used to** my typewriter when they changed them all for computers.
   Are you getting used to your new teeth yet?

150

UNIT 38

Practice 38.1

Look at this example:

Do you like Spain?
— Not really, **I'm not used to** the heat.

Use **(be) used to** to answer the following questions:

1. Do you like Iceland? (the cold)

   Not really. I'm not used to the cold.

2. Do you like working on the farm? (the smell)

   ....

3. Do you like sharing a flat with Bill? (his bad habits)

   ....

4. Does your sister like living so close to the airport? (the noise)

   ....

5. Do the children like the new house? (living in town)

   ....

Practice 38.2

(get) used to is very common in the situation where you want to say that you are not accustomed to a new situation yet!

I **haven't got used to** the heat yet.
I **haven't got used to** living here yet.

Answer the following questions in the same way.

1. Do you like Japan? (the high cost of living)

   ....

2. Are you enjoying your new job? (getting up so early)

   ....

3. How are you getting on with your diet? (eating no sugar)

   ....

4. Have you settled back in England after living abroad for so long? (the new money, driving on the left again)

   ....

   ....

UNIT 38

Practice 38.3

Complete the following situations with (be) used to or (get) used to.

1. Old Bill was 50 before he got married. He was very shy and he liked living alone. He was an individual. But he became lonely and decided it was time for him to get married. When he married Jane, it took him a long time to .... living with someone else, but now after 10 years of married life, they've .... each other.

2. How do you think you would .... living in another country? For example imagine you are a Spaniard and you go to live in Greenland. Just think of all the things you would have to .... — the snow, the cold, the long winters, the short days. I wonder if a Spaniard ever could .... life there.

3. Last year James Rogers lost his job. He had worked in the same firm for 30 years. All his friends worked there. Suddenly, he was without a job, and there was no chance of getting another one in the same town. Apart from weekends and holidays, he had never been at home during the day. How did he get on? The answer is very badly, he found it very difficult to .... the idea of being unemployed. He .... always been .... doing things. Now he had to .... the idea that there was nothing to do. He had always .... earning money. Now it was his wife who had a job, while he sat at home. He could not .... that idea, which he didn't like at all.

Practice 38.4

Complete each of these dialogues. You need an expression which contains (get) used to, but you need to use the appropriate tense. Add any extra words in the correct place.

1. These new glasses are awful!
   — Don't worry. You (soon) ....

2. How's the new computer at work?
   — Awful! I (just) .... the old one!

3. Did you like the food in Japan?
   — Not at first, but I soon .... it.

4. The twins have gone away to University this year, haven't they?
   — Yes, so I .... living on my own again.

5. Do you like your new office?
   — No! I (never) .... working in an open plan office!

6. Are you settled in your new job yet?
   — .... all the travelling isn't easy!

Practice 38.5

Choose 4 of the following ideas and say what YOU could never **get used to.**

eating vegetarian food
being unemployed
a very cold climate

black coffee
living on my own
being famous

strong curries
working in a hospital
living aboad

For example: I could never get used to working at night.

1. ....

2. ....

3. ....

4. ....

Practice 38.6

Here are the reports of two people who went to live and work in different parts of the world — very different from their home country. Fill in **(be) used to** or **(get) used to** in the spaces.

Sue Dickson

Two years ago I went to live and work in Nicaragua. Life there was very different from what I .... back home in the UK. To start with, I had to .... a very different climate. I still haven't been able to .... the heat. I'm .... the rain, but I suppose that's because I'm British! One thing I don't think I'll ever .... properly is the poverty. In Britain we .... seeing poor people, but we don't see children begging in the streets. I'll never .... that. As a child I .... a lovely home and everything I wanted. That's why I'm working with these poor children. I'll never .... living in Britain again.

Peter Craig

Last year my firm sent me to their Belfast office for six months. I live in a little village with one policeman. You can understand that I .... seeing soldiers carrying guns. Even though I stayed for six months I still didn't .... that. Nor could I .... the sound of sirens and helicopters during the night. Of course, the people who live there have no choice. They .... all the things that surprised me. When you live in a place like Northern Ireland, you can't allow the violence to control you. You've got to .... it. You've got to live as if everything was normal. That's what I really couldn't ....

Grammar Summary

I you we they he she it	used to didn't use to	live

Question forms are unusual.

I **used to** smoke.

He **used to** play squash until his accident.

Do you work full time?
▷ Not now, but I **used to** before I had the children.

It's funny. I really enjoy cricket now but I **didn't use to.**

Something which was true for a period in the past but was not true later

Note
Did you use to . . . ? is unusual; we usually say *You used to . . . , didn't you?*

Grammar Comment

1. You can always express **used to** in another way:
   > We **used to** go there on holiday.
   > (We went there on holiday before, but we don't go there now.)

   Used to always refers to activity in the past which is complete. It could refer to a period:
   > I **used to** live there.

   It could refer to a series of events.
   > I **used to** go there on warm Sunday afternoons.

   The most important thing about the past activity is that you see it as a whole, which is finished in the past.

2. Notice the spelling in the question and negative forms:
   > Did you **use** to smoke a lot?
   > She didn't **use** to live there.

   This is because **used to** is a simple past tense. The question form is not very common.

3. Remember not to confuse **used to** with **(be) used to** and **(get) used to**, see Unit 38.

UNIT 39

Practise 39.1

Over the years some places change their names. What did these places use to be called? Match up the modern names with the old ones.

1. Sri Lanka 2. Oslo 3. Leningrad 4. Malawi 5. Bangladesh 6. Zimbabwe 7. Harare 8. Istanbul 9. Cape Kennedy	**used to be called**	a. East Pakistan b. Salisbury c. Cape Canaveral d. Rhodesia e. St. Petersburg f. Constantinople g. Ceylon h. Christiania i. Nyasaland

1	2	3	4	5	6	7	8	9

Practice 39.2

Old Mrs Edwards was 97 on her last birthday. She lives alone and is very fit. Her memory is as good as it ever was. She can remember what life used to be like when she was a young woman. She often talks about it to anyone who will listen. Complete what she says using **(used to)**; sometimes you need the negative.

'When I was young, girls never .... go out on their own. You always went out with friends, because you weren't allowed to be alone with a young man. Oh, no, that never .... be allowed. Before I went out anywhere my father always .... ask where I was going and who I was going with, and when I would be back. And make-up — that was forbidden. Of course, as soon as I got out of the house I .... go behind the house and put it on and then take it off before I went home again. I .... disobey my father except when it came to make-up. My mother .... wear it so I didn't see why I wasn't allowed to as well.

Oh, but life was hard in those days. When I think of when we .... get up in the morning. We .... be up and washed by 6.30! Modern girls just wouldn't do it, would they? And quite right too!

And all the housework — we .... clean out all the fires before 8 o'clock. In fact, we .... have to do all the cleaning by lunchtime.'

Practice 39.3

Write some true things about yourself.

1. When I was young I used to love .... but now I never .... it any more.
2. My mother always used to say how important it was to ....
3. I never used to eat .... but now I love it!
4. I used to think people who .... were very strange, but now they seem quite normal!
5. When I was young nobody used to ...., but now everybody does.

155

Grammar Summary

Tags are very important in spoken English. They are not used in written English.

Say	Mean
It's a lovely day, **isn't it.**	Say something about the weather.
That was a super film, **wasn't it.**	Say something about the film.
That's a good idea, **isn't it.**	Give me your opinion about it.
Things were different then, **weren't they.**	Talk about your memory of the situation.

Tags are not questions. They usually invite the other person to make a comment.

How to make tags

Use the first auxiliary to make the tag. If there is no auxiliary use *do, does* or *did.*

Positive sentence	Negative tag	Negative sentence	Positive tag
It**'s** a beautiful day,	**isn't it.**	It **isn't** a very nice morning,	**is it.**
You**'ve** been to London,	**haven't you.**	You **haven't** been to London,	**have you.**
It **must** have been David,	**mustn't it.**	It **couldn't** have been David,	**could it.**
You **know** Mary,	**don't you.**	They **don't** eat pork,	**do they.**
She **drives** to work,	**doesn't she.**	Your mother **doesn't** speak English,	**does she.**
They **played** well,	**didn't they.**	You **didn't** leave the window open,	**did you.**

Notice these:

There's a post office in Churchill Road, isn't there.

There in the tag too.

You will remember to post that letter, won't you.

The tag for *will* is *won't.*

Let's have a cup of tea, shall we?

The tag for *let's* is *shall we.*

Grammar Comment

When you use tags you should say the whole sentence without a pause between the first part of the sentence and the tag.

In order to reply to a sentence with a tag, you must have heard the auxiliary in the tag. For example, in order to reply:

      Yes, I **do.** Too much, I'm afraid.

you must first have noticed the auxiliary in the tag:

      You **don't** smoke, **do** you?

From the Grammar Summary you can see that the rules for making a tag are very simple and mechanical. But they are not so easy to use when you are having a conversation. They are almost automatic. This means that you must have heard and used them many times before they feel completely natural.

UNIT 40

Practice 40.1

Add the correct tag to the following: Each tag uses part of the verb **(be)**.

1. It's a lovely morning, ..isn't it........
2. The train isn't late, ...
3. Sue isn't very happy, ...
4. Her husband's ill, ...
5. We're leaving early, ...

6. You're not changing your job, ...
7. They're getting married, ...
8. Bill and Sue aren't on holiday, ...
9. There isn't a chance, ...
10. There's a match tonight, ...

Practice 40.2

Add the correct tag to the following. Each tag uses part of the verb **(have)**

1. This experiment hasn't worked, has it.
2. It's been a long time, ...
3. Mary's gone for a month, ...
4. Her husband hasn't gone with her, ...
5. We've seen it all before, ...

6. You haven't seen my comb, ...
7. They haven't got married, ...
8. The children have all got flu, ...
9. There's been a mix-up, ...
10. There hasn't been any news, ...

Practice 40.3

Add the correct tag. Each tag uses part of the verb **(do)**.

1. It doesn't matter, ...
2. The clock just struck one, ...
3. Liz doesn't smoke, ...
4. Andy didn't get a ticket, ...
5. We keep forgetting, ...

6. You live next to the Smiths, ...
7. You saw the accident yourself, ...
8. Your parents never fly, ...
9. The mistakes didn't matter, ...
10. They don't like us, ...

Practice 40.4

Add the correct tag. Each tag uses a modal auxiliary.

1. I really shouldn't have another cake,
   ....
2. We really must be on our way, ...
3. You can give me a ring later, ...
4. Your sister'll take a message, ...
5. We could try a little harder, ...

6. It must've been Karim, ...
7. The car just wouldn't work, ...
8. You won't be ready on time, ...
9. Peter should have his hair cut, ...
10. We really must visit your aunt, ...

Grammar Summary

Most tags ask the other person to *comment*. If you say them like questions they ask the other person to *confirm* what you think:

Say	Mean
You don't smoke, do you?	I don't think you do – is that right?
Sheila isn't married, is she?	I don't think she is – is that right?

The sentence *you* use shows what *you* think:

Paul's been to London, hasn't he?	The speaker thinks Paul *has*.
Paul hasn't been to London, has he?	The speaker thinks Paul *hasn't*.

You don't just *answer* invitation tags, you add some extra information:

You can speak German, can't you.	▷ Yes, a bit. I learned at school.
There's a car park near the theatre, isn't there.	▷ Yes, in Gifford Street.
We haven't got time for a cup to tea, have we.	▷ No, the train goes at ten to.

Grammar Comment

Most tags can be said in two different ways:

a. With the intonation of a question — which expects an answer:

> Mary isn't married, **is she?**
> — Oh yes, she's been married for years.

This is a very common way of asking a question in conversation. It avoids the direct question, which can appear too aggressive.

b. As a statement which expects a comment:

> Mary isn't married, **is she.**
> — No, that's why she's got so much time.

Tag statements are very common in conversation because they encourage the other person to develop the conversation.

It is clear that many cannot be real questions:

> It's a lovely day, **isn't it.**
> This is a very clean place, **isn't it.**

These sentences make social contact in English easier.

It is important to know when to use them and, particularly, how to respond to tags. Often the first speaker does not want an answer, but is inviting a comment. Study these two examples with responses:

> You live in the centre of town, **don't you?**
> — **No,** I think you must've mixed me up with someone else.

> Oh, so you're from Japan, **are you.**
> — Yes, I'm from the north, from Sapporo.

If you only answer tag statements, without adding an extra comment, people may think you are "difficult to talk to".

UNIT 41

Practice 41.1

Here are 6 sentences, each using a tag, and 6 explanations. Match them up.

1. You don't smoke, do you?

2. You smoke, don't you?

3. You played in the Final last year, didn't you?

4. You didn't play in the Final last year, did you?

5. Phil likes Mary, doesn't he?

6. Phil doesn't like Mary, does he?

a. I think you did — am I right?

b. I don't think you do — am I right?

c. I think he does — am I right?

d. I think you do — am I right?

e. I don't think he does — am I right?

f. I don't think you did — am I right?

1	2	3	4	5	6

Practice 41.2

In the right-hand column are 8 tagged statements. On the left are eight meanings. Match up the tags, statements and the meanings. You'll have to be careful!

1. I don't think you should.

2. Please don't.

3. Surely you didn't.

4. I don't think you do.

5. I'm sure you did.

6. I think you ought to.

7. I hope you will.

8. I think you do.

a. You don't, do you?

b. You do, don't you?

c. You will, won't you?

d. You won't, will you?

e. You must, mustn't you?

f. You mustn't, must you?

g. You did, didn't you?

h. You didn't, did you?

1	2	3	4	5	6	7	8

UNIT 41

Practice 41.3

Fill in the verbs in these conversations. One space means one word. (**isn't** and **can't** are one word).

1. Oh hello. How .... you?

    — Fine thanks. Lovely day, ... it?

    Yes, beautiful, ... it?

    — It .... dreadful last week, ... it?

    Yes, it ...., ... it?

2. John .... been to work all week, ... he?

    — No, he .... He .... be in hospital again, can he?

    Well, I hope not. He could be on holiday, ... he?

    — Yes, of course he ....!

3. It's been a long day, ... it?

    — Yes, it ...., ... it?

    There's been so much to do, ... there?

    — Yes, there .... even been time to have a cup of tea. Now, that's

    a good idea, ... it?

    — Not half!

Practice 41.4

Usually we try to offer our opinion so that:

>   it does not sound too negative or unpleasant
>   it does not sound too definite or dogmatic
>   it invites the other person to join in.

This is frequently done by adding a tag.

Put tags on the following sentences. Say each sentence so it *sounds* like a comment, and an invitation to the other person to comment too.

1. You've got to be very careful with young children. *haven't you?* ....
2. Yes, you never know what they're going to say. ....
3. They seem to say the first thing that comes into their heads. ....
4. Though unfortunately it isn't always the most suitable thing. ....
5. No, but it's no use being upset. ....
6. No, it's difficult to see why people are. ....
7. If you've got children yourself you get used to it. ....
8. You're right there! They don't need any encouraging. ....
9. Certainly not, and they don't do any harm. ....
10. Yes, we all need a laugh. We'd be lost without children. ....

These examples sound artificial all together but each sentence, or two or three together *are* natural English conversation if you just add a few words like *"Yes", Mm" "That's quite all right".*

160

UNIT 41

Practice 41.5

One of the most important things to learn about tags is how to respond to them. Match each response with a tag statement.

1. It's marvellous weather, isn't it?

2. The trains are very comfortable, aren't they?

3. Very nice meal, wasn't it?

4. Prices are getting worse and worse, aren't they?

5. You've been to Ireland, haven't you?

6. Paul came with you last year, didn't he?

7. This place could be warmer, couldn't it?

8. I saw you out jogging today, didn't I?

9. There's a meeting tomorrow, isn't there?

10. We're in a hurry, aren't we?

a. Yes, I've never had caviar before.

b. Yes, couldn't be better.

c. Yes, he shared the driving with me.

d. Yes, I wish someone would put the heating on.

e. Oh yes, we can't afford to stop.

f. Yes, I just don't know where it's all going to end.

g. Oh yes, must keep fit.

h. Yes, there is, at 7.30, I think.

i. Yes, I was there on business last year.

j. Yes, they're air-conditioned.

Notice in each case the response has a direct 'answer' **and** a little extra bit of new information, added to develop the conversation.

1	2	3	4	5	6	7	8	9	10

Grammar Summary

Statement	Question		
	Auxiliary	**Subject**	**Verb**
Sentences with one auxiliary			
It was raining.	Was	it	raining?
He's seen the doctor.	Has	he	seen the doctor?
You can read my writing.	Can	you	read my writing?
Sentences with more than one auxiliary — use the first			
She's been waiting a long time.	Has	she	been waiting a long time?
They're going to buy a new car.	Are	they	going to buy a new car?
Sentences with no auxiliary — present simple and past simple — use (do)			
The bus stops in Salisbury Road.	Does	the bus	stop in Salisbury Road?
She caught the plane.	Did	she	catch the plane?

Grammar Comment

The basic rule for asking most questions in English is very simple:

> Change the order of the subject and the first auxiliary.
> If there is no auxiliary, use part of the verb (**do**).

He can come.	—	**Can he** come?
He could have come.	—	**Could he** have come?
He came yesterday.	—	**Did he** come yesterday?

The second part of the rule is the most important and powerful rule of English grammar.

> The verb (do) = **do/don't, does/doesn't, did/didn't.**

This verb brings regularity to the basic structures of English. Most of the basic structures of English — questions, negatives, tags etc — depend on the first auxiliary. Where there is no auxiliary, the auxiliary (**do**) is used in the same way.

Some people have seen (**do**) as an exception. It is more helpful to see it as the auxiliary which makes English so regular.

UNIT 42

Practice 42.1

Here are 8 questions to ask a new friend. The words are mixed up. Write out the questions.

1. we   before   met   have

   ....

2. live   you   do   here   near

   ....

3. to   do   English   you   speak   like

   ....

4. interested   you   in   sport   are

   ....

5. ever   you   abroad   have   been

   ....

6. you   tennis   play   can

   ....

7. single   you   or   are   married

   ....

8. me   would   cinema   to   to   go   the   with   like   you

   ....

Practice 42.2

What were the actual words I said in the following situations?

1. I asked him if it was raining outside.

   I said: ...Is it raining outside..?..

2. I wanted to know if she was cold.

   I said: ....

3. I wondered if you had ever visited London.

   I said: ....

4. I asked if she could speak German.

   I said: ....

5. I asked if you smoked.

   I said: ....

6. I wondered whether he had been here before.

   I said: ....

7. I asked him if he wanted to leave.

   I said: ....

8. I wanted to know if there was a train before 8.

   I said: ....

Grammar Summary

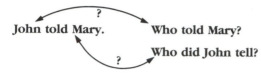

John told Mary.   Who told Mary?

Who did John tell?

1. The question is about the *subject* of the sentence.

2. The question is about the *object* of the sentence.
   The question is made in the usual way. (See **2.** below)

1. Here are some more examples with *who* or *what* as the subject:

Who paid?   **Who** knows about it?
Who told you?   **What** happened?
Who lives next door?   **What** caused the accident?
Who brought Amin to work?

2. Most question word questions are made in this way:

Question word	auxiliary	subject	verb
How many	did	you	buy?
How often	have	you	been there?
How	can	I	get in touch with you?
Which	did	you	choose?
Who	could	we	ask to help?
Why	would	you	like to go?
Which floor	do	you	live on?
Whose car	were	you	driving yesterday?

Grammar Comment

1. We ask question word questions to find out more particular information about **who, what, how, when, where, how much, how many** etc. These questions begin with a special question word. Here is a piece of information:

   > Mary bought that book in Smiths.

   We can ask **one** question about the **subject**:

   > **Who** bought that book?   —   Mary did.
   > (The subject of the question is **who.**)

   The basic pattern for this type of question is:

   > **Question word + verb + object**

   We can ask **two** questions about the object:

   > **What** did Mary buy?   —   That book.
   > **Where** did Mary buy that book?   —   In Smiths.

   The basic pattern for this type of question is:

   > **Question word + auxiliary + subject + verb**

   If you study all the examples in (2) in the Grammar Summary, you will see that question word questions are very regular.
   Remember how important the verb (**do**) is in asking questions. If there is no auxiliary, part of (**do**) is used instead.

2. **Whom** is very rare in question word questions in spoken English; **who** is the normal word.

   > **Whom** did you buy it from?   **Who** did you buy it from?

UNIT 43

Practice 43.1

Link up these words in pairs:

1. why   2. when   3. who   a. carefully   b. tomorrow   c. me
4. where   5. what   6. how   d. nothing   e. outside   f. because

1	2	3	4	5	6

Practice 43.2

Add the correct question word from this list to complete the conversation below.

what   when   why   who   where   which

Rick I'm going to the cinema this evening.

Joe Oh. .... one?

Rick The Majestic.

Joe Are you going alone or with a friend?

Rick With a friend. I don't like going alone.

Joe .... are you going with?

Rick Maria. Carlos and Ann are going too.

Joe .... are you going?

Rick At 7 o'clock

Joe 7 o'clock! That's very early. .... does the film start?

Rick A quarter to 8.

Joe .... are you going so early?

Rick We're going for a hamburger before the film — and afterwards we're going to a party.

Joe .... is the party?

Rick It's at a friend of Maria's.

Joe And .... is the film you're going to see?

Rick "The Name of The Rose". I've heard it's very good.

Joe .... is it about?

Rick I've no idea, but I've heard it's worth seeing.

Joe I think I'd like to see it too.

Rick .... don't you come with us.

Joe But .... will the others say?

Rick Oh, they won't mind.

Joe Right. .... did you say you were meeting?

Rick 7 o'clock, outside the cinema.

Joe See you there at 7 o'clock then!

Joe How are you getting there?

Rick On the bus of course!

UNIT 43

Practice 43.3

Complete the questions. Each space needs one word.

1. .... is the Great Wall of China?
   — It's 3460 kilometres long.
2. .... the oldest living person born?
   — She .... born in 1873.
3. .... does the woman with the longest hair live?
   — In Worcester, USA.
   .... is she called?
   — Diane Witt.
   And .... is her hair?
   — It's 8½ ft long (259cm).
4. .... is the tallest animal?
   — The giraffe.
   .... they live?
   — In the Southern Sahara in Africa.
5. .... heavy was the biggest tomato ever grown?
   — 3.5 kilos!
6. .... hamburgers does McDonald's sell each year?
   — Over 60 billion!
7. .... cheese does a Frenchman eat per year?
   — About 20 kilos.
8. .... eggs were used in the world's largest omelette?
   — 54,763!
   .... do you know?
   — I thought everybody knew that!

Practice 43.4

Here are 8 two-line jokes. First match up the two halves, then learn them!

1. What is the hottest letter of the alphabet?
2. Where can you go dancing in California?
3. What goes "zubb zubb"?
4. What do you do if an elephant sneezes?
5. What is yellow and goes round and round?
6. Which month has 28 days?
7. Why did the boy put a frog in his sister's bed?
8. Why do birds fly south in winter?

a. Because he couldn't catch a mouse.
b. Get out of the way.
c. B — because it makes oil boil.
d. All of them.
e. San Frandisco.
f. Because it's too far to walk.
g. A banana in a washing machine.
h. A bee flying backwards.

1	2	3	4	5	6	7	8

UNIT 43

Practice 43.5

When you were in the bank yesterday, a man came in with a gun and tried to rob it. However, one of the clerks pressed the alarm. The man ran away with nothing. A policeman is asking you some questions. Can you work out what the questions are? He is trying to find out the following:

1. the approximate age of the man

   ....

2. the man's height

   ....

3. the colour of his eyes

   ....

4. the length of his hair

   ....

5 the colour of his hair

   ....

6. the colour of his shoes

   ....

Practice 43.6

Can you work backwards? Find the questions to go with the answers. Notice that each question starts with a question word.

a. In a mosque.
b. Predicts the future.
c. To take your temperature.

d. King Henry VIII did.
e. For admiring yourself!
f. Nobody knows!
g. In wigwams.
h. Eskimos do.
i. Beethoven did.
j. A miner does.
k. In prison.
l. They steal from shops.
m. The USSR did.
n. Burglars do.
o. Leonardo da Vinci.

1. Who invented the wheel?
2. Which criminals break into houses?
3. Which country launched the first satellite into space?
4. What do shoplifters do?
5. Where do Red Indians live?
6. What is a mirror used for?
7. Who wrote "The Moonlight Sonata"?
8. What does a fortune-teller do?
9. Where do Moslems pray?
10. Who painted "The Mona Lisa"?
11. What's a thermometer used for?
12. Who had six wives?
13. Who lives in igloos?
14. Where are criminals kept?
15. Who works underground?

1	2	3	4	5	6	7	8	9	10	11	12	13	14	15

Grammar Summary

As subject or object	**Travelling** makes you tired. **Listening** to music helps me to relax. Mike's hobby is **painting.**
After:	
(do) the	Have you **done the ironing?**
go	They usually **go shopping** on Saturday.
hate	I **hate getting up** early.
love	I **love driving**.
enjoy	Do you **enjoy playing** tennis?
finish	I'll just **finish writing** this letter.
stop (see below)	Jack's **stopped smoking** at last.
suggest	Peter **suggested going** to Ibiza.
need	My hair **needs washing**.
can't help	I **can't help wishing** I hadn't told you.
After:	
go on	He **went on complaining** all evening.
miss	Do you **miss living** in London?
Would you mind . . .	**Would you mind lending** me your pen, please?
(be) used to	I'm **not used to driving** in town.
afraid of	I'm **afraid of flying.**
without	You can't get in **without paying.**
It's worth	**It's worth applying** for a grant.
It's no use . . .	**It's no use arguing.**
It's no good. . .	**It's no good complaining**
instead of	We'll drive **instead of catching** the train.
What about . . .	**What about having** a picnic?
interested in	I'm **not interested in spending** more than £3.

Note
He stopped smoking. = *He smoked but now he doesn't.*
He stopped to smoke. = *He was doing something but stopped so he could have a cigarette.*

Grammar Comment

When it is used as a verbal noun, the **...ing** form is sometimes called the gerund.
You can make a noun from any English verb. Study these examples:

Of a teacher: Her **teaching** is very exciting.
Of a student: Her **reading** is excellent.
Of a band: Their **playing** set everyone alight.
Of a singer: His **singing** is getting worse.
Of a play: The **acting** was very good.

There are many expressions in English which must be followed by the **...ing** form.
When you learn an expression, it is important to learn its structure at the same time.
For example, if you learn the phrase **It's no use,** you must also learn that it is
always followed by the **...ing** form: **It's no use complaining.**
The phrases in the Grammar Summary help you to use the **...ing** form in other
expressions.

UNIT 44

Practice 44.1

Gerund or infinitive?

The words you need to complete this puzzle are either the gerunds (verbal nouns) or the infinitives missing from the sentences below. Choose them from the list on the right.

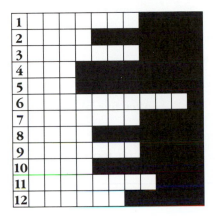

1. At last I've decided to give up smoking cigarettes.   **(pretend)**

2. I really need to .... my hair.   **(come)**

3. I don't like .... money to friends.   **(ring)**

4. Why don't we stop to .... hello to Aunt Mary?   **(say)**

5. We've managed to .... tickets for the show.   **(send)**

6. I wish you would stop .... you know more than you do.   **(lend)**

7. I'll never forget .... the President and his wife.   **(wash)**

8. I hope you won't forget to .... us as soon as you land.   **(visit)**

9. Would you mind .... me to move this case?   **(help)**

10. I never remember to .... my brother a birthday card.   **(meet)**

11. Do you remember .... the old village church?   **(smoke)**

12. I'm really looking forward to .... back.   **(get)**

Some gerund jokes

Doctor, doctor. I can't stop telling lies!
— I don't believe you, of course you can!

How many times have I told you to stop exaggerating?
— I don't know, thousands of times, I suppose.

I want to go to Australia but I can't afford the fare.
— OK. Stop talking and start digging!

UNIT 44

Practice 44.2

Complete these sentences with **...ing** forms. Use these verbs.

do   swim   wait   work   ring   complain   write   waste   go   think

1. We went .... yesterday because it was such a nice day.
2. I haven't finished .... my essay.
3. I hate .... for buses , ... time.
4. I'm having a baby. I stopped .... three weeks ago.
5. It's worth .... to see if there are any tickets left.
6. It's not worth .... after five o'clock.
7. Instead of ...., what about .... something about it!
8. I can't help .... it's a bit too expensive.

Practice 44.3

Fill in the verbs in the **-ing** form.
Jill loves going shopping, but last Saturday everything seemed to go wrong for her.

'As you know I love .... (go) shopping — especially on Saturdays. I usually hate .... (get) up early, but on Saturdays I can't help .... (wake) early, having breakfast, ... (do) the washing up, then .... (get) out to the shops.

But last Saturday everything went wrong! First of all, just as I was about to leave, the phone rang. It was one of my neighbours who asked if I wouldn't mind .... (take) her with me. So, instead of .... (leave) at 9, it was nearer 10 before we set off. Of course, she couldn't help .... (offer) me a cup of coffee. I was afraid of .... (upset) her. I'm not used to .... (drink) coffee at that time of the day. But it was no use .... (refuse).

Half way into town the car broke down! I normally enjoy .... (drive), but when things go wrong, I hate cars. My friend suggested .... (try) to stop another driver and .... (ask) for help. By this time it had started .... (rain). Nobody stopped for us! You can imagine that I was not in a very good mood. And then she started .... (offer) me advice; what about .... (go) to the nearest phone box....it's no good .... (look) under the bonnet. She went on and on .... (complain). Finally, I lost my temper. It's no use .... (make) silly suggestions!, I shouted. So she left in silence to get a bus. As she left, the car started! But what a start to the day!'

170

UNIT 44

Practice 44.4

Complete each of these sentences with a verbal noun (...**ing** form).
Use one of these words in each one.

fly   drive   parachute   play   earn   spend   relax   sing   dance   work

1. .... is the quickest way to travel.
2. .... money is more fun than .... it!
3. .... and .... are both dangerous hobbies, but more people are injured .... football.
4. .... hard makes you tired, but then you can really enjoy ....
5. I prefer .... to ...., so I like ballet more than opera.
6. Dangerous .... kills hundreds of people on the roads every year.

Practice 44.5

Complete this dialogue with verbal nouns (...**ing** forms).

Sally   What about .... to the cinema tomorrow evening with me?

Carol   Well, I'm going .... in the afternoon . . . what time?

Sally   Not before seven, but I don't want to miss .... Dustin Hoffman.

Carol   It's no use .... me to go see and see him. I haven't enjoyed any of his films. I'm not really interested in .... disappointed again.

Sally   Well, instead of .... to the cinema, what about .... a pizza together?

Carol   Great! I miss .... an Italian meal since the 'Roma' closed, but it's worth .... there early. The pizzeria is always busy on Friday evenings, and I hate .... for a table.

Sally   No, I don't think you can get in without .... at the weekends. By the way, would you mind .... me up; my car's out of action at the moment.

Carol   No, that's fine. See you about half past six. I'm hungry now. .... about .... always makes me feel hungry!

Here are some of the verbs you will need:

go   eat   get   have   be   see   shop   ask   pick

Practice 44.6

Write about yourself.

1. (Something you did when you were young).   I really miss ....
2. (Something you like doing).   I love ....
3. (Something you don't like doing).   I hate ....
4. (Something you don't want to waste time on).   It's no use ....

Grammar Comment

1.   Many verbs in English are made of two, or sometimes three, words. Even if you know the meaning of each word, you cannot guess the meaning of the words together.

drop = *fall* or *let fall*   **drop in** = *visit*

These are called phrasal verbs. They are made with a verb and one or more particles (words like prepositions):

put + up/down/on

Phrasal verbs are very common in spoken English. It is impossible to speak or to understand English if you do not know the more common ones. Your English will improve a lot if you try to learn and use them. You need to learn the verb-particle combinations as if they were single words in your vocabulary.
It is quite easy to guess the meaning of some phrasal verbs:

The car **broke down.**	stopped and wouldn't start
Sorry. I **slept in.**	woke up too late

But it is almost impossible to guess the meaning of others. You have to learn them:

Can you **put** us **up**?	give us a bed for the night
Have I **let** you **down**?	disappointed

2.   There are two ways to learn phrasal verbs:
   a. You can take a basic verb and learn all the meanings with different particles, for example:

I **got up** at 7 o'clock.	out of bed
We **got off** at the station.	off the bus
She **got in** at 11.	arrived
What did you **get up to**?	do
etc	

     b. You can learn the particle and all the basic verbs which go with it, for example, all the **up** verbs:

We **brought** you **up** to be polite.	educate at home
I've **given up**!	stopped trying
Look it **up** in a dictionary.	refer to
Please remember to **turn up.**	come
etc	

     It is best to try both ways. Making diagrams like this may help you.

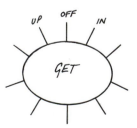 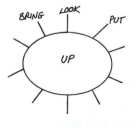

UNIT 45

Practice 45.1

10 verbs with off

Put the correct form of one of these verbs in each of these sentences.

call off	get off	go off	pay off	put off
see off	set off	show off	take off	turn off

1. It's best to .... the train at the harbour station.
2. Our plane didn't .... till 11 o'clock.
3. I hope you remembered to .... the record player.
4. The strike is over. They've .... it ....
5. Let's go to the airport with them to .... them ....
6. What a smell. I think this milk's ....
7. My father's lost his job. He's been ....
8. I can't meet you tomorrow. Can we .... it .... till the day after?
9. Just because you're good at English, there's no need to ....
10. If the main film starts at 7, I think we should .... at 6.30.

Practice 45.2

6 verbs with down

1. If your car **broke down** on the way to work, did it stop completely or just start going more slowly?
2. When a shop **closes down,** does it close for a day, or for ever?
3. If you are **knocked down** by a car, are you very impressed by it, or injured by it?
4. If a good friend **lets** you **down**, are you disappointed or grateful?
5. At what age do most people **settle down** — 12, 26, 55, 70?
6. If you have been **turned down** for a job, do you get the job or not?

Practice 45.3

7 verbs with on

Match the sentences with the explanations below:

1. Are you **carrying on** with your violin lessons?
2. I'm **getting on** all right at college now.
3. **Hold on.** I'm not ready.
4. You must be **having** me **on!** That's a boy!
5. Don't you think you'll need to **put on** your gloves?
6. Excuse me, could I **try** this one **on**, please?
7. How do you **turn** this machine **on**?

a. check clothes
b. wait a moment
c. continue
d. switch on
e. tease/joke
f. wear
g. succeed

1	2	3	4	5	6	7

UNIT 45

Practice 45.4

15 verbs with up

bring up	catch up	get up
give up	grow up	hang up
keep up	look up	pack up
put up	save up	turn up
wake up	wash up	wrap up

1. Let's start .... for a winter holiday!

2. The present was .... in lovely gold paper.

3. The one job I hate in the kitchen is ....

4. Hurry! You go on and I'll .... you ....

5. Look! Rain! Let's .... quickly and get back to the car.

6. It's not loud enough. Please .... it ....

7. Nobody knows the best way to .... children.

8. If only I had my Very Simple Grammar Book, I could .... it ....

9. He's making a lot of money. How long do you think he can .... it ....

10. I wish you would .... and stop acting like a child.

11. I don't know the answer, tell me. I ....!

12. I hate .... on cold winter mornings!

13. ....! You've slept in!

14. I can't get a hotel. Do you know anyone who could .... me ....?

15. If he rings again, don't speak to him. Just ....

Practice 45.5

8 verbs with out

Which sentence is the explanation?

1. We **ate out**.
   a. We had a picnic.
   b. We went to a restaurant.

2. We've **fallen out**.
   a. We've had an argument.
   b. We've decided to leave.

3. I hope nobody **finds out** about it.
   a. I hope nobody discovers what has happened.
   b. I hope nobody says anything.

4. I must **sort out** my papers.
   a. I must throw away all my papers.
   b. I must arrange my papers properly.

5. All the girls in the office **walked out**.
   a. All the girls went on strike.
   b. All the girls went out for a walk.

6. This typewriter is **worn out**.
   a. It is old and almost unusable.
   b. It is old-fashioned.

7. He really **stands out** in a crowd.
   a. He never agrees.
   b. He is very distinguished.

8. Bill's **going out** with Mary.
   a. Bill and Mary have a romantic friendship.
   b. They are leaving together.

174

UNIT 45

Practice 45.6

Match the phrasal verbs in the first columns with the meanings in the second columns.

1. get on	6. put up with	a. cancel	f. continue
2. turn down	7. call off	b. refuse	g. quarrel
3. carry on	8. fall out	c. succeed	h. disappoint
4. put off	9. let down	d. discover	i. delay
5. find out	10. put up	e. tolerate	j. accommodate

1	2	3	4	5	6	7	8	9	10

Practice 45.7

Underline all the phrasal verbs in the following passage:

I had been trying to get through to Bill for days. It wasn't like him not to answer the phone. He was getting on a bit — in his mid-seventies, but it never crossed my mind that he might be ill. He was one of those people who were always young. He looked after people a lot younger than himself. I decided I had to find out.

My car was broken down, but I didn't mind getting the bus — even if it meant a two hour ride over not very good roads. But what would I say if there was nothing wrong — if he was out in his garden, sitting reading the morning paper? Could I pretend that I had just dropped in?

I got off the bus in the village square and walked the quarter of a mile to Bill's cottage. On the way I was looking for him in the face of everyone I passed. I was looking forward to seeing him again. Although he was my father's uncle, he had been more like a grandfather to me, always wise and never telling me off as a boy.

There was no one in the front garden. It looked neat and tidy as if someone had been looking after it every day. My thoughts brightened as I banged on the thick oak door with that big brass knocker which I remember I at last reached two days after my sixth birthday. No reply. Maybe he was out shopping and hadn't got back. I remembered all the times he had promised to write to me, but of course he'd never got round to it — too busy, he always said.

Maybe he hadn't wakened up — after all, it was only 10.30. Maybe.... And then I heard a noise from the back of the house — there was someone in the back garden. Of course — he'd be looking after his pigeons. I remembered he once borrowed a hundred pounds from my father — to buy a new racing pigeon — he never paid it back, but we didn't mind.

I found a young man — in his twenties — in the back garden. 'Is Bill around'? I asked, half-expecting to see Bill come out from his pigeon shed. 'I'm just looking after the place till he gets back from France.'

France! I thought he was having me on. Bill had never been out of the village for 40 years.

'Oh yes. He surprised us all. Married the postmistress last Saturday. Caught the boat train to Paris Saturday night. The whole village was at the station.'

There were 19, how many did you find?

UNIT 46   a, an

Grammar Summary

an in front of a vowel *sound*
in front of **a e i o u**   in *front of h* when it is not sounded

	apple	orange				
an	egg	uncle		**an**	hour	honour
	island					

a in front of all other letters   in front of **u** and **eu** when it sounds like *you*

	bag	girl				
a	child	house		**a**	university	European
	face					

She's **a** dentist.   With a singular (countable) noun
We had **an** argument.
A pound of tomatoes please.

a hundred, **a** thousand, **a** million   With certain numbers

a dozen, **a** couple of, **a** pair of, **a** lot, **a** few, **a** little   With certain quantities
We spent **a** couple of weeks in Spain.
There were **a** lot of people at the game.

30 pence **a** pound   Costs
sixty miles **an** hour   Measurements

Note
a/an is normal, *one* is used for emphasis:
  A: A coke and two lemonades, please.
  B: Two lemonades and two cokes.
  A: No, two lemonades and **one** Coke, please.

Grammar Comment

1. In some languages the word for the first number (1) is the same as the article word. This is not so in English.
One is used with special emphasis:
  Did you say two teas and two coffees?
  — No, two teas and **one** coffee, please.
The usual word for 'one' in spoken English is **a** or **an**.

2. A noun with a countable meaning in English takes **a** or **an,** for example:
  That was **a** good idea.   There's **a** space over there.

3. Remember that in English when you tell someone what your job is, you use **a** or **an**:
  I'm **an** engineer.   I'm **an** accountant.
  I'm **a** secretary.   I'm **a** computer programmer.

4. Notice the use of **a** and **an** in the following phrases:
  What **a** smell!
  What **a** great idea!
  What **an** interesting book!
  It seemed such **a** good idea.
  It was such **a** poor meal that we complained.
  We had such **an** awful time, that we asked for our money back.

UNIT 46

Practice 46.1

Use **a** or **an** in these sentences. Write your answers in words.

1. If you add one to ninety nine, you get ....
2. In Britain another word for twelve is ....
3. Ten times a hundred is ....
4. 1,000,000 in words is .... and a person who owns a million pounds is................ .
5. In town you mustn't drive at more than ....
6. These apples cost ....
7. Have you change for ....
8. The tennis courts cost £2 ....
9. What .... terrible day!
10. Hiring .... bicycle will cost you £2 .... hour or £5 .... day.

5. **30**

6. **40p/lb**

7. **£1**

8. **£2.00 PER HOUR**

Practice 46.2

Look at these examples:

He's **such a** helpful boy.
They're **such** helpful children.

Complete these sentences using **such** or **such a/an.**

1. It was .... awful storm that people's homes were destroyed.
2. Anne went shopping with her grandmother. She's .... helpful girl.
3. Our neighbours are .... noisy people that we can hear them trying to be quiet!
4. The theatre is .... important building that they hope to preserve it.
5. Politicians can be .... funny people that I don't know why we take them so seriously.
6. Your father has led .... interesting life — I could listen to him all evening.
7. Apartheid! I have no idea how people have any time for .... dreadful idea.
8. Some parents have .... peculiar ideas about how to bring up children!
9. Have you ever read .... interesting book as ....
(fill in the name of the most interesting book you have ever read).

Practice 46.3

Look at these examples:

What a nice thing to say!
What horrible teeth!

Complete these sentences using **what** or **what a/an.**

1. .... pretty little girl.
2. .... beautiful babies.
3. .... dreadful old car he has!
4. .... marvellous news!
5. .... boring programme.
6. .... insulting thing to say to you!
7. .... cheek!
8. .... interesting teacher you are!

177

Grammar Summary

Only one spelling: **The** dress, girl, police, children

Two pronunciations: in front of a consonant sound / ðə /   **the** side
                         in front of a vowel sound   / ði: /   **the** apple, **the** engine,
                                                 the other one, **the** umbrella

                                                 the is usually used with:

I left **the** car in George Street.   a person or thing already
(= *my* or *our* car)   identified or known

Which dress did you buy?
▷ **The** blue one.

Can you close **the** door please?

He bought the house next to **the** Post Office.

the China Sea, **the** Ganges, **the** Alps   names of seas, rivers, mountain ranges
Lake Ontario, Windermere   (but *not* lakes)

the Taj Mahal, **the** White House   important buildings
the Eiffel Tower

He plays **the** guitar and **the** piano.   musical instruments

Note

1. Most street names do **not** have *the* in front of them: George Street, but *the* High Street.

2. *The* is not used with **at work, at home, at school, go to work, go home, go to school:**
He goes to school at eight o'clock. What time does he go home?

3. *The* is not used with nouns used with a general meaning: *Milk is good for you.*

Grammar Comment

1.   When it is used with ordinary nouns (not names of unique places, pop groups etc) the meaning of **the** is to make the noun specific and definite. We use it to draw attention to something specific, for example:

       My grandmother goes to church on Sundays.
       — Oh, which one?
       The big church in the centre of town.

That is the easiest and most general rule. There are other rules but most have exceptions, so they are not always very helpful.

2.   To refer to unique nouns (the names of places, lakes, pop groups, organisations etc) It is very difficult to give general rules. It is best to learn the names. Here are some lists to help you.

The West Indies	The British Museum	The Black Sea	Lake Placid
The Soviet Union	The Kremlin	The Mediterranean	Lake Victoria
The Philippines	The Statue of Liberty	The Gulf of Mexico	Lake Michigan
The National Theatre	The Himalayas	The Twenties	The Times
The Bolshoi	The Alps	The early Nineties	The Herald Tribune
The Royal Opera	The Urals	The Swinging Sixties	The Observer
Harrods	Central Park	British Airways	
Woolworths	Piccadilly Circus	Pan Am	
Marks and Spencers	St Peter's Square		

UNIT 47

Practice 47.1

First match up the two parts of each sentence. Then decide whether you need **the** before the second part. Write **the** where you need it.

1. The Pope lives in
2. The American President lives in
3. Mrs Smith lives in
4. Nobody lives in
5. We sailed across
6. We flew over
7. We saw the snow on
8. We climbed
9. The Queen lives in
10. We can meet at

a. .... Alps.
b. .... China Sea.
c. .... Buckingham Palace.
d. .... Vatican.
e. .... White House.
f. .... Piccadilly Circus.
g. .... Eiffel Tower.
h. .... Lake Ontario.
i. .... George Street.
j. .... Taj Mahal.

1	2	3	4	5	6	7	8	9	10

Practice 47.2

Decide which of the following sentences are wrong. Mark them 'X'. When you have checked your answers, draw a line through the wrong examples.

1. We live in the High Street.

2. My brother works in the garage in Queens Road.

3. He washed the hair before he went out.

4. I can play guitar.

5. Why don't you listen to the radio?

6. Did you buy the blue dress after all?

7. What time do you go to the work?

8. I go to school at 8 o'clock.

9. Shall we meet in cinema?

10. Have you ever crossed Atlantic?

11. My parents told me to be at the home by midnight.

12. Do you play piano?

13. When you are growing up, the milk is good for you.

14. I don't like coffee, and especially not the coffee from that machine.

15. I left the car in the George Street.

16. The Edinburgh Castle is the most famous castle in Britain.

17. He bought the cottage next to the post office.

18. I'm not keen on the people next door.

19. Peace is what we need.

20. Fight War, not wars.

UNIT 47

Practice 47.3

Use **the** for the names of:
- abbreviated countries (**the U.K.**)
- groups of islands
- mountain ranges
- oceans and rivers
- newspapers

Don't use **the** for:
- non-abbreviated countries
- single islands
- single mountains
- lakes
- magazines

Now answer these questions. At the same time look for extra rules to add to the lists above.

1. What's the largest desert in the world?

....

2. Which mountain range lies between France and Spain?

....

3. Where can you find the Mona Lisa?

....

4. What's the largest freshwater lake in the world?

....

5. Which river runs through Paris?

....

6. Where in London can you find the statue of Eros?

....

7. Which magazine is read by men all over the world?

....

8. What's the highest mountain in the world?

....

9. Which is the smallest continent?

....

10. Which are the two main newspapers in Britain?

....

11. Which group of islands does Jamaica belong to?

....

12. What's the capital of Afghanistan?

....

13. Which river runs through Rome?

....

14. Where in London is the department store Selfridge's?

....

15. Which is the largest island in the world?

....

16. Give two different names for the most powerful country in the Western world.

....

17. Give two different names for the most powerful country in the Eastern bloc.

....

18. How can we refer to the years 1990-1999?

....

UNIT 47

Practice 47.4

If you think the following should have **the**, write **the** in the space. Write X in front of those which do not need **the**.

1.	....	United Nations	16.	....	St Peter's Square
2.	....	N.A.T.O.	17.	....	Great Wall of China
3.	....	Beatles	18.	....	Mount Everest
4.	....	Mediterranean	19.	....	Rolling Stones
5.	....	Lake Victoria	20.	....	Black Sea
6.	....	U.S.	21.	....	Kremlin
7.	....	Equator	22.	....	Christmas
8.	....	Canaries	23.	....	Himalayas
9.	....	Outer Space	24.	....	Twentieth Century
10.	....	Far East	25.	....	Ganges
11.	....	New York Times	26.	....	Thirties
12.	....	Pacific	27.	....	Warsaw Pact
13.	....	West	28.	....	North Pole
14.	....	British Airways	29.	....	Piccadilly Circus
15.	....	World Bank	30.	....	Milan Cathedral

Practice 47.5

Decide whether to fill in **the** or leave the space empty in the following news report of an air crash.

Yesterday a light aircraft crashed into a lonely hillside on .... border between Italy and Yugoslavia. .... pilot and .... two passengers were killed when .... plane came down in .... thick fog. So far, ... passengers have not been identified. .... pilot, Sr Antonio Ferrara was a prominent Milan industrialist. .... countryside around .... crash site is hilly and .... rescue team from Venice had difficulty in locating .... aircraft. .... plane was found by .... local hunters and their dogs. Several bags containing millions of dollars in used banknotes were found beside .... plane. .... police are investigating.

Grammar Summary

English nouns are divided into two groups:

Countable nouns
Are seen by the speaker in *units*

a glass   **a cup**   **a spoonful**   **a slice**
of water   **of tea**   **of sugar**   **of bread**

Uncountable nouns
Are **not** seen by the speaker in *units*

water   tea   sugar   bread

Countable nouns

– have singular and plural forms

– take singular and plural verbs

> That **boy is** French.
> Those **boys are** French.
> The **timetable changes** tomorrow.
> The **timetables** all **change** tomorrow.

– can have **a/an** and numbers in front of them

> **an** apple   **a** good idea
> **four** apples   **three** good ideas

– have **not many** in front of them

> He has**n't many** friends.
> There were**n't many** people there.

– have **a few** in front of them

> Will you have **a few** more cherries?

Uncountable nouns

– only have one form

– always take a singular verb

> **Music helps** me to relax.
> Their **furniture is** very modern.
> Too much **coffee isn't** good for you.
> The **weather was** beautiful all week.

– never have **a/an** or a number *directly* in front

> weather   information   advice
> furniture   leather

– have **not much** in front of them

> He has**n't much** money.
> We haven't had **much** information yet.

– have **a little** in front of them

> Will you have **a little** more ice-cream?

Note
Much and *many* are used in *negatives* and *questions;* in positive remarks *a lot of* is normally used:

> There were **a lot of** people in town today.
> We had **a lot of** trouble getting here.

Grammar Comment

1. If you **make a mistake** with countable and uncountable nouns, you will not usually be **misunderstood**.

2. Some nouns are always countable and some are always uncountable.
   A lot of common nouns, however, have both a countable and an uncountable meaning, for example:

   > There's **a space** free   How many **times** have you been?
   > There wasn't **any space**.   There wasn't much **time**.

3. Remember that **much** and **many** are often used in negatives and questions in spoken English.
   Spoken English uses **lots of** or **a lot of** in positive sentences.
   In written English or formal spoken English **much** and **many** are more common.

UNIT 48

Practice 48.1

Write the following words under the correct pictures.

sugar	a spoonful of sugar	two sugars
bread	a slice of bread	tea
water	a glass of water	a cup of tea

1. .... 2. .... 3. ....

4. .... 5. .... 6. ....

7. .... 8. .... 9. ....

Now you draw the following ideas in the 3 boxes below:

10. a cake

11. a piece of cake

12. cake

Do not look at the answers until you have tried your best to draw the different pictures. You will find three quite different pictures when you come to check.

UNIT 48

Practice 48.2

Are these nouns usually **countable (C)**, or **uncountable (U)**.

1. boy ...C........	9. chair	17. car ....
2. tea ......U........	10. bed	18. leather ....
3. cup	11. furniture	19. traffic ....
4. water	12. information	20. news ....
5. apple	13. milk	21. video ....
6. fruit	14. person	22. music ....
7. friend	15. bottle	23. cloud ....
8. advice	16. loaf	24. weather ....

Practice 48.3

John and Sue are discussing what to buy for their party. Use **much** and **many** to complete their conversation.

John How .... milk have we got?

Sue I think we've got 2 pints.

John And how .... butter is there?

Sue Oh, we've got plenty of butter, but I don't think there are .... eggs left — maybe only 2 or 3.

John Right, I'll get some more. And have you any idea how .... cheese there is?

Sue A pound. I know there's a pound. So don't get any more.

John And how .... cartons of orange juice did we get? Wasn't it two?

Sue That's right and they're still unopened.

John And how .... is there left of that lettuce?

Sue Oh, most of it. And we've got at least a pound of tomatoes.

John And how .... are there in a pound?

Sue Usually about 8.

John And how .... of that big cucumber is there?

Sue We haven't used it all yet.

John Well, what about drinks? How .... cans shall I get?

Sue We've got 10. Isn't that enough?

John I suppose so. How .... wine is there?

Sue How .... bottles do you think we're going to need?

John Well, I suppose it depends what you mean by 'need'!

184

UNIT 48

Practice 48.4

Match up the following questions and answers. Remember to use **a few** with countable uses and **a little** with uncountable uses:

Write the numbers in the box below.

1. Were there many people there?
2. How much would you like?
3. How many would you like?
4. Did you meet many old friends?
5. Are there many problems?
6. Were there any seats left?
7. Was there much space?
8. Was there any trouble?
9. Have you got any time?
10. Have you any change?

a. Just a few.
b. Just a little.

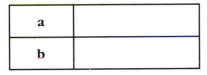

a	
b	

Practice 48.5

Much has an uncountable meaning; **many** has a countable meaning. **A lot of** or **lots of** can be used with either; they are more common than **much** or **many** in positive statements, for example:

> Did you have **much** time to spare?
> — Oh yes, we had **lots of** time.

Fill in **much, many,** or **lots of** in the following:

1. There were .... people at the party, weren't there?
   — Yes, I wasn't expecting so ....
2. I didn't have .... time to spare at the airport.
   — No, I didn't have .... either.
3. I wish I had .... holidays.
   — I sometimes think people have too ....
4. We haven't had .... sun this summer, have we?
   — No there haven't been .... warm days at all.
5. .... people I know are growing their own vegetables.
   — Yes, there are too .... chemicals used these days.
6. There aren't .... trains here in the evening, are there?
   — No, there never were ....
7. .... the people who live here don't come from here.
   — Really, I didn't think there were ....immigrants here.
8. I don't think our boss knows .... about people.
   — I don't think .... bosses know .... about people!
9. Too .... people are killed on the roads every year.
   — Yes and the Government isn't doing .... about it.

185

UNIT 49 **a . . . of . . .**

Grammar Summary

To make countable quantities with uncountable nouns use *a . . . of . . .*

| a | piece
pound
pint
jar
glass
tin | of | information
tomatoes
milk
jam
water
soup | | a | packet
bit
slice
litre
plate
tube | of | cigarettes
luck
toast
oil
spaghetti
toothpaste |

Some words which are countable in some other languages are uncountable in English:

advice   information   news   luggage   knowledge   furniture   health

Some words can be used in two different ways, one countable, one uncountable:

There's *a hair* on your coat.

What *a* lovely *colour!*

Have some more *potatoes.*
▷Just *a few* please.

Her *hair* is beautiful.

Television is very dull without *colour.*

Have some more *potato.*
▷Just *a little* please.

Grammar Comment

1. If we think of objects or ideas, we see some as divided into individual units:
        a book, five people, an idea
    and we see others as undivided:
        water, air, grass

    These are sometimes called 'mass' nouns. Often we can talk about something as mass or divide it into units by thinking of special amounts:

        mass: Don't forget to buy **some toothpaste.**
        unit: Don't forget to buy **a tube of toothpaste.**

        mass: You've got **jam** on your shirt.
        unit: There's **a jar of jam** in the cupboard.

    In the grammar summary and in Unit 48 there are many different ways to talk about individual units of things which we normally see as mass:
        a slice of, a glass of, a tin of, a bit of, a litre of, a handful of

2. **A piece of** is used to talk about one unit of **advice, information, news, luggage, furniture.**
    Study the difference in meaning in this example:
        Could you help me move **this furniture?**
        (This furniture = a lot of different pieces)
        Could you help me move **this piece of furniture?**
        (one particular thing)

186

UNIT 49

Practice 49.1

Match up the words on the left with the food on the right:

1. a litre of
2. a jar of
3. a tin of
4. a piece of
5. a plate of
6. a loaf of
7. a spoonful of
8. a pound of

a. soup
b. sugar
c. butter
d. milk
e. jam
f. muesli
g. bread
h. toast

1	2	3	4	5	6	7	8

Practice 49.2

What do you buy in the following:

1. a bottle of
2. a tube of
3. a jar of

4. a packet of
5. a tin of
6. a bunch of

sauce   cornflakes   flowers   jam   toothpaste   peas

Practice 49.3

There are a few words in English which are uncountable and when we want to talk about 'one' of them, we use **a piece of**. Complete the dialogues below. You will need these words:

information   advice   furniture   good news   luggage

1A I've just had the most wonderful piece of ....

B You haven't won First Prize, have you?

2A Can I give you ....?

B Only if you promise to listen to it yourself!

3A Did the burglars take much?

B Just a piece of antique ....

4A I heard a very interesting .... today.

B About the new company? Yes — very interesting, isn't it?

5A How many .... have you got, sir?

B Just this case and my briefcase.

UNIT 50 *plurals*

Grammar Summary

Most nouns make their plural by adding −**s**.
There are three different pronunciations:

packet	packets	add /s/	after a voiceless sound
hand	hands	add /z/	after a voiced sound (see page 250)
face	faces	add /iz/	after these sounds /s/ /z/ / ʃ / / tʃ / /dʒ/

Some common plurals are different:

woman	**women**	wife	**wives**
man	**men**	knife	**knives**
child	**children**	foot	**feet**
person	**people**	tooth	**teeth**
potato	**potatoes**	baby	**babies**
bus	**buses**	lady	**ladies**
glass	**glasses**	city	**cities**
match	**matches**	sheep	**sheep**

Grammar Comment

1. Most irregular plurals in English are very old-fashioned. Those in the Grammar Summary are the most common.

2. The normal plural of **person** is **people. Persons** is only used in very formal English.

3. There is a group of nouns which all refer to one thing, but end in -s and take plural verbs. Here are the most common:
    shorts, briefs, pants, swimming trunks, trousers, pyjamas, jeans, tights, clothes, spectacles, glasses, scissors

    These **trousers are** too tight.
    The **scissors were** in the kitchen.

    Numbers look plural, but often refer to the amount as a single whole, so the following verb is singular:
    Half a million pounds is a lot to win.
    £20 seems very expensive.
    6 months is a long time to wait.

4. Some words can take a singular or plural verb with slightly different meanings:
    The committee is thinking about your problem.
    (the committee as one body, one group)
    The committee are thinking about your problem.
    (the committee as individual people)

UNIT 50

Practice 50.1

Divide the following plurals into three groups. There are ten words in each group. Number each word 1, 2 or 3:

Group 1 — where s is pronounced /s/
Group 2 — where s is pronounced /z/
Group 3 — where the ending is pronounced /iz/

books	☐	lists	☐	dresses	☐	rules	☐	things	☐
radios	☐	tickets	☐	coaches	☐	peaches	☐	bicycles	☐
drinks	☐	ferries	☐	churches	☐	cups	☐	boxes	☐
matches	☐	chairs	☐	boats	☐	buses	☐	thousands	☐
lights	☐	shirts	☐	horses	☐	trains	☐	cars	☐
faces	☐	insects	☐	houses	☐	heads	☐	maps	☐

Practice 50.2

Here is a list of common nouns which are always plural in form:

**arms   scissors   tights   news   suburbs
trousers   customs   manners   brains   glasses**

Complete the following sentences using these words.

1. The .... from Afghanistan is not very good.
2. I ought to get contact lenses. I keep breaking my ....
3. I hate going through .... — even when I've got nothing to declare!
4. John's .... are not very good. He talks while his mouth is full of food.
5. If you want to cut your nails, you'll find the .... in that drawer.
6. So you think Bill's got .... I don't think he's so intelligent.
7. Women used to wear stockings, but most now wear ....
8. Some schools in Britain still make boys wear short ....
9. No one seems to know where terrorists get their .... from.
10. If I had to work in London, I'd live out in the ....

Practice 50.3

Put the correct plurals in these sentences.

1. '................. and .... first!' shouted the Captain of the Titanic after it hit the iceberg.
2. That was a long walk! My .... are killing me now!
3. '................. who live in glass houses shouldn't throw stones.' (proverb)
4. Was it Henry the Eighth who had six .... or Henry the Sixth who had eight ....?
5. 'Good evening .... and .... Welcome to tonight's meeting.'
6. If you need new .... you go to an optician, but if you want new .... you go to a dentist.

UNIT 51   some, any

Grammar Summary

some is about *part*, or *not all*; **any** is about *all* or *none*.

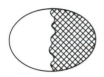

I like **some** fruit.   I don't like **some** fruit.   I like **any** fruit.   I don't like **any** fruit.

any

She doesn't drink **any** alcohol, not even beer.   None

There aren't **any** shops near our flat.

You can take **any** bus from the station.   All

When can you come round?
▷ **Any** day next week.

I like **any** kind of cheese.

Did you take **any** photographs?   "Open" questions

Have you **any** small change, please?

some

Some of the trains stop here but some don't.   Not all

Some people thought it was too expensive.

I like **some** pop music, but not all.

I've bought **some** tea but we need **some** sugar.   General quantity

Would you like us to bring **some** sandwiches with us?

I'd like **some** information about flights to Paris please.

These words are used in the same way:

somebody	**someone**	**something**	**somewhere**
anybody	**anyone**	**anything**	**anywhere**

Grammar Comment

It is unlikely that you will be misunderstood if you make a mistake with **some** or **any**. Because of their meanings, **some** is more common than **any** in positive statements; **any** is more common than **some** in negative statements.
In questions both **some** and **any** are common.

> You must be hungry. Can I get you **something** to eat?
> (This suggests that you have thought about this and possibly have some food ready.)
> Can I get you **anything** to eat?
> (This is a totally 'open' question.)

> Have you **some** idea who could have stolen it?
> (suggests you might have)
> Have you **any** idea who could have stolen it?
> (an 'open' question)

The difference between these questions is very small. It is not decided by the answer you expect. It depends on what you are thinking when you ask the question, whether you need the 'open' idea of **any** or the 'restricted' idea of **some**.

UNIT 51

Practice 51.1

Remember the meaning of **some** and **any**:

$$\textbf{any} = \textbf{all} \text{ or } \textbf{none}$$
$$\textbf{some} = \textbf{not all}, \textbf{part}$$

Read these sentences and mark them:

A = All   **N** = None   **N/A** = Not all

1. I like **any** pop music. ....
2. I don't like **any** pop music. ....
3. I only like **some** pop music. ....
4. **Some** people have blond hair. ....
5. **Some** people have red hair, but not many. ....
6. I love **any**thing with cream on it. ......
7. I hate **some** pop music. ....
8. **Any**body could tell you the answer. ....
9. **Some**body told me a joke this morning. ....
10. **Any**body with any sense knows that! ....

Practice 51.2

Fill in **some** or **any** in the following. Only one is possible in each.

1. .... trains stop here, but .... don't.
2. She doesn't drink .... alcohol, not even beer.
3. You can take .... bus from this stop.
4. .... buses don't stop here.
5. I'm afraid I haven't .... change at all.
6. I like .... punk bands, but not all.
7. .... people think it's important to be able to speak English, but .... think it's a waste of time.
8. I never eat .... thing with sugar in it.
9. Can you come round some time next week? .... day will suit me.
10. .... teachers will tell you that you must never make mistakes when you speak English, but .... think that you can't learn unless you make .... mistakes.

Practice 51.3

Put **some** or **any** in the following. If you think both are possible, write' **both**'.

1. There's ....body outside. I'm sure there is.
   — Oh, don't be silly. If there was ....body there, they would have rung the bell.
2. Have you .... raspberries?
   I'm afraid we haven't .... left. We had .... last week, but ....body came in and bought the lot. We won't be getting .... more till next Friday.
3. I am so hungry. I could eat a horse!
   — Well, don't worry. I'll get you ....thing to eat. I've got so much in the fridge. You could have almost ....thing you want. I've got .... cold meat, ... chicken, ... cheese.
   I think I'd like .... cold meat. And if you have .... bread, that would do fine. Thank you very much.
4. What would you like to drink?
   — Well, if I could have ....thing I liked, I think I'd choose .... really cold milk.

adjectives

Grammar Summary

My wallet is **black**.	Adjectives give more information about a noun.
I've lost a **black** wallet.	
I've lost a **black leather** wallet.	
The boy was **late.**	Singular and plural are the same.
The girls were **late,** too.	
She's a **really nice** person.	Use *very* or *really* to make an adjective stronger.
It's **very cheap.**	

		Comparative	Superlative
Short adjectives			
one syllable	**cheap**	**cheaper**	**the cheapest**
two syllables ending in -y	**early**	**earlier**	**the earliest**
Long adjectives			
two syllables	**careful**	**more careful**	**the most careful**
more syllables	**difficult**	**more difficult**	**the most difficult**
Irregular adjectives			
	good	**better**	**the best**
	bad	**worse**	**the worst**

Grammar Comment

1. It is possible, but unusual, to use more than two adjectives in front of a noun. Study these examples; if you change the order of the adjectives, they sound very strange indeed:

our **new English** teacher	the **flashy white** sports-car
a **new digital** watch	her **lovely red** frock
my **brown tweed** jacket	a **long hard** day
an **old cotton** shirt	a **nice strong** coffee

   The only general guide (it certainly is not a definite rule) is that usually the more specific the adjective is, the closer it comes to the noun. In other words the order is often: general adjective — specific adjective — noun.

2. You can make something sound particularly strong by saying:
   very very dangerous
   really very difficult

3. Some adjectives of two syllables can make their comparative and superlative either with **-er/-est** or with **more/most**:

stupid	**polite**	**common**	**gentle**	**narrow**

   If you are not sure, people will always understand if you use **more/most**.

UNIT 52

Practice 52.1

Look at this example:

> The/train/arrived/on/time/last.
> **The last train arrived on time.**

Arrange the words to make a correct sentence.

1. This/book/was/expensive

   ....

2. The/book/was/on/the/shelf/English

   ....

3. My/coat/was/very/cheap

   ....

4. Her/hair/is/long

   ....

5. They/were/for/the/appointment/early

   ....

6. The/car/crashed/into/the/tree/new/red

   ....

7. Let's/wash/those/dishes/dirty

   ....

8. The/roads/are/in/the/rush/hour/busy

   ....

9. When/does/the/one/leave/first

   ....

10. Curry/is/too/for/me/hot/hot

    ....

Practice 52.2

Put the adjectives in the sentence in the best natural order.

1. We've just seen a ....
   .... car. (lovely, old)

2. Give something to that ....
   .... man. (old, poor)

3. What a lovely .... and
   .... carpet. (white, black)

4. That's a very ....
   .... tie. (expensive, silk)

5. That .... car of
   yours is too noisy. (fast, new)

6. There's a ....
   smell! (funny, burning)

Practice 52.3

Put the adjectives (in brackets) in the correct order in the spaces.

1. I'll be in Moscow in the .... weeks in June. (two, first)
2. The .... days of the holiday were awful! (last, three)
3. There was a lot of fighting in the .... days of the war. (few, last)
4. Why don't we have a break in the .... weeks of May? (middle, two)
5. The .... survivor of the air crash has died. (remaining, last)

UNIT 52

Practice 52.4

Write a description of your favourite or least favourite male relative, for example, an uncle, a cousin, grandfather. Use your own words if you can, or some of the following:

**old   young   tall   short   fat   thin   black   white   yellow   dirty   brown
new   old   torn   broken   lovely   cheap   expensive   awful**

He is .... years old, so he is .... He is very .... He has ....

.... hair, and .... eyes. His nose is very .... He has ....

teeth. He always wears .... clothes. He usually wears .... trousers and

.... shirts, except when he visits our house. Then he wears .... trousers

and .... shirts. He usually has .... shoes and sometimes wears

a .... hat on his head.

Practice 52.5

It is common in English to avoid using negative adjectives, particularly about people. Instead, you use **not very** + **a positive** adjective. For example:

The weather was bad ➧ The weather **wasn't very** good.

Rewrite these sentences using positive adjectives.

1. Jim is short.

    ....

2. Mary is rude.

    ....

3. Their house was dirty.

    ....

4. Jean is very impatient.

    ....

5. The Smiths were unfriendly.

    ....

6. Her clothes looked cheap.

    ....

7. The food tasted awful.

    ....

8. Food was very expensive.

    ....

Practice 52.6

Here are 20 adjectives. There are 10 pairs of opposites. Match them up.

poor	early	noisy	attractive
calm	boring	affluent	modern
sour	ugly	bright	stormy
late	quiet	interesting	sweet
ancient	dull	straight	curly

1. ....

2. ....

3. ....

4. ....

5. ....

6. ....

7. ....

8. ....

9. ....

10. ....

194

UNIT 52

Practice 52.7

Here are 20 adjectives — there are 10 pairs of words of similar meaning. Match them up.

curved	chilly	extrovert	still
rough	pointed	loud	attractive
silky	noisy	cold	rounded
unhappy	sharp	motionless	smooth
outgoing	coarse	good-looking	depressed

1. ....   6. ....

2. ....   7. ....

3. ....   8. ....

4. ....   9. ....

5. ....   10. ....

Practice 52.8

Make compound adjectives by matching one word from each of these groups. Then use the compound adjectives in the sentences below:

loud	sighted
light	tempered
slow	haired
quick	mouthed
white	headed
short	witted

1. I felt quite .... as I climbed to the 25th floor.

2. Although she was old, my grandmother was very .... in conversation.

3. I know I am very impatient. It doesn't take much to make me ....

4. The .... old man walked slowly over the road.

5. He was very .... — he was rude and unpleasant to everybody.

6. The .... lady stared around her. She looked completely lost.

Grammar Summary

Ahmed is **older than** Razi.	Comparative + *than*
The book is **better than** the film.	
This baker is **more expensive than** the one round the corner.	
Have you any **smaller** oranges?	
Have you anything a bit **cheaper?**	
I think yours is **better.**	
Maria is **as old as** Marco.	*as* + adjective + *as*
Gas isn't **as expensive as** electricity.	
Was he **as angry as** he looked?	

Superlatives

Razi is **the tallest** in the class.	*the* + superlative
Gabi is **the most careful** driver I know.	
How much is **the cheapest** flight to Athens?	
The **most expensive** isn't always **the best.**	
Where's **the nearest** toilet, please?	

Grammar Comment

1. Study these examples:
        a. John is older than Peter.
        b. Peter is younger than John.
    The basic meaning of the first two sentences is the same. The choice of the starting-point of the sentence (the topic) forces you to use a particular structure for the rest of the sentence.
    So, although (a) and (b) have the same basic meaning, you use (a) if you want to talk about John, and (b) if you are talking about Peter.
        Bill is **as old** as Mark.
    Note that this does not necessarily mean that Bill and Mark are identical in age. It means that Bill is not younger than Mark. Mark may be a little older than Bill.

2. You can make comparatives and superlatives stronger in the following ways:
        A Ford is **much more expensive.**
        A Volvo is **far more expensive.**
        A Mercedes is **very much more expensive.**
        A Rolls Royce is **by far the most expensive.**

UNIT 53

Practice 53.1

Here are 4 cars. Who do they belong to?

£10,000   £2,000   £1,000   £350

Zoe's car is cheaper than Mick's.   Mick has the most expensive car.
Alex's car is more expensive than Zoe's.   John's car is cheaper than either Alex's or
                                                  Zoe's cars.

Practice 53.2

How old are they?
Study this information and work out how old the people are:
Zoe is 2 years younger than Alex.   Steve is 11 years older than Zoe.
Alex is younger than Steve or John.   Mick is the oldest.
John is 30 years old.   Steve is 3 years younger than Mick.
Mick is 7 years older than John.   Zoe is the youngest.

1. Steve is .... years old.   4. John ....
2. Mick is ....   5. Alex ....
3. Zoe ....

Practice 53.3

Here are the endings of some comparative adjectives. What are they? Fill in the missing letters.

1. _ _ _ l l e r   4. _ _ t t e r   7. _ _ _ _ _ n g e r
2. _ _ l l e r   5. _ _ _ _ p e r   8. _ _ _ n g e r
3. _ _ g h e r   6. _ _ _ _ c k e r   9. _ _ _ r k e r

Practice 53.4

Complete the following. You will need either a comparative or superlative adjective in each.

1. Mount Everest is the .... mountain in the world.

2. The Soviet Union is the .... country in the world, but the country
   with the .... population is China.

3. Going by plane is .... than going by train, but it is also
   ....

4. Although we hear about terrible air crashes, flying is still the .... way
   to travel. It is much .... than walking down the road!

5. Learning a foreign language becomes .... and .... the
   older you get. It is much .... if you start when you are about 7 or 8
   years old.

6. Finland is one of the .... countries in Europe. Don't forget to take
   some warm clothes with you if you go there.

7. The .... picture ever sold was painted by Van Gogh.

8. I suppose it's .... for a German to learn Japanese
   than to learn English.

197

Grammar Summary

Regular

Adjective		Adverb	
slow	careful	slowly	carefully
easy	sensible	easily	sensibly

He's a slow reader.

It's easy to make it yourself.

He reads slowly.   + -ly

You can easily make it yourself.   -y →ily

Irregular

Adjective and adverb the same:

hard	late	early
fast	straight	
harder	earlier	faster

Adjective	Adverb
He has long **straight** hair.	Go **straight** along Cromwell Road . . . .
Let's catch the **late** train.	The train arrived 10 minutes **late.**
She's a **hard** worker.	She works **hard.**

	Adjective	Adverb	
They're a good team.	**good**	**well**	They played well last Saturday.
These are a better buy.	**better**	**better**	Do you feel better now?

These words look like adverbs formed in the usual way but have special meanings:

nearly	= almost	Be careful! You **nearly** spilt your tea.
hardly (any)	= almost none	There's **hardly** any butter left.
lately	= in the near past	I haven't seen her **lately.**
shortly	= in the near future	I'll have to be going home **shortly.**
directly	= immediately	I'll let you know **directly** I hear myself.

Grammar Comment

1. You can make adverbs stronger by using the comparative:

    carefully   You must do your work **more carefully.**

    more carefully   You'll have to do it again **much more carefully.**

    In fact, you'll have to do it **as carefully as possible.**

2. Comparing adverbs is very similar to comparing adjectives:

Adjective	Adverb
Comparative + than	

    Ahmed is **older than** Razi.

    This restaurant is **more expensive than** that one.

    Liverpool played **better** than they did last week.

    She speaks English **more confidently** than her brother.

    Not as . . . as . . .

    Razi isn't **as old as** Ahmed.

    Chinese food isn't **as spicy** as Indian.

    He doesn't speak English **as confidently as** his sister.

    Liverpool didn't play **as well as** they did last week.

UNIT 54

Practice 54.1

Underline the adverbs in the following sentences:

1. It's a very straight road. It goes direct to the station.
2. If you walk straight through the park, it's on your left.
3. You'll be able to do it if you try hard.
4. Life was very hard just after the war.
5. Let's get the early train. I want to be there a bit early.
6. He doesn't need a fast car. He drives too fast with the one he has got now!

Practice 54.2

John and Mick are climbing a mountain. They can see bad weather coming. Complete their dialogue with the adverbs below.

faster   never   shortly   immediately   hardly   fast   almost

John Right, let's go down. The weather is getting worse and worse. We'll
.... get to the top.

Mick OK, but be careful, you .... dropped your hammer.

John It's alright, I've got it, but I can't go on. There's .... any rope left.
Can't you move any ....?

Mick No, it's impossible. I'm going as .... as I can. Have you radio-ed for help?

John Yes of course. I told you I'll let you know .... I hear anything.

Mick Good. Listen, can you hear a helicopter? Yes, there's one on the way.

John Terrific! We'll be rescued ....

Practice 54.3

Look at this example:

His life is dangerous.
— He lives **dangerously.**

Re-write these sentences in a similar way using an adverb ending in **-ly.**

1. Marie is a quick worker.
....

2. Little David is a slow reader.
....

3. Anna is brilliant pianist.
....

4. Eve is a beautiful dancer.
....

5. She's a careful writer.
....

6. This car is a smooth runner.
....

Practice 54.4

Fill in the correct **-ly** adverb in the spaces. Choose from the list.

1. They're very .... married.
2. I'm sorry to say he is .... worse today.
3. This young girl is .... well-qualified for the job.
4. The outbreak of war was .... close.
5. Before the Revolution the rich were .... well-off.
6. The instructions on this packet are .... complicated.
7. We had been .... misled by the pre-course information.
8. He failed the exam because he wrote so ....

disgustingly
badly
carelessly
considerably
dangerously
extremely
unnecessarily
happily

199

Grammar Summary

The rules are very complicated. Here are some useful tips:

1. If you are unsure, put the adverb *at the end* of the sentence.

2. These adverbs of time usually come after **(be)** or after the first auxiliary.

always, often,   Peter is **never** late.
usually, sometimes,   You must **always** lock the door.
never, already   We've **sometimes** had lunch at work.

3. These adverbs make an adjective or adverb stronger or weaker. They come *in front of* the adjective or adverb.

very, too, so,   Richard can swim **very well.**
rather, really, quite,   It's **too far** to walk.
extremely, slightly   It was **quite cold** in the water.
   This is a bad line – it's **extremely difficult** to hear you.

4. **ever**   mainly in questions   Have you **ever** been to Manchester?

5. **enough**   *after* an adjective or adverb   He isn't **strong enough.**
   He didn't work **hard enough.**
   in front of a noun   I haven't **enough money.**

Grammar Comment

The order of words in English is more flexible than many languages. You can put a word at the beginning or the end of a sentence for extra effect. Adverbs usually come in the middle of a sentence, usually after the first auxiliary and before the main verb:

We **always** have tea at 11.
He **sometimes** comes late.
They **usually** say thank you.
My boss **never** complains.
She is **always** buying me flowers.
We must **never** forget.

Study the following pairs where the only verb in the sentence is **(be)**:

I **am never** late. John **always is.**
Mary **is usually** bright and cheerful. Her sister **never is.**

Notice the adverb always comes before the verb in short answers:

We **never are.**   John **always does.**
He **seldom is.**   They **probably have.**

UNIT 55

Practice 55.1

Where does the adverb go?

Mark the best position of the adverb, then write the sentence out in full.

1. Peter is late. (never)
   ....

2. You must look both ways before crossing. (always)
   ....

3. Can you help him — he's not strong. (enough)
   ....

4. Don't keep looking at her. She's shy. (extremely)
   ....

5. I study after midnight. (rarely)
   ....

6. Jane eats meat. (hardly ever)
   ....

7. How much do you pay for lunch? (usually)
   ....

8. I take taxis. (never)
   ....

9. We bump into Jim in the supermarket. (occasionally)
   ....

Practice 55.2

In the following passage all the adverbs are printed in bold. They are then printed below. Study their position. Then mark each one in the following way:

A if it comes after the first auxiliary

B if it comes in front of an adjective or adverb

C if it comes in front of a main verb

I don't think I have **ever** had such a marvellous holiday in my life. It was **absolutely** wonderful. We **never** drive on holiday, but this year we made an exception. I **usually** like to sit on a beach, but this year I decided to discover what southern Spain was **really** like.

We spent four **incredibly** busy days in Seville, then **bravely** decided to hire a car. I had heard that Spanish roads were **very** dangerous, but we found them **unbelievably** quiet. We drove along **almost** deserted country roads, with hundreds of **beautifully** coloured wild flowers on every side. The villages on the coast were **always** clean — **newly** painted for the summer season. The fish in the little beach restaurants were **freshly** caught that morning. The fishermen had **already** landed fish before we had breakfast.

The little towns sitting on the top of hills were never a disappointment. As our car **slowly** climbed in first or second gear and at last we reached the town square, we were glad we had made the effort. We were able to look down over the surrounding countryside, and even as far as the sea — and **smugly** think how lucky we were not to be lying like a **brightly** painted lobster on the hot tourist beaches. What a lovely change from so many other holidays!

1. ever ....
2. absolutely ....
3. never ....
4. usually ....
5. really ....
6. incredibly ....
7. bravely ....
8. very ....
9. unbelievably ....
10. almost ....
11. beautifully ....
12. always ....
13. newly ....
14. freshly ....
15. already ....
16. slowly ....
17. smugly ....
18. brightly ....

Grammar Summary

Subject pronoun	Object pronoun	Possessive adjective	Possessive pronoun	Reflexive pronoun
I	me	my	mine	myself
you	you	your	yours	yourself
we	us	our	ours	ourselves
they	them	their	theirs	themselves
he	him	his	his	himself
she	her	her	hers	herself
it	it	its	its	itself

Use a pronoun instead of a noun when it is clear *who* or *what* you are talking about.

Object pronouns

Would you like to come with **us?**

Do you live near **them?**

Could you send them direct to **me**, please?

after a preposition

Who broke that window?
▷ It wasn't **me**.

after **(be)** instead of a subject pronoun

Can Eva send them to **me**, please?

Tony made it for **her.**

After *to* and *for* with *make, give, send, lend, pass, take, show*

Grammar Comment

1.   If your own language has two different words for '**you**', remember that English has only one. It is normal to use **you** direct to anybody — a friend or a complete stranger.

2.   Do not mix up **her/hers** and **your/yours**:

  I gave the book back to **her**. It was **hers**.
  Are you sure this is **your** pen. I didn't think it was **yours**.

3.   Note the identical pronunciation, but different spelling of **there** and **their**:
  Is that **their** car over **there?**

4.   Most people think of **they** as the 'third person plural' pronoun, and usually it is. But it also has a special use; see Unit 58.

5.   **It** also has a number of special uses; see Unit 59.

UNIT 56

Practice 56.1

Look at these two sentences. They have the same meaning.

> I'm going **on my own.**
> I'm going **by myself.**

Fill in the spaces in the following:

1. You're doing it on .... own.
   You're doing it by ....

2. He's eating on .... own.
   He's eating by ....

3. She lives on .... own.
   She lives by ....

4. It works on .... own.
   It works by ....

5. We make it on .... own.
   We make it by ....

6. They travel on .... own.
   They travel by ....

Practice 56.2

In the following situations fill in one pronoun in each space.

1. You're very welcome to come to the opera with us.
   — Not on .... life!

2. Do you think I'll win?
   —I think it's up to ....

3. Do you like the new anti-smoking campaign?
   — I'm all for ....

4. I wish Jill would stop drinking.
   — Yes, she's .... own worst enemy.

5. Why don't you get a video camera?
   — What do .... think .... am! Made of money?

6. The managers are having a lot of trouble at work with the Unions.
   — It sounds like a '..................... and ....' problem.

7. I'm surprised Bill married someone like Samantha.
   — He's made .... own bed. .... can lie in it!

8. Do you like my new jeans and sweatshirt?
   — Oh yes, ... is very nice, but aren't .... a bit tight?

Practice 56.3

Complete the following with a pronoun ending in **-self** or **-selves.**

1. Don't blame .... It wasn't your fault.

2. You look very pleased with .... Has something nice just happened?

3. My father has just bought .... a new car.

4. I was just going to make .... a cup of tea. Would you like one?

5. I'm very pleased with my video. I don't know why you don't get one
   ....

6. She wasn't very confident, but she surprised .... by passing her test first time.

7. He's just failed his test again, so he's rather sorry for .... at the moment.

8. The train is getting more and more expensive. I'm going to get a car. It'll be quite expensive but it'll soon pay for ....

Grammar Summary

Adjective
Tells you who owns something

My feet hurt!
Is this **your** sweater?
I don't think this is **his** car, is it?
Sheila's left **her** bag somewhere in here.
Our children like **their** school.
What's **your** phone number?

Pronoun
Instead of a possessive adjective and a noun

▷ So do **mine!** = *So do my feet*
▷ Yes, where's **yours?**
▷ No, **his** is over there.
▷ I think this is **hers,** isn't it?
▷ Yes, **ours** like **theirs**, too.
▷ 7726981. What's **yours?**

Reflexive pronouns

He's cut **himself.**

Oh dear! Have you hurt **yourself?**

The subject and the object are the same.

Did you do the decorations **yourself?**
▷ I did the painting **myself,** but that's all.

Can I give you a hand?
▷ No, it's all right thanks. I can do it **myself.**

Used for emphasis

Some special expressions

Help		I live **by myself.**	= I live *on my own.*
Enjoy	**yourself!**	He lives **by himself.**	= He lives *on his own.*
Behave	**yourselves!**	They live **by themselves.**	= They live *on their own.*

Grammar Comment

1. In English we use the possessive adjective to talk about parts of the body:
    > I've hurt **my** foot.
    > **Your** thumb is bleeding.

2. The normal place for the reflexive pronoun is at the end of a sentence:
    > That wasn't very good, was it?
    > — No, I was a bit disappointed **myself.**

    In these examples:
    > I thought the same thing **myself.**
    > She did it **herself.**
    > He wrote the whole book **himself.**

    if you put the reflexive pronoun immediately after the first pronoun, particularly after **I,** you will often sound too formal, so we suggest you avoid sentences like:
    > I **myself** thought the same thing.
    > I **myself** did it.

UNIT 57

Practice 57.1

Mick and Tim have just met. They haven't seen each other since they were at school 15 years ago.

Fill in the spaces with the following pronouns:

mine   your   yours   our   ours   her   his   their   theirs

Tim   You knew I'd got married, didn't you?

Mick   No. Tell me all about .... wife.

Tim   Well, she's an artist actually.

Mick   So is .... What a coincidence!

Tim   Yes, ... wife's work is very popular. .... paintings are quite well-known.

Mick   And .... daughter is the best at art in .... class.

Tim   Is she? I wish I could say the same about .... daughter! But at least .... son is the fastest runner in .... school.

Mick   I think .... son is the slowest in .... school. But of course .... wife and I are very happy with .... children. They really love .... school.

Tim   Well, ... children hate .... They would rather watch TV all the time.

Mick   Look, what's .... phone number? We must meet soon.

Tim   7388921. What's .... ?

Practice 57.2

The most common reflexive pronoun is **yourself.** Fill in the correct verb, and **yourself** in each space.

do   defend   love   control   enjoy   teach   compare   please

1.   I got the paper and paint in the '...........................-It-...........................' shop.
2.   I've bought a '........................... Arabic' course.
3.   Christians believe you should .... your neighbour as ....
4.   There's so much violence around, you have to be able to ....
5.   I'm having a strawberry one. You can ....
6.   Do your best and don't .... with other people.
7.   Have a nice holiday. .... !
8.   Come on, stop crying. ....

Practice 57.3

Use the following pronouns to complete these sentences:

myself   yourself   himself   herself   yourselves

1.   Look at the table — Paul made it ....
2.   Do you repair your car .... or do you send it to the garage?
3.   John hit .... with a hammer when he was fixing the car.
4.   My father lives in that big house by .... He has no friends, and we have all left home.
5.   Children, be quiet, sit down and behave ....
6.   Come in, help .... to food and drink.
7.   May I help .... to a little more salad please?
8.   Does your sister live by .... ?

Grammar Summary

They is used to talk about:

    1. more than one person: *The children are excited – they're going on a trip tomorrow.*

    2. a general group of people:

They are repairing the road.	*they* = the Town Council
They want to increase income tax.	*they* = the Government
They say it's a marvellous film.	*they* = a lot of people
They tell me you are changing your job.	*they* = somebody or some people

They and **their** are also used to talk about *one* person with:

some-	
any-	-body
no-	-one
every-	

Someone has left **their** pen on the desk.

Somebody told you, didn't **they!**

Anybody knows that, don't **they!**

Everyone has to bring **their** own food.

If **anyone** rings while I'm out, please ask **them** to ring back.

Grammar Comment

They is used for:
    a. Two or more people you know.
    b. A group of unknown people.
    c. One person whose sex you do not know.

Here are some examples:
    a. I've spoken to the teachers. **They**'re coming to the disco.
    b. **They**'ve knocked down the old cinema.

Meaning (**c**) may seem unusual to you, but it is perfectly natural and quite common in spoken English:
    c. Look! There's someone climbing out of that window up there. I hope **they**'re careful. It would be terrible if **they** fell.

    If anybody rings, take **their** name and number. Tell **them** I'll ring them back as soon as I can.

    Somebody must have seen it happen, mustn't **they?**

    Anybody could have stolen it, couldn't **they?**

    Nobody mentioned it, did **they?**
    — Well **they** wouldn't, would **they?**

Notice **they** is the normal pronoun for tags and short answers with **nobody, somebody, everybody, anybody.**

UNIT 58

Practice 58.1

Very often **they** is used in sentences of this kind:

They've knocked down the old theatre.
They're going to build a new swimming pool.

Re-write these sentences. Start with **they.**

1. The station has been knocked down.

   ....

2. Taxes are going to be increased.

   ....

3. The price has been put up.

   ....

4. The road is being repaired.

   ....

5. The new airport is being planned.

   ....

Practice 58.2

Fill in **they, them, their** in the following:

1. While we are at the youth hostel, everyone has to make .... own bed.
2. Someone told you, didn't ....?
3. If anyone rings this afternoon, ask .... to leave a message.
4. Someone was here when we were out and left .... keys behind.
5. Anybody in the office would know that, wouldn't ....?
6. ....'re going to re-build the Town Hall, aren't ....
7. Shhhh. I can hear someone coming. Let's go before .... come in.
8. Look! There's someone on that building. I think ....'re going to jump!

Practice 58.3

After each of the following situations, try to write down who **they** refers to.

1. I see they've started digging up the road outside your house.

   They = ...
2. I heard on the news they're thinking of putting interest rates up.

   They = ...
3. They ought to do something about the mess dogs make around here.

   They = ...
4. In Sweden they've got laws about the colour you can paint your house!

   They = ...
5. They ought to raise old age pensions.

   They = ...
6 They've been planning to dig a Channel Tunnel for over 100 years.

   They = ...
7. I'm sorry they don't make women's shoes smaller than size 35.

   They = ...

Can you give a 'rule' for **they**? Can it be **any** group of people?

Grammar Summary

it is used as a pronoun in the usual way: *There is a car park but it's full at the moment.*

it is also used for:

Weather	**It's** raining.	It was snowing.
	It's rather cold.	It was a very warm evening.
Time	**It's** three o'clock.	**It's** the fifth today, isn't it.
	It's getting late.	**It's** time to go.
	It's a long time ago.	**It's** Saturday tomorrow.
Distance	**It's** about two miles.	**It's** not far.
	How far is **it** to Oxford?	**It's** rather a long way.

It is also used as a dummy subject when *is ('s)* is followed by certain adjectives:

It's essential to be there by 7 o'clock.

It's possible to get a bus.

It's lovely to have a day off.

It's best to get a taxi.

It's difficult to believe that.

It's interesting to see new places.

It's not true that he's changing his job.

It's better to phone her.

Note

It's no use asking Peter – he wasn't there.

It's worth asking him – he might know.

Grammar Comment

Note the two spellings and three meanings:

     a. its   = (possessive) : The dog lost **its** way.

     b. it's = it is   : **It's** a lovely dog.

             = it has   : **It's** been a terrible winter.

It is important when you learn a phrase starting with **it**, that you also learn the words which follow. There are a few words which are followed by the **-ing** form; there are many words which are followed by either **to** + **First Form** or **that . . .**

It's	**worth**	try**ing** harder.
It's	**no use**	complain**ing.**
It's	**good**	**to** get out into the country.
It's	**best**	**to** keep quiet.
It's	**difficult**	**to** understand what he means.
It's	**true**	**that** she has a pet snake.
It's	**best**	**that** you arrive 10 minutes early.
It's	**possible**	**that** you'll be promoted.

When you learn a new phrase with **it**, make a note of what can follow.

UNIT 59

Practice 59.1

Fill in **it** and one of the expressions given to complete the sentences below:

essential   possible   lovely   worth   wrong

1. Come in! ....'s .... to see you again.
2. ....'s .... that we have a meeting as soon as possible.
3. Some people think ....'s .... to offer young people alcohol.
4. ....'s .... we've met before but I doubt it.
5. I don't think ....'s .... travelling first class.

silly   difficult   necessary   a pity   no use

6. ....'s always .... to see trees being cut down.
7. ....'s .... to believe how cruel some people can be.
8. ....'s .... crying over spilt milk. (proverb).
9. ....'s .... to check in at least 45 minutes before departure.
10. ....'s .... to cross the road without looking.

best   true   interesting   doesn't matter   right

11. Do you think ....'s .... to watch TV abroad?
12. Is .... to test new cosmetics on animals?
13. Is .... that you keep a diary?
14. .... if you don't win.
15. ....'s .... if you try to speak even if you make mistakes.

Practice 59.2

Fill in **there** + **(be)** or **it** + **(be)** in the following. It's a postcard from a friend on holiday.

This is a lovely place. .... a lot to see and
do. .... a very interesting museum and a
castle. .... on the top of a hill outside town.
.... several lovely beaches. .... very
hot. In fact, ... over 30° at this very
moment. .... too many British people here
and .... lots of Germans.   They are not
popular with Spaniards. .... easy to get
around without speaking Spanish. .... quite a
lot of people who speak excellent English.
.... lovely not to worry about the weather.
And .... great to eat in a different restaurant
every night. .... so many to choose from.
Hope you are well.

Grammar Summary

That train is too early. What time is the next (train) **one.**
The French apples are 50p, but the English (apples) **ones** are only 45p.

Use *one* or *ones* instead of repeating the same noun.

the this/that	one
which	one?

the these/those	ones
which	ones?

I'm going to make a cup of coffee. Would you like **one?**
▷ Mm yes, I'd love **one,** thank you.

Which is your bike?
▷ **The** blue **one, the one** next to the car.

Shall I use these tea-bags?
▷ No, use **the ones** on the shelf, please.

Which one do you prefer?
▷ **That one's** lovely, but I think **this one** will suit me better.

Grammar Comment

We often use the same idea twice in a sentence which contains a **contrast:**
    I like the red dress **but** I'm not keen on the blue **one.**

This is also true when we **compare** two things:
    The house we live in now is **much bigger than** our old **one.**

Often one person in a conversation uses **one(s)** instead of repeating the noun the other person used:
    I'm going to have **a cup of coffee.**
    — Oh, will you make **one** for me too, please?

We are thinking of getting **a dog.**
    — A dog! I wouldn't have **one** in the house — not if you live in town.

We use **one(s)** to avoid repeating a noun. There is a similar way to avoid repeating a verb:

We've already got tickets.	We live in Oxford Road.
— So **have** we.	— So **do** we.

    We are going to buy her a present when she leaves.
    — Really. We're going to buy her **one** too.
or   Oh, we **are** too.

You can see from these examples how you can avoid repeating nouns, verbs, or whole phrases in English.

UNIT 60

Practice 60.1

In each of these sentences you can replace a repeated word with **one(s).** Change the sentences in that way.

1. I'm going to have an ice-cream. Would you like an ice-cream?
2. I'm going to buy a ticket for myself — shall I get a ticket for you too?
3. The pictures I took are OK but the pictures my wife took have come out too dark.
4. The cards from Rome arrived safely but the cards from Venice never arrived.
5. My steak was fine but the steak John had was very tough.
6. The tall man had a beard but the man who took the money was clean-shaven.
7. This new novel is much more amusing than his previous novel.

Practice 60.2

Complete the following dialogues. You will need to use **one(s).**

1. I think we're going to miss our train.
   — When is the next ....?

2. Could I have one of those tarts, please.
   — Now, which .... would you like? The lemon .... are 40p and the raspberry .... are 45p.
   I'll have .... of each, please.

3. I can't remember which is your car.
   — Mine's the white .... over there behind the red ....

4. Shall I use these mugs?
   — No, they're not very clean. Use the .... on the shelf.

5. Have a fruit gum.
   — Do you mind if I have a red ....?
   Yes, I do! The red .... are my favourites. You can have a green ....!
   — But I don't like green ....!
   Well, have an orange .... I'm not so keen on them. I keep the red .... till last. I always eat the black .... first in case any one else gets them!
   — I think you're selfish.
   Only when it comes to fruit gums!

6. I get really frightened when I have to go on a plane.
   — Do you hate all planes?
   Well, most are bad, and some are worse. The big .... are the worst. I'm not as afraid when I'm in a small ....

In these examples you need to add an extra word too:

7. I just love coming back to London.
   — It's the galleries you like best, isn't it.
   Yes, I love them all.
   — But .... do you like best?
   I suppose .... that is my real favourite is the Victoria and Albert.

8. Of all the Royal Family, who do you like best?
   — I think .... I admire most is The Queen herself.
   Yes, she's .... who gets into the news.

there + (be)

Grammar Summary

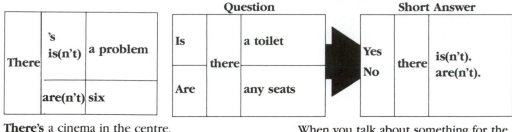

	Question			Short Answer	
There	's is(n't)	a problem	Is		a toilet	Yes No	there	is(n't). are(n't).
	are(n't)	six	Are		any seats

There's a cinema in the centre.

Is there a telephone box in the station?

There are some people waiting outside.

Are there 2 m's in 'recommend'?

There's nothing we can do about it.

There's somebody waiting for you outside.

Is there anywhere to eat near here?

When you talk about something for the first time

There must be a mistake.

There might be a strike.

There can be a lot of rain at this time of year.

There should be a bus in five minutes.

There'll be trouble when he finds out!

With an auxiliary and *be*

There isn't enough room, **is there?**
▷ Oh yes, I think **there is.**

There is repeated in the tag and in the short answer.

Grammar Comment

1. **There + (be)** and **It + (be)** are both used to introduce a new topic into the conversation. As a general guide (but not a definite rule) **there** is followed by a noun, **it** is followed by an adjective:

    There's a letter for you on the table.
    It's very **dark.** I think it's going to rain.

2. **There** can be used with the different forms of the verb (**be**) and with modals:

    There's someone outside.
    There was someone outside.
    There can't be anyone there.
    There must be a mistake.

3. In modern spoken English you will hear both of these:

    There are twenty mistakes.
    There's twenty mistakes.

    There's + a plural is now accepted in spoken English. Notice the short form **'s.**
    There is/was + a plural are not possible.

4. Remember to repeat **there** in tagged statements and short answers.

    There weren't many people there, were **there?**
    There's a hole in it, isn't **there?**

UNIT 61

Practice 61.1

Fill in **there** + **(be)** in the following:

Sue is speaking to John. She has just come back from Spain.

John   So did you have a good time?

Sue   Terrific. I could go back again tomorrow. The main problem was at the
airport. .... so many people you could hardly
move. I couldn't find my bags, and .... nobody
there to help. It was chaos!

John   But .... no policemen around?

Sue   .... nobody to help at all. ....
.... mothers with children — crying. ....
.... old people who couldn't carry their bags — but
.... nobody to help.

John   But at least you had a good holiday, didn't you?

Sue   Oh yes. But when we finally got out of the airport, ...
.... no trains. And .... no information.

John   And you were wishing you had stayed on that beach!

Sue   Exactly!

Practice 61.2

Complete these sentences using the appropriate part of **there** + **(be)** or **it** + **(be)**.

1. .... any apples left?
2. .... cold outside?
3. .... anything good on TV last night?
4. .... much petrol left?
5. .... any chance of a ticket?
6. .... possible?
7. .... far?
8. .... any banks open today?
9. .... a phone near her?
10. .... near enough to walk to?
11. .... enough room for a couple more?
12. .... anybody there yesterday I knew?
13. ....very hot when we arrive?
14. .... many foreigners when you were there?

Practice 61.3

Look at this example:

> **Is there** a monster in Loch Ness?
> — **There** might be.

We often use **there** with modal auxiliaries and **be**. Reply to the following questions with short answers, using **there**, a modal auxiliary and **be**.

1. Is there an underground in Paris?   There must be.
2. Were there Olympic Games in 1924?   ....
3. Will there be Olympic Games in the year 2000?   ....
4. Is there life on the moon?   ....
5. Could there be life on another planet?   ....
6. Must there be two witnesses to a marriage?   ....

213

UNIT 61

Practice 61.4

Here are 5 descriptions of 5 cities. Fill in **there + (be).** Then decide what the cities and countries are.

1. .... a river running though it. .... a very high tower. .... a very famous underground system. .... some very wide streets. .... a famous archway called the Arc de Triomphe. The city is .... It's in ....

2. .... a lot of problems in this city. .... two parts to it. .... a high wall separating the parts. The city is .... It's in ....

3. .... millions of people in this city. .... two oceans near. .... a terrible earthquake there not very long ago. The city is .... It's in ....

4. .... a large castle in the middle of this city. .... a royal palace about a mile from the castle. .... very few English accents, but everyone speaks English. It's an easy place to get a whisky. The city is .... It's in ....

5. .... a lot of cars and a lot of pollution. It is a very old city. .... several hills in the centre of this city. .... a large building called the Acropolis. The city is .... It's in ....

6. .... about 30 million people living here. .... one of the best underground systems in the world. .... lots of modern buildings. .... an Imperial Palace. .... an international airport called Narita. The city is .... It's in ....

Practice 61.5

Match up the following to make five two-line dialogues:

1. I thought there was a cinema here.

   a. There might be. It's not in the programme.

2. Will there be a break?

   b. There must be one somewhere surely.

3. I thought there would be more people here.

   c. There used to be. It's now a supermarket.

4. There are no buses after 10 o'clock.

   d. I feel there should be. It's too far to walk.

5. Isn't there a toilet?

   e. There can be — on Fridays especially.

1	2	3	4	5

UNIT 61

Practice 61.6

Ann's suitcase was stolen when her back was turned at the airport. She is talking to a policeman. She is trying to remember what was in it.

Fill in **there** + **(be)** in the spaces.

Policeman	Now, Miss, can you tell me the contents of your case.
Ann	I'm not quite sure what was in it exactly. It was mostly my holiday clothes.
Policeman	I'm afraid I need more details.
Ann	.... two pairs of shoes. .... a light raincoat and a pair of pyjamas.
Policeman	And what colour were the shoes?
Ann	White. .... six pairs of tights and some underwear. .... a pair of jeans, and, now I remember, ... several T-shirts and blouses. .... a present for a friend, as well.
Policeman	.... anything of any value?
Ann	No, I don't think .... It was mostly clothes. .... a couple of pullovers and a towel.
Policeman	And what was the total value, do you think?
Ann	Oh, that's a difficult question — probably about £200. And the case cost £20 itself.
Policeman	.... anything special about the case — your address, for example?
Ann	Oh, yes, ... two labels, one inside and one outside. Both had my name, address and telephone number.

Practice 61.7

Complete the following situations with your own ideas.

1. At the circus

If you have ever been to a circus you will know .... lots of things to see. There are .... and .... Some people, however, don't believe that .... should .... animals in circuses. They believe it is cruel to train animals just to entertain us.

2. Many years ago

Many years ago before I was born there used to be .... and .... There didn't use to be such things as .... or .... which we now take for granted.

3. My ideal world

If I had my way the world would be a very different place. There would be no .... or .... And there certainly wouldn't be any .... Instead there would be .... and ....

4. The environment

Mankind is ruining the world. Pollution is making the air unfit to breathe, water unfit to drink, and the earth an unsafe place to live in — especially for animals. If we continue polluting our world, there will soon be no .... or .... There will be nowhere left to .... There will be nowhere left to .... There will be ....

this, that, these, those

Grammar Summary

this	these
→○	→○○ ○○○
that	those
→ ○	→ ○○ ○○○

Use:
1. **in front of a noun**
2. **alone when it is clear what you are talking about**

Does **this** bus go to Victoria, please?
Does **this** go to Victoria please?

These strawberries are delicious.
These are delicious.

Things that are physically near.

This is the life!
These science fiction films are a waste of money.

Things which are "psychologically near"; the speaker feels they are near at the moment of speaking.

How much is **that** dress please?
How much is **that** please?

A pound of **those** tomatoes please.
A pound of **those** please.

Things which are physically remote.

That was lucky! I didn't expect **that**.

That kind of person really annoys me.

Is **that** all?

Things which are "psychologically remote" from the speaker at the moment of speaking.

Grammar Comment

This and **these** express nearness to the speaker: near in space, time, relationship. The basic idea is 'here', in my space.

That and **those** express distance from the speaker. The basic idea is 'there', not in my space.

Study the following pairs:

Will you post **these** letters, please?
Where are **those** letters I left here earlier?

What's **this** I hear about you going out with Marie?
What was **that**? I didn't hear what you said.

What time does **this** concert we're going to tonight start?
What was **that** concert like last week?

This is going to be the holiday of our lives!
That was the worst holiday I've ever had!

Notice the nearness is not only physical, it can also be psychological, things which the speaker **feels** are immediate or 'near'.

UNIT 62

Practice 62.1

Complete the following situations using **this**, **that**, **these**, and **those**.

1. What's your new car like?
   — .... one is much more reliable than my old one.

2. Have you been to see that new film everyone's talking about?
   — I'd never go to anything like ....!

3. I don't think Pete should get the job.
   — Oh come on. .... is a terrible thing to say!

4. Just look! Have you seen .... picture in the paper?
   — Oh yes, ... was taken a long time ago.

5. Have you ever been to Rome?
   — Years ago, but .... was one of the best holidays I've ever had.

6. You might not believe ...., but I've given up my job.
   — But ....'s crazy!

7. Hello, Bill, ... is Liz, my new area manager.
   — Hello Liz, pleased to meet you.

8. You look different. Are .... new glasses?
   — Yes they are, as a matter of fact.

9. I remember when beer was ten pence a pint.
   — Ah, ... were the days, my friend!

10. .... shoes cost £50!
    — But they're very nice.

11. Mmmm, ... is the nicest fruit salad I've had for ages.

12. She said she never wanted to see me again so .... was ....!

Practice 62.2

In this argument between two business colleagues fill in **this**, **that**, or **those**.

Edward	Everyone in the Brussels office is thinking of resigning. We have never had a situation like .... before.
Philip	.................'s true, but I don't think it's as serious as you make out.
Edward	So you think .... is a storm in a teacup, do you?
Philip	No, ...'s not what I meant. I know they are unhappy, but I don't think anyone will resign.
Edward	Look — what do you think .... is! It arrived today. It's a letter signed by the five of them.
Philip	Oh, ...'s different.
Edward	Is .... all you can say! Listen to me! .... people in .... office are your responsibility. .... is not a storm in a teacup. .... is a revolution! And the sooner you get over there and do something about it, the better.

Grammar Summary

that, who and **which** introduce more information about a person, thing, or idea.

The woman **that** lives next door is very friendly.	Tells us *which woman.*
Could I speak to the doctor **that** I saw yesterday, please?	Tells us *which doctor.*
The essay **that** won the prize was written by a German student.	Tells us *which essay.*

The person **who** told me had been there himself.

It was the blue car **which** caused the accident.

The thing **that** really surprised me was the price.	Often used with *the thing that . . .*
The thing **that** I really enjoyed was the music.	

That is usual in spoken English.

In written English use: *who* with people   *which* with things.

that, who, which are usually left out if they are the object of the verb that follows.

The man **who** I saw yesterday told me to come at ten o'clock.
→ **The man I saw yesterday told me to come at ten o'clock.**

Can I collect the coat **that** I brought in last week, please?
→ **Can I collect the coat I brought in last week, please?**

Grammar Comment

1. These words are used mostly in written English. The rules are complicated. Unless you need to write English accurately, do not worry if you find these comments difficult.
   There are two kinds of relative clause:

   a. One which **defines what has gone before:**
   The man **who helped me** was called Smith.
   (which man? — the one who helped me)
   You wasted the money **that I lent you.**
   (which money? — the money I lent you)
   These are called defining relative clauses.

   b. One which **adds extra information** about what has gone before:
   Do you remember old Mrs Brown, **who used to live next door?**
   (the clause gives an extra piece of information)
   We're going to Spain, **which will be pretty warm,** I suppose.

'Extra information' clauses must have commas.
Defining relative clauses are not written with commas.
That is **only** used in defining relative clauses.

2. The pronoun can be omitted in defining clauses when it refers to the object of the clause:

   The person **(that) I met in the queue** was the director.
   The woman **(who) I knocked down** was only slightly hurt.

UNIT 63

Practice 63.1

Join the sentences together. Use **who** to refer to people and **which** to refer to everything else.

Example:　　　　I owned the dog. It was run over by that lorry.

　　　　　　　　— I owned the dog **which** was run over by that lorry.

1. It was a black car. It caused the accident.

   ....

2. The thief was a young man. He was wearing a woollen hat.

   ....

3. We turned up early for the performance. It was cancelled.

   ....

4. I used to play in the band. It is now very famous.

   ....

5. I once knew the restaurant owner. He was found drowned in the river.

   ....

6. I saw the policeman. He arrested the murderer.

   ....

7. Who was driving the taxi? It didn't stop at the lights.

   ....

8. When did you stay at that hotel? It was burned to the ground.

   ....

9. Why were you so rude to that old lady? She asked you the way.

   ....

10. When did you write that letter? It caused a lot of trouble.

   ....

In most of these examples **that** can be used instead of **who** or **which; that** is more informal than **who** or **which,** and is more common in spoken English.

Practice 63.2

Look at these two sentences:

> The size surprised me.
> — The thing that really surprised me was the size.

They mean the same, but in the second the speaker uses **The thing that ...** in order to put the words he wants to emphasise — the sizes — at the end. The most important new information of an English sentence is usually at the **end** of the sentence. Change the following sentences in a similar way, starting **The thing that....**

1. I really liked the food.
   ....
2. His letter really pleased me.
   ....
3. We enjoyed the night life.
   ....
4. Her salary really amazed me.
   ....
5. The quietness helped me a lot.
   ....
6. The chance of promotion influenced me most.
   ....

Practice 63.3

Study these two sentences:

1. **I met the man who sent me £1000.**
   In this sentence **who** (referring to **the man**) is the subject of the second part.
   The first part = **I met the man** (Subject, **I**; object, **the man**).
   The second part = **The man sent me £1000** (Subject, **the men**; objects, **me, £1000**).
   You **cannot** miss out **who** in examples like this.

2. I met the man who I sent £1000 to.
   In this sentence **who** (referring to **the man**) is now the object of the second part.
   The first part = **I met the man**
   The second part = **I sent the man £1000.**(I is the subject; **the man** and **£1000** are the objects).

In sentences like this you **can** miss out **who** (or **whom**), so you can say **I met the man I sent £1000 to.**

In the following sentences, cross out **that, who,** and **which** where it is possible to do so.

1. Those people whom you met this morning were very rich.
2. Have you read the book that won the Booker prize?
3. I once slept in a bed that had been slept in by Henry VIII.
4. I lived beside the shop which was bombed.
5. I knew John was the only one who could become boss.
6. I thought Mary was the one who they would promote.
7. I've come to collect the camera which I lost yesterday, and which I heard had been handed in.
8. Is he the guy that everyone's talking about?
9. This is the house that Jack built.
10. I'm sorry to say that you dropped the match which started the fire.
11. I've been thinking about the problem which you told me about.
12. Why didn't you give something to the boy who found your wallet?
13. The number 13 is unlucky for people who believe in luck.
14. We live in an area that used to be full of slums.
15. I only like people who agree with me.

UNIT 63

Practice 63.4

Fill in **that, who,** or **which** in the following sentences:

1. What was the name of the guy .... assassinated President Kennedy?

2. The ship, ... was carrying 2000 people, sank on its first voyage.

3. The worst thing .... happened was losing our suitcase.

4. I've never discovered the name of the person .... found my wallet.

5. My eldest brother, ... lives in Canada, hasn't been home for 25 years.

6. This is the book .... caused all the problems.

7. She's the girl .... used to live next door.

8. There's the house .... Jack built.

9. Where's my pen? You know, the one .... had my name on it.

10. The storm, ... came during the night, destroyed thousands of trees.

Practice 63.5

Join these sentences together in a natural way using a relative pronoun. For example:

> There's the man. He stole my bag.
> — There's the man **who** stole my bag.

1. People cause trouble. They complain.

   ....

2. It was a white Mercedes. It knocked the woman down.

   ....

3. Where are the scissors? I bought them last week.

   ....

4. It must have been Mary. She left the note.

   ....

5. The Government might not win. It has a large majority.

   ....

6. The meeting was very interesting. I thought it was going to be really boring.

   ....

7. The bomb blew up a car. The car was near the bank.

   ....

8. I wish I knew the name of that man. He spoke to me again today.

   ....

Grammar Summary

about	the subject of a conversation idea, book, etc.	Tell me **about** your family. What are you thinking **about?**
at	certain special expressions	**At** home, **at** school, **at** work, **at** university, **at** the cinema, **at** the end of . . . .
by	the person or thing that did something	It was written **by** William Golding. I was shocked **by** what she told me.
	transport	We went **by** train.
for	purpose + noun or . . . *ing* form	Let's go **for** a cup of coffee. This machine's **for** peeling potatoes.
	a general period of time	We were there **for** three weeks. I haven't seen you **for** ages.
from	place of origin	Where is he **from?** They come **from** Sri Lanka.
with	in company	Would you like to come **with** us?
	what you use to do something	He cut himself **with** his pen-knife.

Grammar Comment

Students often think choosing the correct preposition is very confusing. It is much more logical than you might think. Most prepositions have a simple basic meaning. These are given in Units 64-67. The basic meanings can sometimes be shown with diagrams which help more than explaining the prepositions with more words. There are two problems. These are phrasal verbs (see Unit 45) and idioms. When prepositions are used in phrasal verbs or idioms they do not have their basic meaning. You need to learn the **whole** phrasal verb or the whole idiom.

> We drove **over** the new bridge.
> (**over** is a preposition, with its basic meaning)

> He can't **put** things **over** very well.
> (**put over** is a phrasal verb, meaning **explain.** You need to learn it as a single 'word', even though it has two parts.)

> Who's that **over there?**
> I've told you about it **over and over** again.
> (You need to learn these groups of words as idioms, without thinking of the basic meaning of **over.**)

UNIT 64

Practice 64.1

Fill in the following prepositions in these sentences:

about **at** **by** **for** **from** **with**

1. The longest rail tunnel is .... Tappi Saki to Fukushima.
2. He died .... the grand old age of 95.
3. A lot of people have been poisoned .... mushrooms this autumn.
4. All his life he talked .... the life to come.
5. Are you .... or against Nuclear Power?
6. What did you get your sister .... her birthday?
7. Was there anyone important .... the wedding?
8. This whole debate is .... who makes the decisions.
9. I wish you wouldn't play that radio .... full volume.
10. Are you paying cash or .... cheque?
11. To catch the bus we'll have to be ready .... 12 o'clock.
12. I didn't want to be seen so I sat .... the back.
13. You're very welcome to come .... us in our car.
14. You may think you're talking .... the Labour Party, but I think you're only talking .... a small minority.
15. Now, is this .... Handel or .... Mozart?
16. You're surely not going to hitchhike all .... yourself?

Practice 64.2

Fill in the following prepositions in these sentences:

about **at** **by** **for** **from** **with**

1. I was absolutely blue .... cold. I hadn't taken any warm clothes.
2. Can we discuss this .... lunchtime. I'll meet you then.
3. What's the word .... someone who collects stamps? I know it begins with phil . . .
4. I've never bought an avocado. How can you tell a ripe one .... an unripe one?
5. There's something funny .... John. He never gets eye contact with anyone.
6. .... Edinburgh, we took the train to Aberdeen.
7. I'll be in the Canaries .... October till mid-December.
8. Divide 63 .... 7 and you get 9!
9. We've lived in the same house .... the past 25 years.
10. I'm not very good .... foreign languages, but I am quite good .... maths and science.
11. You sound as if you're .... Australia.
12. We all watched the film .... tears in our eyes.
13. It's not a book .... Graham Greene, it's a book .... him. Someone else wrote it.
14. If you don't want to go on your own, why not take someone .... you?
15. .... time to time I worry .... the future. What's going to happen?
16. I got this lovely sweater .... Peter .... my birthday.

223

Grammar Summary

On
- **Friday** — Day
- **Wednesday morning** — Day + *morning, afternoon,*
- **Wednesday night** — *evening, night*
- **the sixteenth of March** — Date
- **Christmas Day** — Special Day

At
- **two o'clock** — Time
- **Christmas** — Festival
- **lunchtime** — Mealtimes
- **the weekend**
- **night**

In
- **Spring** — Season
- **1947** — Year
- **August** — Month
- **the morning**
- **the evening**

Sometimes *during* and *in* have the same meaning: *in the night* is very unusual; *during the night* is normal.

Periods

- **For three weeks** — General period
- **In three weeks** — Period starting from now
- **Three weeks ago** — Period ending now

Note
ago goes *after* the period.

Sometimes we talk about a *point*
a *period* between two points

at 2 o'clock

We arrived **at** 2 o'clock.

about 2 o'clock

We'll be there **about** 2 o'clock.

before 2 o'clock

The doctor can't see you **before** 2 o'clock.

after 2 o'clock

I'll be in my office **after** 2 o'clock.

until 2 o'clock = not before 2

I won't be there **until** 2 o'clock.

by 2 o'clock = *any* point *before* or *at* 2

Will we be there **by** 2 o'clock?

since 2 o'clock

I haven't seen her **since** 2 o'clock.

(looking back to a point in the past, with a perfect form of the verb.)

from 2 o'clock

They are open **from** 2 o'clock.

Grammar Comment

Prepositions of time are very regular and easy to understand. The diagrams will help you to understand what the different prepositions mean.

UNIT 65

Practice 65.1

Fill in the correct preposition:

1. We met .... exactly 7 o'clock.
2. We hadn't met .... 16 years.
3. The last time we met was .... June 1968.
4. In fact, we haven't met .... my wedding.
5. I remember it well. It was .... Midsummer's Day.
6. We are leaving .... a few days' time.
7. Is New Year's Day .... a Tuesday this year?
8. I'll see you .... the sixteenth, ... the evening.
9. I'll see you .... Wednesday morning .... 10 o'clock, then.
10. Shall we meet .... lunchtime tomorrow?

Practice 65.2

Match up these three prepositions with the phrases on the right:

	a.	1990	h.	Christmas Day
	b.	Easter	i.	five o'clock
1. on	c.	Thursday	j.	lunchtime
2. in	d.	night	k.	the afternoon
3. at	e.	the morning	l.	the twentieth century
	f.	July	m.	Sunday night
	g.	July the thirteenth	n.	midnight

a	b	c	d	e	f	g	h	i	j	k	l	m	n

Practice 65.3

Fill in the prepositions of time in the following:

1. It was .... the Spring of 1945 that my parents met for the first time. They didn't get married .... 1955!
2. There were a lot of refugees .... the Second World War.
3. I'd hate to work .... night. My best work is done .... the morning.
4. This year my birthday is .... Friday the thirteenth.
5. I'm only free .... weekends .... August.
6. There can be a lot of rain .... August and September, but October is generally quite dry.
7. The road works will start .... three weeks and they'll last .... about three weeks.
8. If we arrive .... 2 o'clock in the morning, what will we do .... 9, when the shops open?
9. 'Sugar .... the morning, sugar .... the evening, sugar .... suppertime' was a pop song .... the early sixties.
10. .... 1970 the cost of living was only a fraction of what it was .... 1988.

UNIT 65

Practice 65.4

Fill in the prepositions:

Sue is writing to an old school friend telling her about a visit she has just had.

Dear Jill

You'll never guess who has just been visiting me! Mary Bruce! I was in the garden ....Saturday morning when the phone went, and it was Mary. She's over from Canada .... two months. Remember, she went out there .... 1975 as a nurse and she hasn't been back .... then. Her mother is ill, so she's going to look after her .... a while. So, she came over .... Sunday afternoon and has been staying with me .... the past two days. She's just left. We stayed up each night .... 2 in the morning talking! She told me all about her life and how she couldn't get a job .... two months when she first went out there. But then she got a super job in a big hospital and she's been there .... the last 12 years. At first she had to work .... night, but now she works .... 9 .... 6, and she never works .... weekends. She's very lucky only working .... the day. It would be terrific if the three of us could meet. Are you free .... Friday 15th? We could all meet .... the morning and go off for lunch somewhere. Give me a buzz .... 7 any evening. That's when I finish work. Looking forward to hearing from you.

Sue.

Practice 65.5

Fill in the correct prepositions.

1. I broke my leg three weeks .... The doctor says I have to be off work .... six weeks, so I won't be back .... another three weeks. And I'm going on holiday .... a month, so I'll only be back at work .... a week before I'm off .... another two weeks.

2. I usually do my shopping .... Friday evening but yesterday I went .... the afternoon. That was a mistake! I know town is busy .... lunchtime, but I thought it would be quiet ....the afternoons, except .... the weekends, of course. Anyway, next time if I can't go .... the evening I'll go the next morning or do without!

A preposition joke

I haven't slept for days.
Neither have I. I usually sleep at night.

UNIT 65

Practice 65.6

Without looking back at the drawings, can you draw each of the prepositions in **bold** in the following sentences:

1. I haven't lived in Birmingham **since** 1984.
2. We can have a chat **after** the meeting.
3. We won't be home **until** 7 o'clock.
4. The banks are open **from** 9.30 in the morning.

5. We won't get back **before** the end of May.
6. Can we meet **about** 5.30?
7. I think I'll be in my office **by** 8.30.
8. Why don't we meet **at** 7.30?

Draw them on these lines:

1. _____ 5. _____

2. _____ 6. _____

3. _____ 7. _____

4. _____ 8. _____

Grammar Summary

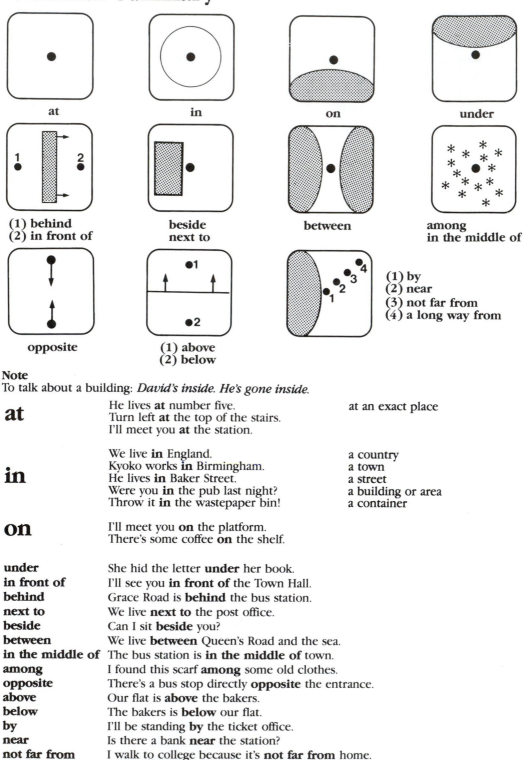

Note

To talk about a building: *David's inside. He's gone inside.*

at	He lives **at** number five.	at an exact place
	Turn left **at** the top of the stairs.	
	I'll meet you **at** the station.	
in	We live **in** England.	a country
	Kyoko works **in** Birmingham.	a town
	He lives **in** Baker Street.	a street
	Were you **in** the pub last night?	a building or area
	Throw it **in** the wastepaper bin!	a container
on	I'll meet you **on** the platform.	
	There's some coffee **on** the shelf.	

under	She hid the letter **under** her book.
in front of	I'll see you **in front of** the Town Hall.
behind	Grace Road is **behind** the bus station.
next to	We live **next to** the post office.
beside	Can I sit **beside** you?
between	We live **between** Queen's Road and the sea.
in the middle of	The bus station is **in the middle of** town.
among	I found this scarf **among** some old clothes.
opposite	There's a bus stop directly **opposite** the entrance.
above	Our flat is **above** the bakers.
below	The bakers is **below** our flat.
by	I'll be standing **by** the ticket office.
near	Is there a bank **near** the station?
not far from	I walk to college because it's **not far from** home.
a long way from	We live **a long way from** the shops.

UNIT 66

Practice 66.1

These numbers contain the secret number and the key number. The treasure is hidden in a box under one of the numbers. You will be able to find the number if you follow the instructions.

```
2 3 5 7 9 8 9 7 6 3
2 4 6 3 5 4 6 8 8 4
4 6 4 8 0 2 7 5 3 1
7 3 8 4 0 1 5 8 3 6
0 2 8 4 9 2 3 6 2 4
1 4 8 9 7 6 3 9 2 1
9 2 5 2 9 0 5 1 9 2
```

Start with 2 that is between 0 and 7.
Go to 6 which is three places below the 2.
Now move to 1 on the right of 6.
Move to 4 immediately above.
The treasure is hidden under the number beside the 4.
What number hides the treasure?

But you need the key! Go back to the number you started with and move as far as you can to the left. Move down to the bottom then along to the right. The key is under the number between two 2's.

Circle the numbers hiding the treasure and the key.

Practice 66.2

Where do they live?

Karen, Maria, Abdul, Carol, Steve, and Razi are all neighbours in a terrace of houses. Here is information for you to work out which house belongs to which person. The houses are numbered 1, 2 .. 6, starting at the left.

Steve lives 2 houses along from Karen.
Karen and Razi live next to each other.

Abdul has the biggest house at the end of the terrace. It's number 6.
Maria lives between Abdul and Razi.

Karen lives at number .....   Maria lives at ....   Abdul ....

Carol ....   Steve ....   Razi ....

Practice 66.3

Fill in the prepositions in the following sentences.

1. The Prime Minister always lives .... No 10 Downing Street.
2. I work .... a restaurant .... the old part of town.
3. I was the only passenger .... the plane travelling first class.
4. Our offices are .... the tenth floor.
5. There was a lot of discussion about whether the Tunnel should be .... the sea-bed or .... top of it.
6. Little groups of lost and injured children were found wandering .... the ruins.
7. At the meal I found myself sitting .... the priest. I had him .... one side and my mother-in-law .... the other.
8. During the eight hours .... the train, I could not avoid looking straight into the eyes of the woman sitting .... me. I knew I would see her again.
9. We lived on the ground floor. The Browns were in the flat .... us. They were .... the Greens who had the second floor flat.
10. My wife and the nurse sat .... the back seat, with the baby .... them.
11. Many people think that Britain is .... the times and old-fashioned.
12. My marks in the exam were, I'm sorry to say, ... average. Everyone was surprised because I've always been quite a bit .... average.

prepositions - where to?

Grammar Summary

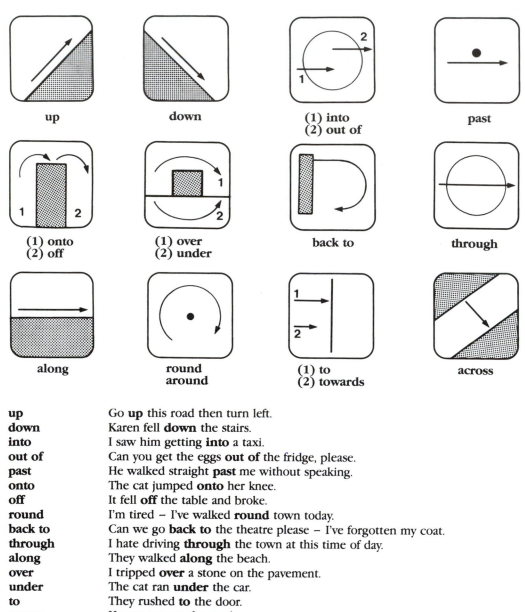

up	down	(1) into (2) out of	past
(1) onto (2) off	(1) over (2) under	back to	through
along	round around	(1) to (2) towards	across

up	Go **up** this road then turn left.
down	Karen fell **down** the stairs.
into	I saw him getting **into** a taxi.
out of	Can you get the eggs **out of** the fridge, please.
past	He walked straight **past** me without speaking.
onto	The cat jumped **onto** her knee.
off	It fell **off** the table and broke.
round	I'm tired – I've walked **round** town today.
back to	Can we go **back to** the theatre please – I've forgotten my coat.
through	I hate driving **through** the town at this time of day.
along	They walked **along** the beach.
over	I tripped **over** a stone on the pavement.
under	The cat ran **under** the car.
to	They rushed **to** the door.
across	He ran **across** the road.

Grammar Comment

One general point can help you to choose the right preposition of place — there is a clear difference between prepositions for 'where' and those for 'where to'. The prepositions which tell us 'where' are **static,** and often occur with static verbs — **be, stand, lies.** The 'where to' group occurs with verbs of **motion** — **run, walk, jump** etc.

UNIT 67

Practice 67.1

Look at the pictures. They show what happened when some cows broke out of their field and ran through the village. Fill in the correct preposition.

1. The cows are going .... the shop.
2. The shopkeeper is running .... the shop.
3. The tins have fallen .... the shelf.
4. The boy tripped .... the cat.
5. The old lady ran .... the road.
6. The policeman ran .... the road.
7. The girls crawled .... the table.
8. The cat ran .... in circles.

Practice 67.2

Fill in the prepositions in these sentences.

1. On the way to Japan we had to fly .... Siberia.
2. Alan walked right .... me without recognising me.
3. Wreckage from the plane was scattered .... a wide area.
4. I don't understand anyone who wants to walk .... the Antarctic ice-cap.
5. The toilet is straight .... that door, then .... the stairs on the left.
6. Half-way to the station, we realised we had forgotten the tickets. We had to go all the way .... the house for them.
7. Get .... your bicycle! You're not allowed here. It's been pedestrianised.
8. We drove .... and .... the area trying to remember where Pete lived. In the end we went to a phone box and rang him!
9. Why is the car damaged? I'll tell you. I was driving .... a narrow country road in Devon, when a cow ran .... a field and I ran out of road!
10. .... the rugged rock, the ragged rascal ran a rapid race.

The last sentence is a famous English tongue twister.

Grammar Summary

A conjunction joins two ideas:

A:	Tea **or** coffee?	**or**	joins alternatives
B:	Tea, please.		
A:	Sugar **and** milk?	**and**	joins two *similar* ideas
B:	Milk **but** no sugar, thank you.	**but**	joins two *different* or *opposite* ideas

or, and, but   1. come between the ideas they join.
                2. can join two sentences.

so gives the *result* of the first part of the sentence. It is the second part of the sentence.

> The class was boring, **so** I left.   The rent is too high, **so** we are moving.

so that gives the *purpose* for something. It is usually the second part of the sentence.

> I need a nursery place **so that** I can go to work.

> You'd better write it down **so that** you don't forget.

With these words the two parts of the sentence can come in either order with the same meaning:
> **Because** we were late, we took a taxi.   **If** she comes, I'll tell her.
> We took a taxi **because** we were late.   I'll tell her, **if** she comes.

if gives the *condition* for the other part of the sentence to be true.
> I'll do it **if** you'll help me.

> **If** anyone rings, can you ask them to call back, please?

although *contrasts* two ideas.
> **Although** he's got good qualifications, he can't get a job.

> I'm going to get one, **although** they are very expensive.

because gives the *reason* for something; answers the question *Why?*
> **Because** we were late, we took a taxi.

> I didn't come **because** it was raining.

These words show the *connection in time;* answer the question *When?*

as	The lorry hit us **as** we were turning the corner.
when	I'll tell her **when** I see her.
while	They arrived **while** we were trying to phone them!
since	Where have you been living **since** you came to England?
till/until	Could you keep an eye on things **until** I get back, please?
before	I hope he gets here **before** the train leaves.
after	I'll see you here **after** I've been to the bank.
as soon as	Phone us **as soon as** your plane gets in.

Grammar Comment

1. The difference between **when** and **while** is that **while** emphasises the fact that the two actions happened at the same time:
> The band played **while** the ship went down.
> **When** I came into the room, she left.

2. **Since** has two meanings:
> Time   — I haven't smoked **since** I was ill in 1986.
> Reason — **Since** you're going into town, could you get me some stamps.

Usually the **since** clause comes first in sentences where it gives the reason.

UNIT 68

Practice 68.1

How many people caught the train?

Sue arrived at the station as the train left.

Steve arrived at the station when the train left.

Alex arrived at the station before the train left.

John arrived at the station after the train left.

Answer: ....

Practice 68.2

Use **and, but,** or **because** in the spaces.

1. If this TV doesn't work, bring it back .... we'll give you your money back.

2. I'd like to stop working .... I've got too much work still to do.

3. I'd love to come to the cinema with you .... I saw that film last night!

4. My father rang me .... he was worried about me.

5. We tried to get tickets .... it was full.

6. Her ambition is to run in a marathon .... to visit China.

7. He looked everywhere for the cat .... his wife was fond of it.

Practice 68.3

Use **if, although, because** in the spaces.

1. I promise not to tell him .... I see him.

2. I bought an umbrella .... it started to rain.

3. I bought an umbrella .... the weather was lovely.

4. I recognised my cousin straightaway .... it was years since I'd seen her.

5. He's going to study in Paris .... he passes his exams.

6. He went on Concorde .... he had to get there in time for the meeting.

7. I'll travel on Concorde .... I can get to the airport on time.

8. .... I've got good qualifications, I can't get a job.

Conjunction joke

Teacher to boy on first day at school:
Teacher Aren't you going home now?
Boy   My father says I have to stay at school until I'm 18.

UNIT 68

Practice 68.4

Choose the correct conjunction to complete the sentences below:

>   so   so that   although   when   while
>   since   until   before   after   as soon as

1. .... we were doing the dishes in the kitchen, the burglar was stealing the video from the front room!

2. .... I heard his accent, I knew immediately who he was.

3. The war hadn't finished .... Bill went to China.

4. The police will never stop .... they find the man who killed all those children.

5. Have a cup of tea .... you go.

6. I wish you'd stop talking .... we can hear what the others have to say.

7. .... I had the operation, I never felt better in my life.

8. .... you won't even consider giving me a wage rise, I'll have to find another job.

9. Petrol has got too expensive, ... we're selling the car.

10. .... Fernandez passed his English exam, he can hardly say a word.

Practice 68.5

Make 6 sentences using the table below. There is only one solution, so all the sentences make sense.

I'll try to phone you at 6	or	at 7.
	but	it might be half past.
	so that	we can discuss the problem.
	if	I can find a phone box.
	although	it might be a bit later.
	as soon as	I finish work.

Practice 68.6

Fill in the spaces using one of these conjunctions.

>   when   because   if   although
>   then   as   not only . . . but also

A survey was published recently, suggesting that many wives are suffering because of their husband's work. .... the accuracy of the survey is questionable, apparently six out of ten wives say that romance has disappeared from their lives. .... their husbands are more interested in climbing higher in their careers, they spend less time at home. .... you have a workaholic husband, ... you should think clearly about what to do. St Valentine's Day is important .... it gives couples a chance to be romantic. Romance is .... about giving your wife a bunch of flowers, ... about kissing her goodbye .... you leave for work in the morning.

234

UNIT 68

Practice 68.7

Fill in the spaces using these conjunctions.

in case   as if   whoever   once   even though
wherever   suppose   whether . . . or not

.... you are, ... you live, you must be interested in the future of this planet.

.... you are a conservationist ...., you have no choice. Man is acting .... this beautiful and wonderful world we live in had an endless supply of energy, fuel, oxygen, food, and all the other things we need to survive. .... that were the case, it would still be no reason to waste and pollute the way we are doing at the present. .... the world has huge amounts of everything we need, people are still dying of hunger all over the world. Only a small proportion of the world's population has clean water to drink. .... you think I am joking, whole forests are disappearing in South America and thousands of trees are dying in Western Europe. .... you wake up to this problem, you will become a conservationist.

Practice 68.8

Complete these sentences with one of these words or phrases:

as   when   while   since   until   before   after   as soon as

You will need to use each one once. There is only one way to complete all the sentences so that they all make sense.

1. I'll ring you .... I get home.

2. We can't do anything .... the doctor arrives.

3. I rang you .... I heard because I knew it was urgent.

4. Have you settled down .... you retired?

5. He walked in .... the clock struck ten; it was perfectly timed.

6. We might as well have a cup of tea .... we are waiting.

7. I'll give you a lift if I get home .... you set off.

8. We arrived .... everyone else had left. It was deserted.

Grammar Summary

If can be used with many different structures. Here are the most common.
It is usually possible to have the *if* part of the sentence as the first or the second half of the sentence:

If Sara's late, she never apologises.   **If** she worked harder, she'd pass.
Sara never apologises **if** she's late.   She'd pass **if** she worked harder.

General conditions

Present simple   **Present simple**

Sara never apologises	**if**	she is late.
He gets angry		you argue with him.
How long does milk keep		you haven't got a fridge?

Likely conditions: things which are very likely to happen.

'll (will)   **Present simple**

The doctor'll see you	**if**	you come at nine.
I'll ask Ali		I see him.
We'll miss the bus		we don't hurry.
They won't come		the weather's bad.

Unlikely conditions: things which might happen, but probably not.

'd (would)   **Past simple**

She'd pass	**if**	she worked harder.
He wouldn't be happy		he lived on his own.

Impossible conditions

'd have + third form   **Past perfect (had + third form)**

I'd have told you	**if**	I had known myself.
We'd have been there on time		we'd caught the earlier bus.

Instructions, advice

Imperative   **Present simple**

Stay in bed tomorrow	**if**	you don't feel better.
Get the early train		you want to get there in time.

If can also join sentences with a modal auxiliary. Here are some examples:

What should I do **if** the baby cries?

Can I see the manager **if** I come back later?

Grammar Comment

1. In the Grammar Summary, sentences with **if**, sometimes called conditional sentences, are grouped in different ways. These are to help you learn some of the most common patterns. There are many other patterns which are not as common.

2. The following are both correct in spoken English:

     If I were you . . .   **If I was you . . .**

3. **If** is not the only way to give conditions in English. Some of the other words with a similar meaning are:

     providing/provided,   **on condition that,**   **as long as**

You can go, **providing/as long as** you're home by ten o'clock.

These words are usually stronger than **if,** and emphasise the condition.

UNIT 69

Practice 69.1

Match up the two halves of the sentences. Write them out in full. The sentences you make are true.

1. Mick never apologises		I don't do my homework.
2. You can't be a first-class athlete		it's below zero.
3. Water freezes	**if**	I come by bus.
4. I always arrive early		he is late.
5. My teacher is annoyed		you smoke.

1. ....
2. ....
3. ....
4. ....
5. ....

Practice 69.2

Match up the two halves of the sentences. The following are very likely to happen.

1. The plane will be late		she works hard.
2. Zoe will pass her exams		we go to London.
3. We'll be very tired	**if**	it's very windy.
4. I'll meet you at 3		I finish in time.
5. Mick will be famous		he appears on TV.

1. ....
2. ....
3. ....
4. ....
5. ....

Practice 69.3

Match up the two halves of the sentences. The following are unlikely to happen.

1. Andrew wouldn't be happy		he visited Britain.
2. He would visit New York		he lived alone.
3. He wouldn't be late so often	**if**	he had enough money.
4. He would speak better English		he went to bed earlier.
5. He wouldn't be so tired		he bought a watch.

1. ....
2. ....
3. ....
4. ....
5. ....

UNIT 69

Practice 69.4

Match up the two halves of the sentences. The following are impossible conditions.

1. I'd have bought a new car
2. I wouldn't have told you
3. Diana would have got up earlier
4. Mick would have helped you
5. You wouldn't have had that accident

if

a. you'd been more careful.
b. she'd known the train left at 7.
c. you'd asked him.
d. I'd been able to afford one.
e. I'd known you were going to be upset.

1	2	3	4	5

Practice 69.5

Read the text, then complete the sentences below.

Mary went to Leeds for the day. When she caught the bus, the sun was shining, so she never thought to take a raincoat. But what a terrible day she had! Everything that could go wrong, went wrong. The weather changed at lunchtime and the afternoon was very wet. She had a bad fall on the stairs in a store. Someone stole her purse — probably, she thinks, when her back was turned when she was talking to a friend she met. The bus on the way home was an hour late — it broke down. Her family were annoyed she was so late.

1. If Mary had taken her raincoat, ...

2. If she'd listened to the weather forecast, ...

3. If only she'd taken the lift in the store, ...

4. If she hadn't turned her back, ...

5. If the bus hadn't broken down, ...

6. If she'd been home on time, ...

Practice 69.6

There has been a terrible flood in the Sudan. It has been raining for weeks. Lots of homes have been destroyed. People are dying. Make sentences starting with **if** to say what needs to be done. There are suggested answers in the key.

1. If .... aid .... die.
   ....

2. If .... more doctors .... children.
   ....

3. If .... tents .... nowhere to sleep.
   ....

4. If .... food .... starve.
   ....

5. If .... rain .... worse.
   ....

UNIT 69

Practice 69.7

Match the two halves of these conditionals to make natural sentences. Usually there are several possibilities. List **all** the possible sentences in the table below.
Put √ if the combination is possible, × if it is not.

1. If you are ill
2. If you are seriously ill
3. If you get any worse
4. If you got any worse
5. If you had got any worse

a. go to the doctor.
b. they'd have taken you into hospital.
c. you'll have to see the doctor.
d. you'd have to see the doctor.
e. they take you into hospital.

	a	b	c	d	e
1					
2					
3					
4					
5					

Practice 69.8

It is July. There has been no rain for two months. Every day the temperature is above 30°C. People are not used to such warm weather. Make sentences starting with **if** to describe the situation.

1. If .... warmer .... stop work.

   ....

2. If .... continues .... shortage of water.

   ....

3. If .... cooler .... old people .... die.

   ....

4. If .... rain .... harvest .... ruin.

   ....

5. If .... harvest .... farmers ... lose money.

   ....

Practice 69.9

A girl is being interviewed for a new job by the interviewer. They are discussing exactly when she could start.
Fill in the verb forms. You may need to use **not** in some of the examples.

Interviewer Well, we'd like you to start on September 1st. Would that suit you?

Interviewee Well, if I leave before the middle of September, I .... (lose) all my holiday pay. And if I .... (lose) that, I .... (be able) to afford to buy a car.

Interviewer And if you .... (have) a car, I'm afraid we can't offer you the job.

Interviewee So, I'm in an impossible position. I really want the job. If I .... (get) it, I .... (know) what I'm going to do.

Interviewer We can't give you a car. If we .... (give) a car to you, we .... (have to) give one to all our employees — and we couldn't afford to do that!

Interviewee Everything .... (be) all right if I could start on the 7th of September. I have a week's holiday to come.

Interviewer If you .... (be) sure that you can start on the 7th, I'm sure that .... (be) fine.

Grammar Summary

1	one	first		30	thirty		thirtieth
2	two	second		40	forty		fortieth
3	three	third		50	fifty		fiftieth
4	four	fourth		60	sixty		sixtieth
5	five	fifth		70	seventy		seventieth
6	six	sixth		80	eighty		eightieth
7	seven	seventh		90	ninety		ninetieth
8	eight	eighth		100	a hundred		hundreth
9	nine	ninth		200	two hundred		two hundredth
10	ten	tenth		1000	a thousand		thousandth
11	eleven	eleventh		1,000,000	a million		millionth
12	twelve	twelfth					
13	thirteen	thirteenth					
14	fourteen	fourteenth					
15	fifteen	fifteenth					
16	sixteen	sixteenth					
17	seventeen	seventeenth					
18	eighteen	eighteenth					
19	nineteen	nineteenth					
20	twenty	twentieth					
21	twenty-one	twenty-first					
22	twenty-two	twenty-second					

Write	Say		Say	Write
$\frac{1}{2}$	a half		point five	.5
$\frac{1}{4}$	a quarter		point two five	.25
$\frac{3}{4}$	three quarters		point seven five	.75
$1\frac{1}{2}$	one and a half			
$\frac{1}{6}$	one sixth			
			three point two	3.2

Grammar Comment

1. Notice how you say the following:
   - 101st customer = the hundred and first customer
   - 550th anniversary = the five hundred and fiftieth anniversary
   - 1300th person = the thirteen hundredth person

2. We write ½, ¼, ⅜, but we say **a half, a quarter, three eighths.**

3. Remember the different ways of saying 0:

   zero = the number zero
           zero degrees centigrade
           The results range from 25 down to **zero.**

   oh = It happended in 1909. (nineteen — **oh** — nine)
        = My phone number is 35 80 70 (three five, eight **oh**, seven **oh**)

   nought = a less common way of talking about the number; but used in decimals: 0.5cc (**nought** point five cc's)

4. Do not use plural-**s** with an exact number of hundreds, thousands, or millions:

          five hundred   **two thousand**   **ten million**

5. Telephone numbers are usually given in the following ways in British English:
   0273 - 736344   = **oh two seven three, seven three, six three, double four.**
   or
   08 - 55 67 84   = **oh eight, double five, six seven, eight four**
   Telephone numbers in Britain are never given *fifty five/ sixty seven/ eighty four.

UNIT 70

Practice 70.1

Write the following numbers out in full — using the exact words you would use to say them.

1. 101 .....*a hundred and one*..
2. 563 ....
3. 999 ....
4. 1487 ....
5. 250,000 ....
6. 5¼ ....
7. 3⅛ ....
8. 3.142 ....

Fill in the spaces in the following:

9. .... plus a quarter is three quarters.
10. At least .... of the world is covered in water. (Answer = 7/10)

Practice 70.2

Complete the following with a number. Write your answer in words.

1. We live in a .... dimensional world.
2. There are .... players in a football team.
3. I'm sorry things are a bit untidy. We're all at .... and .... at the moment.
4. This train seems to be late .... times out of ....
5. At first I was confused, but then I put .... and .... together.
6. ....'s company, ...'s a crowd.
7. He's a great player. He gives .... percent in every game.
8. Protests flooded in from the .... corners of the world.
9. We split the prize money .... , and I've already spent my half.
10. Life begins at ....

Practice 70.3

Complete the following with ordinal numbers (**third, sixth** etc). Write your answers in words.

1. I believe the Government should increase its aid to the .... World.
2. We shouldn't treat immigrants as ....-class citizens.
3. The Americans celebrate Independence Day on the .... of July.
4. More progress has been made in the .... century than in the whole of history.
5. In the last sixty years the Olympic 100m record has improved by four .... of a second.
6. They're good friends. They've been on .... name terms for years.
7. Applications will be dealt with on a .... come, ... served basis.
8. Most people have a special party for their .... birthday.

Grammar Summary

Have you the time, please?

What time is it, please?
▷ It's twenty-five to seven.

It's | exactly
just
about
nearly | three o'clock.

(clock face diagram)

five to — o'clock — five past
ten to — ten past
a quarter to 9 — a quarter past
twenty to — twenty past
twenty-five to — twenty-five past
half past

What time does it start?

What time does the York train leave, please?

The train leaves at six forty-seven.

There's a train at fifteen forty.

I'll see you about sixish.
-ish gives an approximate time.

Days
Monday
Tuesday
Wednesday
Thursday
Friday
Saturday
Sunday

Seasons
Spring
Summer
Autumn
Winter

Months
January   July
February   August
March   September
April   October
May   November
June   December

Write: **Say:**
15th July   the fifteenth of July
21.4.54   the twenty-first of April, nineteen fifty-four.

Grammar Comment

1. A common way of asking the correct time is:

    What time do you make it?

2. Both of the following are correct:

    the first of April   **April the first**

3. In spoken English **half five** means **half *past* five.**

4. In spoken English it is common to leave out the hour when this is understood, for example:

    I'll meet you at **twenty five past,** OK?
    It didn't start till **ten past.**

5. You usually use **-ish** with full hours, to give approximate times:

    I'll be home about **three-ish.**
    It is also possible to say:
    I think it begins about **half past eightish.**

6. When the 24 hour clock is used in timetables, times are said in the following way:

    09.15 = **nine fifteen**
    12.00 = **twelve noon**
    13.45 = **thirteen forty five**
    17.00 = **seventeen hundred hours**

UNIT 71

Practice 71.1

Fill in the names of the months in the following well-known English rhyme.

Thirty days hath ...., ..., ... **and** ....,

All the rest have 31, except .... **alone,**

Which has 28 days clear — and 29 each Leap Year.

Practice 71.2

Fill in the times in the following problems. Write them in words.

1. If you arrive at the station at twenty to three, twenty five minutes late for your train, when did it leave?

    Answer: ....

2. School starts at 9 in the morning. Lessons are forty minutes long with a ten minute break between each one. When does the third lesson of the day end?

    Answer: ....

3. It's a quarter to four. What time will it be in twenty minutes?

    Answer: ....

4. Your train leaves at 11.45 pm. Can you think of three different ways of saying that?

    Answer: ....

    ....

    ....

Practice 71.3

Find out, then write out in full the following Zodiac periods.

For example:
   Aquarius is from the twentieth of January to the eighteenth of February.

1. Libra is from .... to ....

2. Taurus is from .... to ....

3. Cancer is from .... to ....

4. My sign is .... It starts on .... and finishes on ....

Grammar Summary

Past

A long time ago
 Six or seven years ago
  A few years ago
   A couple of years ago
    Eighteen months ago
    Last year
     A few months/weeks ago
     Recently
     The other week
     Last week
      A few days ago
      The other day
       The day before yesterday
       Yesterday
        Yesterday evening
        Last night
       Now

Now

In the morning
 Tomorrow morning
 Tomorrow
  The day after tomorrow
  In a day or two
   In a couple of days
   Next Saturday
    Next Sunday evening
    In a few days time
    Soon
     Next week
      A week on Thursday
      Next month
       In a few weeks time
       Next year
        In a couple of years
       Future

Grammar Comment

1.   It is possible to say **the other day/week/month** but not *the other year*.

2.   Another word for **two weeks** is **a fortnight**:
        I've been ill. I've been off work for **a fortnight.**

3.   If you mean: you say:
       exactly one week from today   **a week today**
       exactly one week from tomorrow   **a week tomorrow**
       exactly one week from Friday   **a week on Friday**

UNIT 72

Practice 72.1

Fill in phrases from the lists opposite to complete these sentences.

1. It was such a .... that I met my uncle, I'm sure I wouldn't recognise him.

2. Let's see. Today is Friday, so .... before .... was Wednesday.

3. If today is Thursday, that means that .... after .... is Saturday.

4. I posted the parcel today, so I'm sure you'll be getting it .... a .... days .... It usually only takes two days.

5. If this is December 1999, July 1998 was .... ago.

6. That reminds me. I met John in the supermarket .... other .... He wasn't looking well at all.

7. It's .... couple .... years .... now since I moved here.

8. Just think! .... weeks .... we'll be lying on a beach in the South Pacific.

Practice 72.2

Put the following phrases in order. Number 1 will be the furthest in the past. Number 10 will be the furthest in the future.

in a few years   **last June**   **years ago**

the other week   **some years ago**   **eighteen months ago**

in a couple of months   **the other day**   **the day after tomorrow**

in an hour or two

1. ....

2. ....

3. ....

4. ....

5. ....

6. ....

7. ....

8. ....

9. ....

10. ....

Grammar Summary

At the beginning of a word

un-	the opposite of	*unmarried*
non-	not	*non-smoker*
anti-	against	*anti-American*
pro-	in favour of	*pro-American*
pre-	before	*pre-war*
post-	after	*post-1960*
ex-	former	*ex-President*
re-	do again	*re-start*
mis-	wrongly	*mis-understand*
over-	too much	*over-confident*

At the end of a word

-ness	adjective → noun	*darkness*
-able	verb → adjective	*washable*
-en	adjective → verb	*brighten*
-less	without	*homeless*
-ful	a quantity	*cupful*
-ish	approximately	*youngish*

Grammar Comment

1. Prefixes and suffixes are very useful if you need to express an idea and there is no word for it. Here are some modern and more creative examples:

   Your idea is a **non-starter.**
   The party was a **non-event.**
   Our school is a **non-profit-making** organisation.
   You are **anti-anything** I suggest, aren't you?
   The computer will have to be **re-programmed.**
   The firm is badly **mis-managed.**

2. Some prefixes are more common with some parts of speech than others:
   un- is used with adjectives and verbs, but not with nouns.
   Anti- is commonest with adjectives. Here are some more useful words which use prefixes:

   un-fasten, un-do, re-think, re-write, mis-manage, mis-direct, over-pay, over-eat

   anti-war, anti-apartheid, pro-French, pro-nuclear, pre-war, pre-Christian, post-war, post-1980

   non-drinker, non-driver, ex-King, ex-teacher

3. Prefixes and suffixes are often used to help us to invent new words to say what we mean in a very convenient way:

   I can't do anything at the moment. I'm **car-less.**
   I've spent a long time looking for a scarf, but the colour is **un-matchable.** I can't find anything that matches it.

If you want to say something and you don't know a particular word, don't be afraid to invent a word. Prefixes and suffixes can help you. The word you invent may not be a correct "real" word, but people will often understand you, and that is the most important thing.

UNIT 73

Practice 73.1

The three most important negative prefixes in English are:

un-	**un**happy
dis-	**dis**approve
mis-	**mis**interpret

Complete the following sentences using a word which starts with one of these prefixes.

1. In some countries men and women receive .... pay. What do you think of the idea of equal pay for equal work?
2. I was sure I had locked the back door, but when we got back home, I found it ....
3. John and his wife usually agree, but when it comes to money matters, they always ....
4. We found people in country areas very friendly, but the people we spoke to in the cities were very ....
5. I always thought that Bill was totally honest, so when I found out that he had been ...., I was very shocked.
6. The shop said the toy was ...., but it didn't take the children long to break it!
7. I've always found Mary very kind, so I'm surprised that you said she was .... to you.
8. I like nearly all fruit, but I have to say that I .... bananas.
9. I was sure I had understood what you meant, but I obviously .... you badly. I'm sorry.
10. I hope that peace and order will come out of the present situation of terrorism and ....
11. At first we were satisfied with our hotel, but as it became noisier and noisier, we grew more and more ....
12. You can bring cooked meat into Britain, but you can't bring in .... meat.
13. Some of your ideas are helpful, but I'm sorry to say that some are ....
14. Last year's festival was very ...., but this year's is much better organised.
15. Twelve runners qualified for the 100 metres, but two were .... for using drugs.
16. Why don't we stress the similarities between us, instead of the ....?
17. No sooner had we packed, than we had to .... again. The plane was delayed for 24 hours.
18. The opponents of factory farming say it is .... The natural thing is for animals to be outside, running free.

Practice 73.2

If someone is *without a home,* they are **homeless.**
What is the word for:

1.	Without a child	....	5.	Without thought	....
2.	Without hope	....	6.	Without a friend	....
3.	Without power	....	7.	Without care	....
4.	Without fear	....	8.	Without meaning	....

247

Practice 73.3

Although the two most common ways of making opposites in English are to use **un-** or **dis-**, there are other prefixes:

in-   il-   im-   ir-

There are no definite rules for which words take which prefixes. Do you know the opposites of these common words? Use the prefixes above.

1. possible ....
2. complete ....
3. responsible ....
4. direct ....
5. sincere ....
6. legitimate ....

7. mature ....
8. correct ....
9. relevant ....
10. accurate ....
11. visible ....
12. logical ....

13. experienced ....
14. practical ....
15. capable ....
16. sensitive ....
17. legal ....
18. convenient ....

Practice 73.4

Use the following prefixes to make words to fit the explanations:

over-   mis-   anti-   non-   re-
pro-   pre-   ex-   post-

a. too enthusiastic
b. the former king
c. in favour of war

d. not a driver
e. do again
f. before 1900

g. place wrongly
h. after 1980
i. against nuclear

Now use these words in the following sentences:

1. The .... demonstration marched as far as the power station itself.
2. I can't give you a lift. I'm afraid I'm a ....
3. This work isn't good enough. You'll have to .... it — and this time be more careful.
4. .... women were expected to stay at home.
5. I don't know where I've put your book. I must have .... it.
6. Calm down! Take it easy! He's only a pop singer. There's no need to be ....
7. The .... comes to England quite a lot to visit his relatives in Buckingham Palace.
8. The Conservative Party became more popular in the .... period.
9. I thought you were a pacifist. How can you say that you would have been .... in 1945?

Practice 73.5

Make four words of your own with each of these prefixes. They can be real words, or words you think you need — new, invented words. People often invent new words using prefixes.

1. **anti-**
2. **pro-**
3. **ex-**

....
....
....
....

UNIT 73

Practice 73.6

Some adjectives can be made into nouns by adding **-ness**. For example:

       dark — **darkness**   loud — **loudness**

Make nouns from the following adjectives and use them in the sentences below:

cheerful ....   ill ....   happy ....

smooth ....   kind ....   weak ....

dark ....   sad ....   rough ....

1. I really appreciated your .... when I was in hospital. It was so nice to have a visitor.

2. Can you find .... in money or possessions?

3. You could tell how expensive her coat was by the .... of the leather.

4. Chocolates are my biggest .... What's yours?

5. Did you see the .... on the faces of the children dying of hunger in the Sudan?

6. We were still looking for somewhere to stay the night when .... fell.

7. There are still lots of .... which have no cure.

8. The journey was very uncomfortable. I was surprised by the .... of the road.

9. The best thing about the survivors of the train crash was their ....

Practice 73.7

Some verbs can be made into adjectives by adding **-able**.
For example:
    You can wash these trousers. You don't have to have them dry-cleaned.
    They are **washable.**

Make adjectives from these verbs, then use them in the sentences below. In some of the examples you will also need the prefix **un-**.

break ....   accept ....   wash ....

love ....   laugh ....   control ....

recognise ....   believe ....

1. When the cat had six kittens, we didn't want to give any of them away. They were so ....

2. I wanted at least £200 for my moped. When he offered me £50, I told him his offer was .... and ....

3. After he had been attacked, Bill's face was hardly ....

4. Some plastics are almost ...., except at very low temperatures.

5. This jumper is .... only in cold water.

6. For one man to win both the 100 metres and the marathon is totally

     ....

7. The car was .... when it hit the patch of ice.

Grammar Summary

All vowel sounds are voiced. There are two kinds of consonant sound in English:

Voiced
You can feel vibration

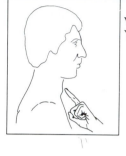

Voiceless
You can feel no vibration

These are pairs:

Voiced sounds:	/b/ bin	/v/ view	/ ð / with	/d/ said	/z/ zoo	/ ʒ / television	/dʒ/ bridge	/g/ go
Voiceless sounds:	/p/ pin	/f/ few	/ θ / think	/t/ set	/s/ say	/ ʃ / fish	/tʃ/ church	/k/ come
These are voiced:	/m/ men	/n/ now	/ ŋ / sing	/l/ long	/r/ red			

There are three other sounds: /h/, house; /j/ yellow; /w/ wear, but these never come at the end of words.

Past simple (second form)

The past simple is usually made by adding **-ed**. There are three pronunciations:

/t/   after a voiceless sound: *walked*
/d/   after a voiced sound: *opened*
/id/   after a /t/ or /d/ sound: *waited*

Grammar Comment

If an English word ends with **-s**, it can mean one of five things:

1. The word is plural — **books**
2. It is possessive — my sister**'s** bike.
3. It means **is** — It**'s** sunny.
4. It means **has** — Pete**'s** been to the shops.
5. 3rd person-**s** — It **costs** a lot.

The rules for the pronunciation of the final **-s** are always the same. Here is a table with more examples:

	/s/	/z/	/iz/
plural	books	questions	houses
possessives	Nick's book	John's book.	Liz's house
is	Nick's reading.	John's reading.	Liz's moving.
has	Nick's been reading.	John's been reading.	Liz's moved house.
3rd person -s	Nick likes reading.	John reads a lot.	She passes every day.

UNIT 74

Practice 74.1

Remember that the 3rd person **-s** ending can have three different pronunciations:

1.   /s/   speaks
2.   /z/   lives
3.   /iz/   dances

Say the following verbs. Write them in the correct groups below.

breaks	begins	buys	catches	costs	chooses	drinks	eats
enjoys	freezes	feels	flies	goes	hurts	leaves	reaches
	rests	rushes	remembers	talks	walks	passes	

Group 1 /s/

1. ....
2. ....
3. ....
4. ....
5. ....
6. ....
7. ....
8. ....

Group 2 /z/

1. ....
2. ....
3. ....
4. ....
5. ....
6. ....
7. ....
8. ....

Group 3 /iz/

1. ....
2. ....
3. ....
4. ....
5. ....
6. ....

Practice 74.2

Think of a regular verb starting with each letter of the alphabet. We have done the most difficult ones for you. Write down and say the past simple tense of each one. Write the pronunciation of the **-ed**; is it /**t**/, /**d**/ or /**id**/?

a	....	n	....
b	....	o	....
c	....	p	....
d	....	q	....queued.... /d/
e	....	r	....
f	....	s	....
g	....	t	....
h	....	u	....
i	....	v	....
j	....	w	....
k	....	x	....x-rayed.... /d/
l	....	y	....
m	....	z	....zipped.... /t/

If you cannot think of a word for a particular letter, use your dictionary.

Grammar Summary

Possession ('s or s')

's	singular	**Ravi's** car is a Ford.
		Whose bag is that? ▷ It's **Jean's.**
's	irregular plural nouns	The **children's** room is on the left.
s'	regular plural nouns	The **boys'** room is at the top of the stairs.
		The **students'** work wasn't very good.

Spelling

-ch -sh **-x -s -o**	add **e**	before **-s**	watch box tomato	→ → →	wat**ches** bo**xes** toma**toes**
-e	~~e~~	before **-ed** **-es** **-est**	like bake late	→ → →	lik**ed** bak**es** lat**est**
-y	**y→ie** **y→i**	before **-s** before **-ed** **-er** **-est** **-ly**	fly try easy lazy happy	→ → → → →	fl**ies** tr**ied** eas**ier** laz**iest** happ**ily**
Short vowel **+ consonant**	**double** **letter**	before **-er** **-est** **-ing** **-ed**	begin big stop permit	→ → → →	begin**ner** big**gest** stop**ping** permit**ted**

Grammar Comment

When you learn a new word, it is best to learn its meaning, pronunciation, and spelling, at the same time. There are very few useful rules to help you spell English words correctly. These rules have exceptions and many people feel that they are not useful. The only rule worth giving is: learn the spelling when you learn the word! If you read a lot of English, you will find that your spelling will improve and you will be able to guess the spelling of new words.

There are a few words which British and American English spell differently, for example: colour/color; pyjamas/pajamas. The differences are few and never lead to misunderstanding.

UNIT 75

Practice 75.1

The apostrophe in English is '. Put the apostrophe in the correct place in the following sentences; is it **'s**, or **s'**?

1. Johns book is in the bookcase.

2. The mens toilet is round the corner.

3. The boys money was in their rooms.

4. He put his wifes suitcase on the rack.

5. My parents house is being sold.

6. The Prime Ministers secretary phoned.

7. The ladys hat ended up in the river.

8. The towns main attraction is the beach.

9. How many birds nests did you find?

10. What is Petes brothers first name?

Practice 75.2

Give the plural of the following words. For example: watch — watches

1. box ....
2. lady ....
3. tomato ....
4. fly ....
5. lily ....

6. potato ....
7. boss ....
8. match ....
9. baby ....
10. speech ....

Practice 75.3

Choose the correct spelling in the following sentences. Cross out the wrong spelling.

1. Smoking is not permited/permitted.

2. You should have written/writen.

3. We're going swimming/swiming.

4. Are you puting/putting on your best clothes?

5. It just got biger/bigger and biger/bigger!

6. The Purple Coconut Disco is livelyer/livelier than most.

7. They are happily/happyly married.

8. What are you getting/geting for your birthday?

9. Were you stopped/stopped at the traffic lights?

10. I'm hoping/hopping it's going to be a boy.

253

Grammar Summary

Advising

I'd complain **if I were you.**
You ought to take a couple of days off.

ought to suggests a stronger, more objective opinion.

Agreeing

I'm looking forward to the weekend.
▷ **So am I.**

Repeat the same auxiliary in the answer

I love chocolate.
▷**So do I.**

No auxiliary, use **(do)** in the answer

I don't like football on television.
▷ **Neither do I.**

Use *neither* to agree with a negative remark

Apologising

I'm sorry.
▷ I'm sorry.

Not really anyone's fault
– *both* say the same

I AM sorry.
▷ That's quite all right.

Stress on **am** – a real apology

Excuse me, could you change a pound please?

Excuse me before you disturb a stranger

Excuse me, please.

You want to pass someone

Have you got the tickets yet?
▷ **I'm afraid not.**

Use *I'm afraid* to 'soften' a negative or unhelpful answer

Could I speak to John please?
▷ **I'm afraid** he's out at the moment.

Asking for something

A pound of apples, **please.**
Could you pass the salt, **please.**

These sound unfriendly without *please*

Asking someone to do something

Could you spell it, **please.**
Will you ask him to ring me, **please.**

Always *please* at the end

Would you mind opening the door, **please.**

Would you mind . . . ing for people you don't know

Asking for permission

May I borrow your pen?

Personal

Do you mind if I smoke?
▷ I'd rather you didn't.

Is it all right if I park here?
▷ No, I'm afraid parking isn't allowed.

More objective

Grammar Comment

In Units 76, 77, and 78 many of the grammatical structures presented in earlier units are presented and practised in situations. It is important to understand that many of the phrases do not change. If you change them, even a little, you can change the meaning a lot.

If you study all the phrases carefully, you will realise how important two areas of grammar are when you use English in situations: auxiliaries and modals. The difference between the short and full form of auxiliaries is very important. When you read through the phrases, underline all auxiliaries and modals. Say the phrases again and again so that you are happy with the way you pronounce them.

UNIT 76

Practice 76.1

Complete these dialogues using the language presented in the Basic Functions.

1. The watch I bought yesterday isn't working.
   — .... take it back to the shop if I .... you.

2. I feel on top of the world today.
   — So .... I.

3. ...., could you change a pound, ...?
   — .... I've got no change.

4. Have you remembered my book?
   — Oh, goodness! .... I haven't.

5. .... I have another cup of tea, ...?
   — Certainly.

6. .... you .... helping me with these bags, ...?
   — Certainly. I'll take the heavy one.

7. Would .... the window, please.
   — Certainly. It is rather warm in here, isn't it.

Practice 76.2

Agree with the following remarks. Use **So . . . . I** or **Neither . . . . I**

1. I can water-ski.

   .So can I...

2. I'm interested in tennis.

   ....

3. I can play badminton.

   ....

4. I love windsurfing.

   ....

5. I'd like to go riding.

   ....

6. I feel like going to the disco.

   ....

7. I'm not very interested in football.

   ....

8. I don't really like tea.

   ....

UNIT 77 basic functions (2)

Grammar Summary

Complaining

I **HAVE** been waiting twenty minutes.
It **WAS** only yesterday I bought it.
You **DID** promise to help me.

Stress the auxiliary to show you are annoyed

Correcting

I think you've made a mistake.
I think it should be £2.80, not £3.80.

Usually with *I think*

I think it was 1982, **wasn't it?**
I think the train goes at ten past, **doesn't it.**

Often with a tag

Inviting

Would you like to have lunch with us?
▷ Oh thank you. I'd love to.
  That's very kind of you, but I'm afraid I can't.

Offering

Would you like a cake?
▷ Thank you. I'd love one.

Offering something

Let me carry that for you.
We'll do the washing up.
Shall we pick you up at the station?

Offering help

Can I give you a hand?
▷ Thank you. That's very kind of you.
  It's all right thank you. I can manage.

General offer to help

Have a cake!
Help yourself.

Use the first form of the verb

Refusing to do something

I **won't** work on that machine. It's dangerous.
He **won't** tell me.

Suggesting

Why don't you get a taxi?
You could send it air mail.

To the other person

Let's go now or we'll be late.
Let's go on Saturday evening.
Why don't we buy her a pen?

Doing something *together*

Sympathising

Oh dear. What a nuisance
Oh dear. I AM sorry to hear that.

Something not very important
More serious. Stress **am.**

Thanking

Thank you.
Thanks very much.

Not important

Thank you. That **IS** kind of you.
Thank you. That makes things **MUCH** easier.
Thank you. That **WILL** be a help.

When you are grateful stress one word strongly

Warning

Be careful!
Look out!

General

Mind the floor, it's slippery.
Don't forget to take a coat.

256

UNIT 77

Practice 77.1

Complete these dialogues using the language presented in the Basic Functions.

1. Excuse me, do you .... if I park here?

   — You can, but it's against the law.

2. Oh, come on! We can't wait all day. I .... asked you for the bill three times already.

   — ...., sir. Here it is.

3. The train leaves at five to six.

   — I .... it's ten to.

4. .... you .... to come round for coffee tomorrow?

   — .... love to. .... much.

5. .... you like to come with me?

   — That's very .... you, but .... I can't.

6. .... a biscuit.

   — Oh, thanks.

7. .... me hold that for you.

   — Oh, it's all right, ... I can ....

8. .... don't you take the ferry?

   — Never again! Not after the last time!

9. Why .... we meet outside the disco?

   — .... a good idea.

10. Shall we go on Friday?

    — .... go on Saturday instead.

11. Did you hear that I've got to have an operation?

    — Oh dear. .... to .... that.

12. Well, I hope you enjoyed the meal.

    — Yes, it was lovely. ....

13. The weather forecast is awful. .... your umbrella.

    — Don't worry. I won't.

Grammar Summary

Checking English
Could you say that again, please?
What does this mean, please?
I don't understand this.
How do you spell . . . ?
How do you pronounce this, please?
Is this correct, please?

Directions in the street
Excuse me, could you tell me where . . . is, please?
Excuse me, is there a . . . near here, please?
Turn left/right.
Take the (second) turning on the left/right.
It's on the left/right.
It's straight ahead.
Go straight along/down/up here.
It's on the corner of Brook Street and Park Lane.

Asking the time
Have you the time please?
What time do you make it, please?

When someone is going away
Have a good holiday.
Have a good trip.
Have a safe journey.

Introducing yourself
I don't think we've met before. I'm *(David Jones)*.

On the phone
May I speak to . . . please?
▷ Speaking.
Just a moment, please.
Can I take a message?
I'll ask him/her to ring you.
Sorry. I've got the wrong number.

Sending a greeting to someone
Give my regards to . . .
Remember me to . . .

On someone's birthday
Many happy returns.
Happy birthday.

On (or just after) January 1st.
Happy New Year.
▷ Thank you. The same to you.

Someone has passed an exam, got a job, won something
Congratulations!

When someone gets engaged
Congratulations. I hope you'll be very happy.

Grammar Comment

The phrases in this unit are useful in very special situations. For example, the two phrases for what you say on someone's birthday are the **only** two possible. You cannot guess some of the phrases on this page. You simply have to learn them exactly as they are printed.

You must learn them so that you say them automatically when you are in that particular situation. Notice particulary how often **please** comes **at the end** of any request. Some people say this is the single most important word to use when you are speaking English!

UNIT 78

Practice 78.1

What do you say when:

1. You don't know what something means.

   — What .... this .... please?

2. You don't know where the Police station is?

   — .... me, could .... tell me ....

   .... , please?

3. You want to know the time.

   — Excuse ...., what .... do you .... it, ... ?

4. Someone is going away.

   — .... a good trip.

5. You want to introduce yourself.

   — Hello, I .... think we've .... before. I'm ....

   ....

6. You get the wrong number on the phone.

   — .... I've got ....

7. You leave and want to send a greeting to someone.

   — Give my .... your parents.

8. It is someone's birthday.

   — Many ....

9. It is January 1st.

   — ....

10. A friend gets engaged.

    — .... I hope you'll .... very ....

Practice 78.2

Which of the useful phrases did the person say who received these answers?

1. .... It's about half past five.

2. .... A - double D - R - E - double S,

3. .... Thanks. I hope you enjoy Spain, too.

4. .... No, it's to, not at.

5. .... Speaking.

6. .... How do you do.

Remember when you meet someone formally for the first time, people often say
How do you do. This is not a question, because the reply is also *How do you do!*

KEY

In many of the practices the answers given are the correct and only answers. In a large number of the practices, there is more than one correct answer. The answers given for these practices are suggestions. If your answer is different from the answer in this key — and you think your answer is possible — ask your teacher for an opinion. If you can, it is always better to discuss the answers with someone else.

1.1

1. will 2. are 3. must 4. would 5. does 6. were 7. have 8. won't 9. is 10. do 11. can 12. will 13. didn't 14. did 15. should 16. are 17. may 18. won't 19. has 20. doesn't

1.2

have, can, are, could, didn't, would, would, didn't, might, don't, don't, have, can, are, must, am, can't

1.3

has dropped, could it belong, are you going, Shall I take, might belong, must be, will make, should do, don't I keep it, could buy, would buy, might cost, would have, have always wanted, can use, am I going to do, didn't have, was coming, was going, don't know, Shall I take, can have

1.4

1. He couldn't drive. 2. It isn't raining. 3. I can't play tennis. 4. You shouldn't go. 5. We weren't thinking of going. 6. They aren't waiting outside. 7. John doesn't drive to work. 8. I don't believe you. 9. I don't like cheese. 10. They didn't come to the party.

1.5

1. Can we go early? 2. Is she getting married? 3. Were you speaking to John? 4. Would he like to go? 5. Does Bob get the 7.55 train? 6. Do I know Chris? 7. Does Britain still use miles, not kilometres? 8. Do banks usually close in the afternoon?

1.6

1. Do we need some more milk? 2. Does he play for Liverpool? 3. Does it look like rain? 4. Did they say it was going to rain? 5. Did she take her umbrella? 6. Does school start again next Monday? 7. Does it take longer by train? 8. Does money make people happy?

1.7

1. Have you met Ann before? 2. Do you know my colleague, Ann Carson? 3. Would John lend us one? 4. Do they sell them in the market? 5. Could we borrow one from John? 6. Does it look like rain?

1.8

1. I don't think I understand exactly what you mean. 2. I don't want to have an early dinner this evening. 3. I wouldn't ask Paul if I were you. 4. We won't see him before the weekend. 5. The boss doesn't understand the problem. 6. I don't sleep very well nowadays.

1.9

First dialogue: Is Jane taking . . . it isn't tomorrow . . . it can't be tomorrow . . . has she been worried . . . she mustn't worry . . . has she got . . . she hasn't done enough . . . she won't pass . . . she isn't worried. Second dialogue: Does Jane take . . . she doesn't take it . . . they don't work . . . does she worry about it . . . worrying doesn't help . . . does she have . . . she doesn't do . . . they don't pass . . . she doesn't worry.

2.1

1. . . . weren't they. 2. . . . was it. 3. . . . can't he. 4. . . . don't they. 5. . . . doesn't he. 6. . . . don't you. 7. . . . doesn't it. 8. . . . doesn't he.

2.2

1. Yes, I have. 2. No, I didn't. 3. Yes, she does. 4. No, I don't. 5. Yes, they are. 6. No, they won't.

2.3

1. Oh, have you? 2. Oh, is it? 3. Oh, does he? 4. Oh, did you? 5. Oh, was she? 6. Oh, is there?

2.4

1. We HAVE been waiting half an hour! 2. I DO like Mary a lot! 3. You DID promise 4. I WILL not come!
5. It HAS been raining a lot! 6. I DO love the sun! 7. We DID ring three times! 8. We DID warn you!

3.1

1. I am coming. 2. You're right. 3. We are not very pleased. 4. She's married. 5. It is not very expensive.
6. We've been here before. 7. They have not done it yet. 8. He's changed his job. 9. She has not changed at bit. 10. We'd met them before. 11. It does not matter. 12. I don't care. 13. She did not write back.
14. They won't be there. 15. I will speak to her. 16. I'd like to leave.

3.2

1. is 2. has 3. is 4. has 5. is 6. has 7. is 8. has 9. has 10. is

3.3

1. I don't think he is. 2. I don't think you do. 3. I don't think she has. 4. I don't think there is. 5. I don't think he did. 6. I don't think you would. 7. I don't think it will. 8. I don't think we do. 9. I don't think we have. 10. I don't think I would. 11. I don't think it was. 12. I don't think it did.

3.4

Across 2. am 4. are 5. is 7. are not 8. would
Down 1. have 3. has 5. is not 6. had 8. will not

3.5

1. a 2. b 3. b 4. a 5. b 6. a 7. b 8. a 9. b 10. a 11. b 12. b

4.1

1. What temperature does water boil at? 2. Which river flows through Paris? 3. What animal lives in China and eats bamboo? 4. Where does the Pope live? 5. Does light travel faster than sound? 6. Where do kangaroos come from? 7. Which islands lie in the middle of the Atlantic? 8. How long does it take to fly from London to New York in Concorde? 9. What does 'likely' mean? 10. Do horses sleep standing up?
The answers are: 1. e 2. d 3. f 4. i 5. a 6. b 7. h 8. j 9. c 10. g

4.2

get up early, jog around, don't believe you, do next, play football, cycle with my brother, have new bikes, cycle at least 30 kms, what do you do, don't play football, am lazy, stay at home and watch TV, do you go out then, get up quite late, go to the beach, don't go swimming, don't understand you, swim in the sea, cycle at least 10 kms, don't understand you, feel much happier.

4.3

Here are some suggestions. There are many more possible sentences:
They do/They don't/They do it/They don't do it/You like it/Do you like it/Do they know/Does it do that/
It doesn't do that/You like to/You like one/Do you like to etc.

4.4

Here are suggested answers. Sometimes two descriptions can fit one sentence.
1. a 2. d 3. b. 4. b 5. b 6. b 7. c 8. a 9. d 10. c 11. d 12. d

4.5

1. d 2. f 3. c 4. g 5. b 6. a 7. h 8. i 9. j 10. e

4.6

John is a teacher. Mick is a musician. Diana is a gardener.

4.7

1. d 2. c 3. b 4. a
(i) 4 (ii) 3 (iii) 1 (iv) 2

4.8

1. c 2. f 3. h 4. j 5. i 6. e 7. a 8. g 9. b 10. d

4.9

Ask your teacher to look at your answers.

5.1

1. Yes, I am. 2. No, I'm not. 3. Yes, you are. 4. No, you aren't. 5. Yes, she is. 6. No, he isn't. 7. Yes, it is. 8. Yes, we are. 9. No, we aren't. 10. Yes, they are.

5.2

1. Are you thinking of leaving? 2. Are you looking for the way out? 3. Mary's trying to learn to play the piano. 4. Is your father still working? 5. it's raining again! 6. We're going to New York. 7. Are you and your sister getting the same train? 8. Our teachers are planning a party. Are you joking?

5.3

1. c 2. d 3. e 4. b 5. a

5.4

1. c 2. a 3. b 4. b 5. c 6. a 7. a 8. b 9. c 10. c

5.5

Here are the obvious answers. There are more. Discuss your answers with other students and your teacher.
1. b 2. d 3. f 4. h

5.6

A Are you playing tennis . . . B I'm working . . . A And are you working . . . B I'm not playing . . . A I'm beginning to get . . . B I'm studying . . . A You're killing yourself . . . B I'm taking . . . A I'm trying to get into . . . I'm looking forward to playing . . .

Examples of the different types are: A I'm beginning to get that idea! B I'm not playing much tennis this year. C Are you working at the weekend?

5.7

1. I'm thinking. 2. I'm trying to make . . . 3. . . . you are learning to drive. 4. . . . they are watching the television. 5. She is leaving . . . 6. . . . the bell is ringing. 7. I'm going to sleep. 8. Why is Jim wearing a coat? Is he expecting rain? 9. . . . you are doing . . . you are trying to get in to. 10. Are you thinking what I'm thinking?

5.8

Ask your teacher to look at your sentences.

5.9

I'm learning to drive . . . Sheila is learning to drive . . . I'm keeping it a secret . . . I'm thinking of changing my job . . . What are you thinking of doing . . . I'm applying for job . . . who is teaching you . . . I'm having lessons . . . my brother is taking me out . . . Richard is coming . . . how is Richard getting on . . . he is getting stronger . . . he is starting work again . . . I'm having a lesson.

5.10

1. Mick is buying a flat near his new job. 2. He is selling his old car because he is planning to walk to work. 3. Are you getting tired? 4. Why aren't you watching the TV? 5. Is Zoe going on holiday to Italy next year? 6. No, I think she is staying at home.

a — 3,4   b — 1,2   c — 5,6

5.11

1. he is working 2. who is speaking 3. she is playing 4. what are you doing 5. I'm looking 6. I'm hoping 7. Sue and I are going out 8. my parents are coming
The uses are: a — 2,3,6,   b — 1,4,5,   c — 7,8

6.1

The correct answers are: 1. a 2. a 3. a 4. b 5. a 6. a 7. a 8. b

6.2

1. Where do you live? 2. Where are you staying? (Which hotel are you staying at?) 3. What do you do? 4. What are you doing? (What on earth are you doing? — if you are very surprised.)

6.3

1. c 2. d 3. a 4. f 5. e 6. b 7. g

6.4

1. We usually go to France every summer, but this summer we're going to Tunisia. 2. I usually get the bus, but today I'm walking to work. 3. I play tennis on Tuesdays, but this month I'm playing on Wednesdays instead. 4. Karim usually works on the night shift, but this winter she is working on the morning shift.

6.5

1. I'm going crazy. I go to Spain every summer. 2. I'm seeing John off at the airport this evening. I see what you mean. 3. I think I'll go home now. I'm thinking of having an early lunch. 4. I start crosswords but never finish them. I'm starting to forget people's names. 5. I usually have supper about 10. I'm having a party this Saturday. 6. I always do my homework as soon as I get home. Today I'm doing my homework before I go home. 7. I speak German well, but no French at all. I'm speaking. 8. I think I'm getting a cold. I get colds every winter. 9. I catch the 8.55 bus every day. I'm catching the sleeper to Glasgow this evening. 10. I'm enjoying myself, aren't you? I only enjoy discos when the music is extra-loud.

7.1

1. I missed 2. I talked 3. Steve cycled 4. John found . . . took 5. Zoe forgot 6. Sarah bought 7. the doctor told 8. He asked 9. I didn't see 10. Where did you go 11. What did you take 12. Did you see 13. Did you dance 14. Did you enjoy

7.2

Where else did you go?/What else did you buy?/Where else did you visit?/Who else did you meet?/What else did you eat?/What did you enjoy most?

7.3

1. died, exploded 2. collided, died 3. found, lived 4. fell, hoped 5. became, celebrated, spent 6. caused, flooded 7. went, came 8. won, beat, lasted

7.4

Left box: broke, ate, cost, tore, told, came, shot, stood.
Right box: kept, did, got, needed, sat, hid ate, rose.

7.5

1. e 2. b 3. f 4. c 5. a 6. d

7.6

1. regretted 2. hesitated 3. borrowed 4. believed 5. finished 6. happened 7. answered 8. opened 9. remembered 10. talked 11. liked 12. believed 13. walked 14. cheated 15. opened 16. damaged
You may have found others.

7.7

1. What did you do? 2. How did you get there? 3. Did he drive fast? 4. Why did he drive so fast? 5. What did you see? 6. Did you go straight home after the film?

8.1

1. No, he wasn't. He was still working! 2. I wasn't. Rob was driving. I was looking at the map. 3. Yes, they were. 4. You were. It was annoying everyone. 5. Yes, I was. And I was trying to ring you. 6. Yes, he was. 7. Yes, it was. It was raining very heavily. 8. Yes, you were!

8.2

1. Tom lost his wallet while he was visiting London. 2. Liz met a friend while she was waiting for the train. 3. The aeroplane crashed while it was taking off. 4. Peter ran out of petrol while he was driving to London.

8.3

1. Where were you living in 1976? In London.
2. Who were you going out with in 1977? Mary.
3. Where were you working in 1978? In London.
4. Where were you working in 1982? In New York.
5. Were you living in a small flat in 1983? No, in a large apartment.
6. Who were you going out with in 1984? Liz.
7. Were you working at Barclays before you went to America? No, I was working at the Bank of England.
8. Were you living with friends while you were working in New York? No, I had my own apartment.

8.4

Q1—R3, Q2—R6, Q3—R5, Q4—R7, Q5—R1, Q6—R8, Q7—R4, Q8—R2

9.1

1. I was watching . . . when you rang. 2. We were cleaning . . . when we found. 3. My mother was tidying . . . when she found. 4. We were walking . . . when we thought 5. How many people were queueing . . . when the tickets ran out. 6. Where were you going when I passed you 7. What was I doing before you interrupted me 8. I was shopping and I bumped into the man 9. Were your friends waiting for you when you arrived 10. I was thinking of writing to you when I heard 11. I was feeding . . . when one jumped 12. I was phoning . . . when my dad came in and asked me who I was speaking to . . . when he discovered that I was making . . .

9.2

Here are some possibilities. Talk to your teacher about others.
1 d,f,g,h   2 e,f,   3 a,c   4 a,b,   5 a,b,h

9.3

1. I was watching television. 2. No, I didn't. I decided . . . 3. Was it late when you went to see her? — I left home about 9.30. 4. What was she doing when you got there? — She was writing letters. 5. And how long did you stay? 6. And when did you get home? 7. It only took you 20 minutes. Why did it take you twice as long . . . What were you doing between . . . — I was trying to get my car to start.
8. And how long did it take you to get it started? 9. Did you come straight home? — No, I went upstairs . . 10. What did she say . . . — Well, I never got in . . . she was sleeping so she didn't hear me . . . so I went straight home. 11. Did anybody see you working . . . 12. and your girlfriend didn't see you either? — No, she was sleeping. 13. Somebody saw your car . . . You were sitting inside reading . . . you came out and opened the boot. Two men armed with guns ran out of the bank. The three of you drove off at high speed. While you were sitting outside in the car, they were robbing the bank!
14. Somebody saw your car . . . We spoke to your girlfriend. We know that you saw her yesterday evening, but you didn't leave at 11.30. You left at 11.20. And she was not sleeping at 11.50. She was writing some more letters.

9.4

I had my first experience . . . It was about 11 o'clock . . . I was in my hotel room and was taking my clothes off when I thought I heard someone . . . the whole room began to shake . . . the hotel was shaking . . . I was staying on the third floor . . . I ran out of the room and started to go . . . all the lights went out. While I was going down the stairs, I met someone who shouted . . . I did as he said. When I got there . . . they told me to stay under the stairs and we didn't come out until we thought the earthquake was over.

9.5

1. I saw Alan 2. What was he doing there? 3. He said he was meeting a friend from Portugal. Later I thought I saw Diana . . . 4. What was she doing there? 5. she was buying lots . . . as we saw each other, I suddenly caught sight of Steve. 6. What was he doing there? 7. He drove past too fast, I don't think he noticed.

9.6

In numbers 1 — 7 it is the b sentence which is the really natural one. In 8a the lights went from green to red. In 8b they changed from red to green.

9.7

1. I was thinking of going out when you called. 2. We met while we were studying in Liverpool. 3. When she was travelling on the underground, someone stole her bag. 4. The theif took the money when the staff were having lunch. 5. Steve was driving to London when he remembered to phone Alex.

9.8

1. were living 2. was shining 3. were enjoying 4. was looking 5. saw 6. opened 7. told 8. was leaving 9. was putting 10. was crying 11. walked 12. stopped 13. jumped 14. was thinking 15. landed 16. was smiling

10.1

The hidden forms are: given, had, fit, ran, caught, slept, understood, stood, forgot, forgotten, got, cost, gave, heard, thrown, torn, told, drove, felt, won, drank, sold, hurt, stuck, chose and the two you must read upwards were cut and set.

10.2

1. thought, bought, fought, taught, brought 2. flew, knew, threw, grew, drew 3. broke, woke 4. cost, cut, hit, hurt, let, put, set, shut, split

10.3

1. began 2. bitten 3. broken 4. brought 5. caught 6. chose 7. came 8. bought, cost

10.4

1. drunk 2. drove 3. eaten 4. fell 5. found 6. forgiven, forgotten 7. froze 8. gave

10.5

1. grew, grew 2. heard 3. hid 4. kept 5. knew 6. lent, got 7. left 8. lost

10.6

sat, saw, got, took, seen, shone, taught, sold, lit, stole, stolen

10.7

1. meant 2. met 3. paid 4. rang 5. ran 6. seen, saw 7. sold, bought 8. sent 9. set 10. shone

10.8

1. shot 2. shown 3. slept 4. wrote 5. spent 6. stood, came 7. lost, stolen 8. stuck, frozen 9. took 10. taught 11. torn 12. told 13. understood, wrote 14. woke, went

11.1

1. Bill has . . . Dave hasn't 2. . . . who has . . . 3. Three people have 4. Only one person hasn't . . .
5. Ellen and Andy have . . . Andy hasn't 6. . . . who has . . . 7. Nobody has . . . 8. Two people have . . .
9. Sue and Dave have . . . neither has . . . 10. Sue and Ellen have . . .
Ask your teacher to look at your answers to nos 11 and 12.

11.2

1. b 2. c 3. a

11.3

1. She's just had a baby. 2. He's just crashed his car. (had a crash.) 3. He's just fallen asleep. 4. They've just had a fight. 5. It's just taken off. 6. He's just won. (the race) 7. They've just got married. 8. He's just got an electric shock.
If your answers were not exactly the same as the ones given, ask your teacher. You could be right.

11.4

2. A I've already bought my ticket. B Have you? So have I.
3. A I've spent all my money. B Have you? So have I.
4. A I've met your brother's new girlfriend. B Have you? So have I.
5. A I've got very wet. B Have you? So have I.
6. A I've bought a CD player. B Have you? So have I.

11.5

1. Have you ever been to Sri Lanka? 2. He's just had some very good news. 3. I've never wanted to be rich. 4. Haven't you finished yet? 5. We've always been very good friends. 6. People have often mistaken me for John Wayne. 7. I've already locked the door. 8. It hasn't rained very much lately.

11.6

1. We have built . . . 2. We have created . . . 3. We have brought down . . . 4. We have reduced . . .
5. We have given . . . 6. We have modernised . . . 7. We have employed . . . 8. We have made . . .
9. We have helped . . . 10. They have made . . . 11. They have destroyed . . . 12. They have forgotten . . .
13. They have damaged . . . 14. They have shaken . . . 15. They have cut . . . 16. They have forgotten . . .
17. They haven't taken . . . 18. They have left . . .

11.7

1. I've just passed my exam. 2. I've just broken my leg. 3. I've rung her twice. She must be out.
4. I'm afraid I've already seen it. 5. I've never seen it before. 6. I've brought sandwiches with me.
7. I haven't passed my test yet. 8. I've hurt my foot. (leg) 9. I've sold it and bought a new one.
10. Yes, I've just got engaged.

12.1

1. 've 2. haven't 3. 've 4. haven't 5. 's 6. hasn't 7. 've 8. haven't 9. 've 10. haven't

12.2

1. I've been living in Leeds. I've been working in a furniture factory. 2. I've been living in Australia. I've been working on a farm. 3. I've been living in Dublin. I've been working in a travel agents. 4. I've been living at home. I haven't had a job. (I haven't been working.) 5. I've been living in Aberdeen. I've been working in a hospital. 6. I've been living in London. I've been working in a theatre. 7. I've been living in Cornwall. I've been working in a hotel. 8. I've been living in Paris. I've been working in an international bank.

12.3

1. She's been crying. 2. They've been watching a film. 3. He's been swimming. 4. They've been running. 5. They've been playing tennis. 6. It's been raining. 7. He's been having a bath. 8. He's been sleeping.

12.4

1. Who's been sitting on my chair? 2. Who's been eating my porridge? 3. Who's been sleeping in my bed?

12.5

1. How long have you been working there? 2. What exactly have you been doing there? 3. How much have you been earning? 4. How many hours a week have you been working? 5. Have you been enjoying your work? 6. Why have you decided to leave your old job? 7. Why have you applied for this job?

13.1

The following are the possible sentences: 1. I've just been swimming. 2. Have you heard your results yet? 3. Have you bought a new car yet? 4. You've grown since I last saw you! 5. I've passed my exam! 6. I've lost my new pen. 7. I've started to learn to drive. 8. I think I've broken my arm!

13.2

1. a 2. a 3. b 4. b 5. a 6. b

13.3

The following are very unlikely: 1. b 2. b 3. b 4. b

13.4

1. They've been saving up for a holiday for months. They've gone to China. 2. He's been going out with Jane for 5 years. He's asked her to marry him. She's refused! 3. They've been digging in these hills for years. They've found it at last. 4. I've been trying to learn Esperanto for six months. I've given up! I've decided to learn to play golf instead! 5. We've been planning to have a big party. We've decided to have it on the 16th. We've invited 50 people. We haven't invited anyone from the office! 6. I've been looking for my pen. Somebody has stolen it.

13.5

1. b 2. a 3. a 4. b 5. a 6. b 7. b 8. a 9. a 10. b 11. a 12. b 13. b 14. a 15. b 16. a 17. b 18. a

14.1

1. Yes, I did. 2. No, I haven't. 3. Yes, I have. 4. Yes, I did. 5. Yes, I did. 6. No, I haven't. 7. Yes, I have. 8. Yes, I did. 9. Yes, she has. 10. No, she didn't.

14.2

We haven't seen Tom — yet / since last weekend / for ages / for 20 years.
We saw Tom — at Christmas / on the 26th / yesterday / last week.

14.3

1. b 2. a 3. a 4. b 5. b 6. a 7. a 8. b 9. b 10. a

14.4

1. I started to read Death on the Nile on holiday. I've only read the first two chapters so far. 2. I bought 10 peaches this morning. I've eaten 9 already. 3. Bill won £5000 in a lottery. He's spent most of it already. 4. Jill did French at school. She's forgotten most of it by now. 5. Pete left home last Tuesday. He's hitch-hiked over 200 miles in the last three days. 6. Some friends of mine bought an old car for £50. They've travelled all over Europe in it in the past year. 7. I started my homework after dinner. It's almost bedtime and I've hardly done anything yet! 8. I bought a new pad of paper yesterday. I've almost used it all up already!
The links with Now are expressed by the following words:
1. so far 2. already 3. already 4. by now 5. in the last three days 6. in the past year 7. yet 8. already

14.5

1. Have you ever been involved . . . Yes, I have actually. I had a very bad accident . . . I broke both legs.
2. Have you every been to the top . . . Yes, I have . . . When I was in Paris. I went to the top . . .
3. Have you ever won . . . No, I haven't, but once I won £10 . . . 4. Have you ever found anything . . . Yes, I once found a diamond ring. I found it . . . I took it to the police. I never heard . . . 5. Have you ever lost anything . . . Yes, I took my watch off . . . when I went back . . . 6. Have you ever felt really ill? . . . The first time was when we went to France . . . the second time was when we came back! 7. Have you ever had a fight with anyone? . . . Yes, I had a fight . . . we argued about . . . 8. Have you ever done something . . . I did something really silly last summer . . . I wore a winter coat and carried an umbrella. Everyone asked me why. I said I thought it was going to rain.

14.6

Ask your teacher to look at your answers.

14.7

1. j, m   2. f, k   3. d, n   4. b, q   5. h, l   6. g, s   7. i, t   8. c, o   9. e, p   10. a, r

15.1

1. been 2. blown 3. planted 4. grown 5. reached 6. climbed 7. hidden 8. come 9. taken 10. burnt 11. survived 12. reminded

15.2

1. I had never driven before. 2. I had never flown before. 3. I had never given a speech before.
4. I had never skied before. 5. I hadn't played tennis before. (I'd never played tennis before.) 6. I had never sung in public before.

15.3

1. I'd never tasted Mexican food until I met Maria. 2. I'd never spoken Spanish until I met Maria. 3. I'd never listened to Spanish music until I met Maria. 4. I'd never visited Mexico city until . . . 5. I'd never crossed the Atlantic until . . . 6. I'd never fallen in love until . . . 7. I'd never enjoyed life so much . . . 8. I'd never lived abroad . . .

15.4

1. Mary said she'd gone on her own. 2. Bill said he'd enjoyed the film a lot. 3. Pete said he'd walked home. 4. Diana said John had given her a lift. 5. James said it had cost £50. 6. Jean said she had expected to be on time. 7. Brian said he had thought he was right. 8. Liz said Mike had spoken to her about the problem. 9. Mr Black said he had waited until the shop closed. (had closed) 10. The policewoman said she hadn't seen exactly who did what. (who had done what.)

16.1

1. h   2. d   3. f   4. a   5. g   6. b   7. e   8. c

16.2

1. He's going to give up smoking. 2. She's going to stop eating sweets. 3. He's going to have his hair cut. 4. She's going to help old people. 5. She's going to work harder. 6. He's going to start jogging.
Check your answers with your teacher.

16.3

1. He's going to teach himself to play the guitar. (He's going to learn to play the guitar). 2. He's going to write letters. 3. He's going to read a lot. 4. He's going to play tennis. 5. He's going to swim. 6. He's going to explore the area. 7. He's going to listen to music. 8. He's going to get up early. 9. He's going to play chess. 10. He's going to teach himself Chinese. (He's going to learn Chinese.)

16.4

The following are suggestions. Ask your teacher to look at your sentences: 1. I'm going to get up late tomorrow. 2. I'm going to have something to eat. 3. I think we're **going to** run out of petrol soon. 4. I'm going to be late. 5. You're going to spill it. 6. I'm going to ring the police. 7. I think the weather is going to clear up. 8. I feel as if I am going to go to sleep.

16.5

1. The first is correct. The second sounds very aggressive. 2. The first sounds more natural. 3. The second sounds more natural – the use of **going to** suggests a considered decision. 4. The second is natural because the decision is made on the evidence now – that I am so far behind with my work. 5. The second is the more natural because it is a decision at the moment of speaking. 6. The first is more natural. It is an immediate reaction to the ringing of the phone. 7. The first is the more natural for the same reason as no 6 8. The second is more natural because the speaker has evidence now that forces him to make the decision.

17.1

Liz — Why won't you speak to me? Tom — I just won't! Liz — I'll tell you why I'm angry if you'll tell me why you're angry. Tom — Well, I won't tell YOU anything. Liz — But why won't you? Tom — Why won't I? You want me to tell you why I won't speak to you! I'll tell you something, I'll never speak to you again! And that is final! Liz — I think you will! Tom — No, I won't!

17.2

1. Will you marry me? Yes, Steve, I will. 2. I'll get the doctor. 3. The lock won't open. I'll boil some water . . . 4. I'll see you . . . 5. You'll get home . . . 6. When do you think you'll get your results? I think they'll be in the post tomorrow. 7. I'll speak to him . . . 8. I'll close the window. 9. Why won't you give me a lift? . . . My car won't start. 10. I'll take a look at it.

17.3

I'm playing against Liz . . . then I'm going to the disco . . . I'm staying at my parents . . . I'm having lunch . . . We are having some relatives . . . I'm planning to escape . . . and then I'm starting my summer holiday . . . I'm leaving for the north . . . I'm hiring a car . . . the ghosts are waiting for you!

17.4

1. Who are you going with? 2. Where are you going? 3. Why are you going there? 4. How are you getting there? 5. Where are you staying? 6. Why aren't you coming with us?

17.5

. . . we arrive in Paris . . . we stay in Paris . . . we fly to Rome . . . it leaves quite early . . . we stay 2 nights . . . we take the train to Venice . . . we fly to Athens . . . we spend the weekend in Athens . . . we go for an early morning walk . . . we take the Olympic Airways flight . . . we stay for 3 nights . . . we leave at 7.30 for London where we stay till the Sunday . . . Today we fly direct . . . but when we come back from London, the plane touches down in New York.

17.6

Ask your teacher to look at your answers.

17.7

1. d 2. f 3. a 4. c 5. b 6. e

17.8

But what are we going to do? (or what will we do) . . . Where are we going to find somewhere else to live? (or where will we find) . . . We'll find somewhere. I'll ring the landlord. 2. I'm going shopping with a friend . . . she is having a party that evening . . . I'll ring you later and tell you what I'm going to do. (or what I'm doing). 3. I'm going to Exeter tomorrow . . . when the 11 o'clock gets in . . . You'll have to change . . . It arrives at 1.35 . . . when does it arrive ? . . . You'll have to change twice! (or you have to) 4. I know you are meeting that man tonight . . . tonight I am playing (or going to play) cards . . . by midnight you will be on the night train.

18.1

Break two eggs and put them in a bowl. Beat them and add salt and pepper to taste. Heat a frying pan with a little butter or oil, then pour the egg in. Make sure the bottom of the omelette doesn't burn. Turn it over when the bottom is cooked.

18.2

Take the outer tyre off . . . Loosen the valve and remove the inner tube . . . Fill a large bowl . . . put the inner tube . . . mark the hole and dry it . . . stick the patch . . . leave it . . . replace the inner tube . . . be careful . . .

18.3

Go straight up here to the traffic lights. Cross over and carry on up until you come to the roundabout. Turn right then go along as far as the next roundabout. Turn left there then first right. Lawrence Road is the second street on the left. Ask somone if you get lost but it's really very easy to find.

18.4

Come in, both of you. Take your coats off. Now, come into the sitting-room . . . Come in, make yourselves at home. Come and sit near the fire . . . John, get Carol and Peter . . . John, put the light on . . . use the green towel . . . Now, Carol, wait until I get back . . . Come on Carol, tell us everything. Don't say a word . . . Keep them guessing . . . Don't take any notice of him. Don't worry about him! I'm so curious, so tell us the news . . . Don't be impatient. Wait for Peter, and wait until I've got everybody a drink. Relax, Carol . . .

18.5

1. mix 2. add, mix, add 3. put, leave 4. put 5. bake, remove 6. allow

18.6

1. Let's not tell Jim. 2. Let's not worry how much it costs. 3. Let's not go swimming. 4. Let's not spend more than £5. 5. Let's not wait for the bus. Let's walk instead. 6. Let's not go to France. Let's go to Spain instead. 7. Let's not buy her a book. Let's get some flowers instead. 8. Let's not waste time. Let's get on with it.

18.7

1. e 2. a 3. f 4. c 5. g 6. b 7. d 8. h

19.1

The following are the more natural: 1. a 2. a 3. a 4. a 5. a

19.2

1. Mr Jones was killed by his wife in a fit of anger. 2. Over 50 people were killed the guerillas. 3. Most of the top floor was destroyed by the bomb. 4. How much were you paid? 5. The rebuilding was begun in 1975. 6. 20 demonstrators were arrested by the police. 7. The job was finished by 10 o'clock. 8. The road has been closed to through-traffic.

19.3

1. Was the building completed in time? No, it wasn't.
2. Has Jill been told about it yet? Yes, she has.
3. Were you taught well when you were at school? No, I wasn't.
4. Are you often misunderstood when you speak English? I'm afraid I am.
5. Has your car been found yet? Yes, thank goodness, it has.
6. Are girls given the same opportunities as boys?
7. Are foreign languages taught to most students?
8. Has the countryside been spoilt by pollution?
9. Have many motorways been built?

19.4

1. built 2. made 3. invited 4. given 5. sent 6. been thanked 7. been fixed 8. was written 9. was pulled down 10. was opened

19.5

1. found 2. buried 3. driven 4. felt 5. destroyed 6. born 7. split, destroyed 8. killed

19.6

1. He was murdered. 2. I was pushed. 3. I was sacked. 4. I was asked to leave. 5. I was taught by John Williams.

19.7

Fire engine — was treated . . . was sent. Soldier shot — was shot . . . was said. Thief — was arrested. Meat thief — was eaten. Birthday bag — was arrested. £15m — was spent. Police magazine — has been knocked down. Tractor — was run over.

19.8

The books have been moved. The pear has been eaten. The blind has been closed. The vase has been broken. The door has been opened. The candle has been lit. The armchair has been torn. The television has been turned off.

20.1

1. auxiliary 2. auxiliary 3. full verb 4. auxiliary 5. auxiliary 6. full verb 7. auxiliary 8. full verb 9. auxiliary 10. have = auxiliary, had = full verb

20.2

1. have 2. have 3. have 4. had 5. have 6. is having 7. are having 8. are having 9. have had 10. having 11. have or had 12. have 13. have 14. have, have 15. have 16. have 17. are having 18. was having, had

21.1

been, be, been, are, are, were, was, are, are, are, are, is, be
Total: 13 forms

21.2

be, is, is, are, were, be, is, is, be, is, be

21.3

1. I'm hungry. 2. I'm sleepy. 3. I'm late. 4. We're early. 5. I'm thirsty. 6. Why are you afraid?
7. . . . if you're careful. 8. He's very funny. 9. . . . I was very upset. 10. . . . we were completely
exhausted. 11. How old were you . . . 12. How long is . . .

22.1

1. aux 2. aux 3. aux 4. aux 5. full 6. aux 7. aux 8. aux 9. did = aux, do = full 10. full 11. didn't = aux,
did = aux 12. don't = aux, do = full

22.2

1. Most people know how to read and write, but some don't. 2. Most people like small children, but some
don't. 3. Some people speak another language fluently, but most don't. 4. Most people read a paper every
day, but some don't. 5. Most people own a television set, but some don't. 6. Most people enjoy travelling,
but some don't. 7. Some people believe the earth is flat, but most don't. 8. Most people used to believe the
earth was flat, but some didn't.

22.3

1. b. I don't speak German. c. Do you speak German? d. My brother speaks German. e. My sister doesn't
speak German. f. Does your brother speak German? g. We didn't speak German yesterday. h. Did you speak
German yesterday?
2. b. I don't take the train. c. Do you take the train? d. My brother takes the train. e. My sister doesn't take
the train. f. Does your brother take the train? g. We didn't take the train yesterday. h. Did you take the
train yesterday?
3. b. I don't visit her. c. Do you visit her? d. My brother visits her. e. My sister doesn't visit her. f. Does
your brother visit her? g. We didn't visit her yesterday. h. Did you visit her yesterday?

22.4

1. do 2. do 3. do, do 4. do 5. doing 6. does 7. has done 8. do 9. did (or have done), do, have done, did
10. are you doing

22.5

1. do 2. don't 3. do 4. don't 5. don't 6. do 7. don't 8. do

22.6

doesn't, doesn't, does, do, did, does, do, did, doesn't, doesn't, didn't, do, did, do, don't, don't

22.7

1. Don't . . . do 2. do . . . do 3. did you do . . . 4. to do 5. did . . . done 6. have done 7. doing 8. does

22.8

1. did 2. do 3. did 4. do, don't 5. does, don't 6. don't 7. did, do 8. did 9. do 10. did 11. do 12. did,
didn't, didn't 13. does 14. didn't 15. does 16. don't 17. do 18. don't, don't 19. doesn't 20. did, do

23.1

The following are the most natural, but there are other possibilities: 1. should 2. can 3. must 4. could,
would 5. will, would 6. may, might 7. shall, shall 8. can, may 9. must, might

23.2

1. can/could/may/shall/should/must 2. could/may/might/should/will/must 3. could/may/might/should 4. must
5. could/may/might/must 6. could/should/will/would/must 7. could/would 8. could/may/might
9. can/could/will/would

24.1

1. He can fly. 2. She can sing. 3. He can cook. 4. He can ski. 5. She can ride a bike. 6. He can play tennis.
7. She can windsurf. 8. It can swim. 9. It can talk.

24.2

1. can't 2. can 3. he can't 4. she can 5. I can't 6. they can 7. I can't 8. can

270

24.3

1. Can I pay by credit card? 2. Can I dial direct to . . . ? 3. Can I use the same ticket? 4. Can I change my ticket? 5. Can you use a word-processor? 6. Can I help you? 7. Can you lend me a pound? 8. Can you read German? 9. Can you baby-sit for me?
The uses are: 1. a 2. a 3. a 4. a 5. a 6. c 7. b 8. a 9. b

24.4

1. You can't be hungry. 2. He can't be French. 3. You can't be tired. 4. He can't be very careful. 5. She can't be coming. 6. They can't be at home.

24.5

If you replace **can** with **could** there is little difference in meaning in the following: 2, 3, 4, 6, 7, 9 11 (2nd use), 13, 14. **could** is impossible in the following: 8, 10.

25.1

could, could, couldn't, couldn't, could, could, couldn't, couldn't, could

25.2

1. You could take the train. 2. You could take your own. 3. You could book a sleeper. 4. You could read some good books. 5. You could ask a friend. 5. You could stay at home.

25.3

1. Jim could speak . . . 2. Mary couldn't speak . . . 3. Jim could play the piano . . . 4. Mary couldn't read . . . 5. Mary couldn't swim . . .

26.1

1. can, may 2. may 3. may 4. can 5. can't 6. may 7. may 8. may 9. can 10. can, may, can, can, may

26.2

1. b 2. a 3. b 4. a 5. b 6. a 7. a 8. b

27.1

1. Pete might be coming. 2. It might rain. 3. I might be sick. 4. She might be right. 5. That might have been the doorbell. 6. We might have been wrong.

27.2

1. It might have. 2. There might be. 3. I might have. 4. I might be. 5. I might be able to. 6. It might have. 7. There might be. 8. you might have to.

27.3

Similar = 1, 3, 4 Different = 2, 5

28.1

1. I will if you will. 2. I'll get . . . you'll have 3. Who'll be there? I won't but my brother will. 4. I'll ring . . . and so will I. 5. . . . will you . . . I'll tell no one. 6. I'll just go . . . You'll miss . . . I'll catch . . .

28.2

1. c 2. f 3. a 4. b 5. e 6. d

28.3

1. I'll open the window. 2. I'll post them for you. 3. I'll lend you mine. 4. I'll make a cup of tea. 5. I'll scream. 6. I'll give you a lift. 7. I'll open . . . 8. I'll be off then, I'll be in touch in a few days.

29.1

The natural sentences are: 1. a 2. a 3. b 4. b 5. c

29.2

1. Shall we leave before it gets busy? 2. Will you open the window, please? 3. Shall we dance? 4. Shall I call the doctor for you? 5. Will you get me a coffee, please? 6. Shall I get a ticket for you? 7. Shall I help you with your luggage? 8. Shall we have an ice-cream? 9. Shall I bring some sandwiches? 10. Will you give me a lift?

30.1

1. b 2. a 3. d 4. c

30.2

1. b 2. c 3. d 4. a

30.3

1. I'd close the door . . . 2. I'd go up to the top floor . . . 3. I'd start going down . . . 4. I'd hang out . . . 5. I'd start praying . . .

30.4

1. I'd rather get the earlier bus. 2. I'd prefer to have a sandwich. 3. We'd prefer to have meal. 4. I'd prefer to speak to the manager. 5. Who'd rather have tea? 6. I'd rather fly.

30.5

1. That would be lovely. 2. That would be ridiculous. 3. That would be surprising. 4. That would be annoying. 5. That would be awful.

30.6

1. would take 2. would please 3. would be 4. would drive 5. would get 6. would object 7. would stop 8. would help 9. would go 10. would read

30.7

1. Would you like a cup of coffee? 2. I don't think you would like it. 3. What would you do in my position? 4. Perhaps an aspirin would help. 5. Would you mind if I came? 6. Why wouldn't they let you in? 7. If I were you, I would do that. 8. Nobody would know, would they?

31.1

1. You should ring the police. 2. You should ask for it back. 3. You should take it back. 4. You shouldn't smoke so much. 5. You shouldn't read so much. 6. You shouldn't work so late at night. 7. You shouldn't eat so much. 8. You should ask for a rise. 9. You should have a holiday. 10. You should complain to the maker. 11. You shouldn't give them so much. 12. You shouldn't complain so much.

32.1

1. punished 2. fined 3. abolished 4. imprisoned 5. banned

32.2

1. should, ought 2. should, ought 3. ought, ought 4. ought, should 5. ought, ought 6. should, ought 7. should, ought 8. ought, should, shouldn't

32.3

1. I think he ought to go. 2. You ought not to have said that. 3. Do you think we ought to tell her? 4. What do you think we ought to do about it?

33.1

1. b 2. e 3. h 4. g 5. d 6. f 7. a 8. c (also possible are 6. c and 8. f)

33.2

1. Then she must be Swiss. 2. You can't be serious. 3. You must be joking. 4. Then he must have been the director. 5. Oh, it must have been raining . . . 6. You can't be. 7. Then she must be leaving early. 8. Then it can't be worth going to.

33.3

1a must 1b mustn't 2a mustn't 2b must 3a must 3b mustn't 4a mustn't 4b must

34.1

1. we have to check in by 7.30! 2. you have to take them 3 times a day . . . you have to take them before meals. 3. you have to report to the secretary. 4. you have to ring the agents first. 5. you have to leave it at reception.

34.2

1. Do you have to get a visa . . . but you have to get one for Poland. 2. Did you have to fill in a form . . . Yes, we did, but at least we didn't have to wait long . . . 3. How much do you have to earn before . . . Everyone has to pay tax. 4. John had to pay . . . we only had to pay half fare . . . 5. What grades did you have to get before you got into university . . . they said I had to get . . .

34.3

1. I'll have to reply . . . 2. I'll have to stop . . . 3. You'll have to give me . . . 4. That boy will have to start (or boy'll) 5. We'll have to . . . 6. You'll have to . . . 7. You'll have to have . . . 8. I'll have to buy . . .

34.4

1. a—y, b—x 2. a—x, b—y 3. a—x, b—y 4. a—y, b—x 5. a—y, b—x 6. a—y, b—x 7. a—x, b—y 8. a—y, b—x

35.1

1. You mustn't be there till 7.30. 2. You mustn't drink it! 3. You don't have to pay on this bus. 4. You mustn't wash it. 5. We mustn't. 6. You don't have to. 7. You mustn't. 8. he mustn't.

35.2

1. mustn't 2. don't have to 3. mustn't 4. don't have to 5. mustn't, you don't have to 6. mustn't 7. mustn't 8. mustn't 9. mustn't, don't have to.

35.3

Mary-mustn't, Dick-don't have to, Dick-don't have to, Mary-mustn't, Dick-don't have to, don't have to, Mary-don't have to, mustn't

35.4

1. d 2. f 3. a 4. b 5. c 6. e 7. h 8. g

35.5

1. d You can, but you don't have to. 2. a Well, you mustn't let it worry you. 3. f I know. I mustn't forget. 4. c Well, you don't have to have a credit card. 5. e You mustn't say things like that! 6. b Well, they don't have to lend you anything. 7. You don't have to buy me a present, but you mustn't forget to send me a card!

36.1

1. It's got to be seen to be believed. 2. If you've got to go, you've got to go. 3. What have you got to do tonight? 4. I've got to get to the bank before they close.

36.2

1. You've got to be there before 7.30. 2. He's got to get up by 8 o'clock. 3. You've got to stay in bed until the fever has gone. 4. It's got to be finished by tomorrow afternoon. 5. You've got to buy the tickets at least two weeks before departure. 6. I've got to take two in the morning and three at night. 7. You've got to wait for the Leeds train to arrive.

37.1

1. Maria's got long dark hair. (or has got) 2. I've got a car, but I haven't got a bike. 3. He's got . . . 4. Have you got change . . . 5. . . . you've got an appointment 6. . . . have you got change . . . 7. I've got a meeting . . . 8. I've got so much to do . . . 9. You've got a lovely car . . . you've got a big petrol bill, too. 10. We haven't got any children . . . 11. Have you got a phone? 12. . . . haven't got enough to eat.

37.2

Compare your answers with other students.

37.3

1. Have you got a minute to spare? 2. Have you got an appointment? 3. Have you got my number? 4. Have you got a cold? 5. Have you got the time?

37.4

1. I've got a stone in my shoe. 2. I've got a cold. 3. She's got flu. 4. I've got two still to write. 5. She's got two boys and a girl. 6. He's got a Mini and an Audi. 7. They've got a beautiful smell. 8. It's got six rooms. 9. I've got enough! 10. They've got too much.

37.5

1. She's got . . . 2. He's got . . . 3. She's got . . . 4. He's got . . . 5. She's got . . . 6. He's got . . . 7. She's got . . . 8. He hasn't got . . . 9. Her country has got . . . 10. His country has got . . . 11. Her children have got . . . 12. His children haven't got . . . 13. She's got . . . 14. He hasn't got . . .

38.1

1. I'm not used to the cold. 2. I'm not used to the smell. 3. I'm not used to his bad habits. 4. She's not used to the noise. 5. They're not used to living in town.

38.2

1. I haven't got used to the high cost of living yet. 2. I haven't got used to getting up so early yet.
3. I haven't got used to eating no sugar yet. 4. I haven't got used to the new money and I haven't got used to driving on the left again.

38.3

1. . . . it took him a long time to get used to living with someone else . . . they've got used to living with each other. 2. . . . you would get used to living . . . you would have to get used to . . . I wonder if a Spaniard ever could get used to life there. 3. . . . he found it very difficult to get used to the idea of being unemployed. He had always been used to doing things. Now he had to get used to the idea . . . He had always been used to earning money . . . He could not get used to that idea . . .

38.4

1. You'll soon get used to them. 2. I'd just got used to the old one. 3. I soon got used to it. 4. Yes, so I'll have to get used to living on my own again. 5. I'll never get used to working . . . 6. Getting used to all the travelling isn't easy!

38.5

Ask your teacher to look at your answers.

38.6

Sue Dickson: Two years ago I went to live and work in Nicaragua. Life there was very different from what I was used to back home in the UK. To start with, I had to get used to a very different climate. I still haven't been able to get used to the heat. I'm getting used to the rain, but I suppose that's because I'm British! One thing I don't think I'll ever get used to properly is the poverty. In Britain we are used to seeing poor people, but we don't see children begging in the streets. I'll never get used to that. As a child I was used to a lovely home and everything I wanted. That's why I'm working with these poor children. I'll never get used to living in Britain again.
Peter Craig: . . . You can understand that I'm not used to seeing soldiers carrying guns. Even though I stayed for six months I still didn't get used to that. Nor could I get used to the sound of sirens . . . They have got used to all the things (or they were used to all the things) . . . You've got to get used to it . . . That's what I really couldn't get used to.

39.1

1. g   2. h   3. e   4. i   5. a   6. d   7. b   8. f   9. c

39.2

. . . girls never used to go out . . . that never used to be allowed . . . my father always used to ask . . . I used to go behind . . . I didn't use to disobey . . . my mother used to wear it . . . when we used to get up . . . we used to be up and washed . . . we used to clean out . . . we used to have to do all the cleaning . . .

39.3

Ask your teacher to look at your answers.

40.1

1. isn't it 2. is it 3. is she 4. isn't he 5. aren't we 6. are you 7. aren't they 8. are they 9. is there 10. isn't there

40.2

1. has it 2. hasn't it 3. hasn't she 4. has he 5. haven't we 6. have you 7. have they 8. haven't they 9. hasn't there 10. has there

40.3

1. does it 2. didn't it 3. does she 4. did he 5. don't we 6. don't you 7. didn't you 8. do they 9. did they 10. do they

40.4

1. should I 2. mustn't we 3. can't you 4. won't she 5. couldn't we 6. mustn't it 7. would it 8. will you 9. shouldn't he 10. mustn't we

41.1

1. b   2. d   3. a   4. f   5. c   6. e

41.2

1. f   2. d   3. h   4. a   5. g   6. e   7. c   8. b

41.3

1. How are you . . . Lovely day, isn't it . . . yes, beautiful, isn't it . . . It was dreadful last week, wasn't it . . . Yes, it was, wasn't it.
2. John hasn't been to work all week, has he . . . No he hasn't. He can't be in hospital **again**, can he . . . He could be on holiday, couldn't he . . . yes, of course he could!
3. It's been a long day, hasn't it . . . Yes, it has, hasn't it . . . there's been so much to do, hasn't there . . . Yes, there hasn't even been time . . . that's a good idea, isn't it.

41.4

1. haven't you 2. do you 3. don't they 4. is it 5. is it 6. isn't it 7. don't you 8. do they 9. do they 10. wouldn't we

41.5

1. b 2. j 3. a 4. f 5. i 6. c 7. d 8. g 9. h 10. e

42.1

1. Have we met before? 2. Do you live near here? 3. Do you like to speak English? 4. Are you interested in sport? 5. Have you ever been abroad? 6. Can you play tennis? 7. Are you single or married? 8. Would you like to go to the cinema with me?

42.2

1. Is it raining outside? 2. Are you cold? 3. Have you ever visited London? 4. Can you speak German? 5. Do you smoke? 6. Have you been here before? 7. Do you want to leave? 8. Is there a train before 8?

43.1

1—f 2—b 3—c 4—e 5—d 6—a

43.2

which one . . . who are you going with . . . when are you going . . . when does the film start . . . why are you going so early . . . where is the party . . . what is the film . . . what is it about . . . why don't you come . . . but what will the others say . . . when did you say . . .

43.3

1. How long 2. When was, was 3. Where, what, how long 4. Which, where do 5. How 6. How many 7. How much 8. How many, how

43.4

1. c 2. e 3. h 4. b 5. g 6. d 7. a 8. f

43.5

1. What was the approximate age of the man? (or How old was the man approximately?) 2. How tall was the man? 3. What colour were his eyes? 4. How long was his hair 5. What colour was his hair? 6. What colour were his shoes?

43.6

1. f 2. n 3. m 4. l 5. g 6. e 7. i 8. b 9. a 10. o 11. c 12. d 13. h 14. k 15. j

44.1

1. smoking 2. wash 3. lending 4. say 5. get 6. pretending 7. meeting 8. ring 9. helping 10. send 11. visiting 12. coming

44.2

1. swimming 2. writing 3. waiting, wasting, 4. working 5. ringing 6. working 7. complaining, doing 8. thinking

44.3

going, getting, waking, doing, getting, taking, leaving, offering, upsetting, drinking, refusing, driving, trying, asking, raining, offering, going, looking, complaining, making

44.4

1. Flying 2. Spending, making 3. Flying and parachuting, playing 4. Working, relaxing 5. dancing, singing 6. driving

44.5

What about going . . . I'm going shopping . . . miss seeing . . . it's no use asking me . . . interested in being disappointed . . . instead of going to the cinema, what about having a pizza . . . I miss having . . . it's worth getting there early . . . I hate waiting for a table . . . without booking at the weekends . . . would you mind picking me up . . . Talking about eating always makes me feel hungry!

44.6

Ask your teacher to look at your answers.

45.1

1. get off 2. take off 3. turn off 4. called it off 5. see them off 6. gone off 7. paid off 8. put it off 9. show off 10. set off

45.2

1. It stopped completely. 2. It closes for ever. 3. You are injured by it, possibly even killed. 4. You are disappointed. 5. Around 26. 6. You do not get the job.

45.3

1. c 2. g 3. b 4. e 5. f 6. a 7. d

45.4

1. saving up 2. wrapped up 3. washing up 4. catch you up 5. pack up 6. turn it up 7. bring up 8. look it up 9. keep it up 10. grow up 11. give up 12. getting up 13. Wake up 14. put me up 15. hang up

45.5

1. b 2. a 3. a 4. b 5. a 6. a 7. b 8. a

45.6

1. c 2. b 3. f 4. i 5. d 6. e 7. a 8. g 9. h 10. j

45.7

get through, getting on, looked after, find out, broken down, dropped in, got off, looking for, looking forward to, telling me off, looking after, got back, got round to, wakened up, looking after, paid back, looking after, gets back, having me on

46.1

1. a hundred 2. a dozen 3. a thousand 4. a million, a millionaire 5. thirty miles an hour 6. 40 pence a pound. 7. a pound 8. an hour 9. a 10. a, an, a

46.2

1. such an 2. such a 3. such 4. such an 5. such 6. such an 7. such a 8. such 9. such an

46.3

1. what a 2. what 3. what a 4. what 5. what a 6. what an 7. what 8. what an

47.1

1. d the 2. e the 3. i 4. j the 5. h 6. b the 7. a the 8. g the 9. c 10. f

47.2

The following sentences are wrong: 1,3,4,7,9,10,11,12,13,15,16

47.3

1. The Sahara 2. The Pyrenees 3. In the Louvre in Paris 4. The Caspian Sea 5. The Seine 6. In Piccadilly Circus 7. Playboy 8. Mount Everest 9. Europe 10. Choose from the quality papers: The Times, The Independent, The Daily Telegraph, The Guardian; or the most popular: The Sun, The Daily Mirror, or the biggest selling Sunday paper — The News of The World. 11. The West Indies 12. Kabul 13. The Tiber 14. On Oxford Street 15. Australia! — if you think it's an island — otherwise, Greenland. 16. The United States/America 17. The Soviet Union/The U.S.S.R. 18. The Nineties

47.4

1. the 2. X 3. the 4. the 5. X 6. the 7. the 8. the 9. X 10. the 11. the 12. the 13. the 14. X 15. the 16. X 17. the 18. X 19. the 20. the 21. the 22. X 23. the 24. the 25. the 26. the 27. the 28. the 29. X 30. X

47.5

. . . the border . . . the pilot and two passengers . . . the plane came down in thick fog . . . the passengers . . . the pilot . . . the countryside around the crash site . . . the rescue team . . . the aircraft . . . the plane was found by local hunters . . . the plane . . . the police . . .

48.1

1. water 2. a glass of water 3. tea 4. bread 5. a slice of bread 6. a cup of tea 7. sugar 8. a spoonful of sugar 9. two sugars
Ask your teacher to look at your drawings for numbers 10,11, and 12.

48.2

Note that the following answers give the usual use of the nouns. 1. c 2. u 3. c 4. u 5. c 6. u 7. c 8. u 9. c 10. c 11. u 12. u 13. u 14. c 15. c 16. c 17. c 18. u 19. u 20. u 21. c 22. u 23. c 24. u

48.3

How much milk . . . how much butter . . . many eggs . . . how much cheese . . . how many cartons . . . how much is there . . . how many are there . . . how much of that big cucumber . . . how many cans . . . how much wine . . . how many bottles . . .

48.4

1. a 2. b 3. a 4. a 5. a 6. a 7. b 8. b 9. b 10. b

48.5

1. lots of, many 2. much, much 3. lots of, many 4. much, many 5. lots of, many 6. many, many 7. lots of, many 8. much, many, much 9. many, much

49.1

1. d 2. e 3. a 4. h 5. f 6. g 7. b 8. c

49.2

1. sauce 2. toothpaste 3. jam 4. cornflakes 5. peas 6. flowers

49.3

1. good news 2. a piece of advice 3. furniture 4. piece of information 5. pieces of luggage

50.1

books 1, radios 2, drinks 1, matches 3, lights 1, faces 3, lists 1, tickets 1, ferries 2, chairs 2, shirts 1, insects 1, dresses 3, coaches 3, churches 3, boats 1, horses 3, houses 3, rules 2, peaches 3, cups 1, buses 3, trains 2, heads 2, things 2, bicycles 2, boxes 3, thousands 2, cars 2, maps 1

50.2

1. news 2. glasses 3. customs 4. manners 5. scissors 6. brains 7. tights 8. trousers 9. arms 10. suburbs

50.3

1. Women and children 2. feet 3. People 4. wives, wives 5. ladies and gentlemen 6. glasses, teeth

51.1

1. A 2. N 3. N/A 4. N/A 5. N/A 6. A 7. N/A 8. A 9. N/A 10. A

51.2

1. some, some 2. any 3. any 4. some 5. any 6. some 7. some, some 8. any 9. any 10. some, some, some

51.3

1. some, both 2. both, any, some, some, both 3. some, any, some, some, some, some, both 4. both, some

52.1

1. This book was expensive. 2. The English book was on the shelf. 3. My coat was very cheap. 4. Her hair is long. 5. They were early for the appointment. 6. The new red car crashed into the tree. 7. Let's wash those dirty dishes. 8. The roads are busy in the rush hour. 9. When does the first one leave? 10. Hot curry is too hot for me.

52.2

1. a lovely old car 2. that poor old man 3. a lovely black and white carpet 4. a very expensive silk tie 5. that fast new car 6. a funny burning smell

52.3

1. the first two weeks 2. the last three days 3. the last few days 4. the middle two weeks 5. the last remaining survivor

52.4

Ask your teacher to look at your choice of adjectives.

52.5

1. Jim isn't very tall. 2. Mary isn't very polite 3. Their house wasn't very clean. 4. Jean isn't very patient. 5. The Smiths weren't very friendly. 6. Her clothes didn't look very expensive. 7. The food didn't taste very good. (or nice) 8. Food wasn't very cheap.

52.6

poor—affluent, calm—stormy, sour—sweet, late—early, ancient—modern, boring—interesting, ugly—attractive, quiet—noisy, dull—bright, straight—curly

52.7

curved—rounded, rough—coarse, silky—smooth, unhappy—depressed, outgoing—extrovert, chilly—cold, pointed—sharp, noisy—loud, motionless—still, good-looking—attractive

52.8

1. light-headed 2. quick-witted 3. short-tempered 4. white-haired 5. loud-mouthed 6. short-sighted

53.1

£10,000 = Mick, £2,000 = Alex, £1,500 = Zoe, £350 = John

53.2

Steve is 34. Mick is 37, Zoe is 23. John is 30. Alex is 25.

53.3

1. smaller 2. taller 3. higher 4. better 5. cheaper 6. quicker 7. stronger 8. longer 9. darker

53.4

1. highest 2. largest, biggest (or biggest, largest) 3. faster, more expensive. 4. safest, safer 5. harder and harder (or more and more difficult), easier 6. coldest, (or most northerly) 7. most expensive 8. more difficult

54.1

1. very, direct 2. straight 3. hard 4. very, just 5. there, early (2nd use), (some people would also say that **a bit** is used as an adverb) 6. too, fast (2nd use), now
Do not worry if you did not find all these adverbs. Many people cannot agree exactly what an adverb is.

54.2

. . . never get . . . almost dropped . . . hardly any . . . any faster . . . as fast as I can . . . immediately . . . shortly.

54.3

1. She works quickly. 2. He reads slowly. 3. She plays brilliantly. 4. She dances beautifully. 5. She writes carefully. 6. It runs smoothly.

54.4

1. happily 2. considerably 3. extremely 4. dangerously 5. disgustingly 6. unnecessarily 7. badly 8. carelessly

55.1

1. Peter is never late. 2. You must always . . . 3. He's not strong enough. 4. She's extemely shy. 5. I rarely study after midnight. 6. Jane hardly ever eats meat. 7. How much do you usually pay for lunch? 8. I never take taxis. 9. We occasionally bump into Jim . . .

278

55.2

1. a and c 2. b 3. c 4. c 5. b 6. b 7. c 8. b 9. b 10. b 11. b 12. b 13. b 14. a and c 15. a and c 16. c 17. c 18. b

56.1

1. on your own, by yourself 2. on his own, by himself 3. on her own, by herself 4. on its own, by itself 5. on our own, by ourselves 6. on their own, by themselves

56.2

1. your 2. you 3. it 4. her 5. you think I 6. them and us 7. his, He 8. it, they

56.3

1. yourself 2. yourself 3. himself 4. myself 5. yourself 6. herself 7. himself 8. itself

57.1

. . . your wife . . . so is mine . . . my wife's work . . . her paintings . . . my daughter(or our daughter) . . . her class . . . about my daughter . . . my(our) son . . . his school . . .my(our) son . . . his school . . . my wife . . . our children . . . their school . . . our children . . . theirs . . . your phone number . . . yours

57.2

1. Do-It-Yourself 2. Teach Yourself 3. love your neighbour as yourself 4. defend yourself 5. please yourself 6. compare yourself 7. Enjoy yourself 8. Control yourself

57.3

1. himself 2. yourself 3. himself 4. himself 5. yourselves 6. yourself 7. myself 8. herself

58.1

1. They've knocked down the station. 2. They're going to increase taxes. 3. They've put the price up. 4. They're repairing the road. 5. They're planning the new airport.

58.2

1. their 2. they 3. them 4. their 5. they 6. They, they 7. they 8. they

58.3

The following are suggested answers. Discuss your answers with your teacher.
1. the local authority or the road menders 2. banks 3. the police or the local authority 4. the government 5. the government 6. the authorities 7. shoe manufacturers
Rule: **They** is used for a general, but exactly defined, group of people, eg the authorities.

59.1

1. It's lovely . . . 2. It's essential . . . 3. . . . it's wrong . . . 4. It's possible . . . 5. . . . it's worth . . . 6. . . . It's always a pity . . . 7. It's difficult . . . 8. It's no use . . . 9. It's necessary . . . 10. It's silly . . . 11. . . . it's interesting . . . 12. Is it right . . . 13. Is it true . . . 14. It doesn't matter . . . 15. It's best . . .

59.2

There's a lot to see . . . There's a very interesting museum . . . It's on the top . . . There are several . . . It's very hot . . . it's over 30 . . . There are too many . . . there are lots of . . . It's easy . . . There are quite a lot . . . It's lovely . . . it's great . . . There are so many . . .

60.1

1. Would you like one? 2. shall I get one for you too? 3. . . . but the ones my wife took . . . 4. . . . but the ones from Venice never arrived. 5. . . . but the one John had was very tough. 6. . . . but the one who took the money . . . 7. . . . more amusing than his previous one.

60.2

1. When is the next one? 2. . . . which one would you like? The lemon ones are 40p and the raspberry ones are 45p . . . I'll have one of each, please. 3. Mine's the white one over there behind the red one. 4. Use the one on the shelf. 5. Do you mind if I have a red one? . . . The red ones are my favourites. You can have a green one! . . . I don't like green ones . . . have an orange one . . . I keep the red ones till last . . . I always eat the black ones first. 6. The big ones are the worst . . . when I'm in a small one. 7. But which one do you like best ? . . . I suppose the one that is my real favourite . . . 8. I think the one I admire the most . . . she's the one who gets into the news.

61.1

There were so many people . . . and there was nobody there to help . . . but were there no policemen . . . there was nobody . . . there were mothers . . . there were old people . . . but there was nobody to help . . . there were no trains . . . and there was no information . . .

61.2

1. Are there . . . 2. Is it . . . 3. Was there . . . 4. Is there . . . 5. Is there . . . 6. Is it . . . 7. Is it . . . 8. Are there . . . 9. Is there . . . 10. Is it . . . 11. Is there . . . 12. Was there . . . 13. Will it be . . . 14. Were there . . .

61.3

The following are suggested answers. Ask your teacher to look at your answers.
1. There must be. 2. There must have been. 3. There will be. 4. There can't be. 5. There could be. 6. There must be. (at least, there must be in Britain)

61.4

1. There is a river . . . There is a very high tower . . . There is a famous . . . There are some . . . There is a famous archway. The city is Paris. It's in France.
2. There are a lot of problems . . . There are two parts . . . There is a high wall . . . The city is Berlin. It's in Germany.
3. There are millions of people . . . There are two oceans near . . . There was a terrible earthquake . . . The city is Mexico City. It's in Mexico.
4. There is a large castle . . . There is a royal palace . . . There are very few English accents . . . The city is Edinburgh. It's in Scotland.
5. There are a lot of cars . . . There are several hills . . . There is a large building . . . The city is Athens. It's in Greece.
6. There are about 30 million people . . . There is one of the best underground systems . . . There are lots of modern buildings . . . There is an Imperial Palace . . . There is an international airport . . . The city is Tokyo. It's in Japan.

61.5

1. c 2. a 3. e 4. d 5. b

61.6

There were two pairs . . . There was a light raincoat . . . There were six pairs of tights . . . There was a pair of jeans . . . there were several T-shirts . . . There was a present . . . Was there anything of any value? I don't think there was . . . There were a couple of pullovers . . . Was there anything special about the case . . . there were two labels.

61.7

Ask your teacher to look at your answers.

62.1

1. This 2. that 3. that 4. this, that 5. that 6. this, that 7. this 8. these 9. those 10. These 11. this 12. that was that

62.2

. . . a situation like this before . . . That's true . . . this is a storm . . . no, that's not what I meant . . . what do you think this is . . . Oh, that's different . . . Is that all you can say . . . those people in that office . . . this is not a storm . . . this is a revolution . . .

63.1

1. It was a black car which caused the accident. 2. The thief was a young man who was wearing a woollen hat. 3. We turned up early for the performance which was cancelled. 4. I used to play in the band which is now very famous. 5. I once knew the restaurant owner who was found drowned in the river. 6. I saw the policeman who arrested the murderer. 7. Who was driving the taxi which didn't stop at the lights? 8. When did you stay at that hotel which burned to the ground? 9. Why were you so rude so that old lady who asked you the way? 10. When did you write that letter which caused a lot of trouble?

63.2

1. The thing that I really liked was the food. 2. The things that really pleased me was his letter. 3. The thing that we really enjoyed was the night life. 4. The thing that really amazed me was her salary. 5. The thing that helped me a lot was the quietness. 6. The thing that influenced me most was the chance of promotion.

63.3

1. Those people you met this morning were very rich. 2. same 3. same 4. same 5. same 6. I thought Mary was the one they would promote. 7. I've come to collect the camera I lost yesterday, and which I heard had been handed in. 8. Is he the guy everyone's talking about? 9. This is the house Jack built. 10. I'm sorry to say you dropped the match which started the fire. 11. I've been thinking about the problem you told me about. 12. same 13. same 14. same 15. same

63.4

1. who 2. which 3. that 4. who 5. who 6. which(or that) 7. who 8. that(or which) 9. that (or which) 10. which

63.5

1. People who complain cause trouble. 2. It was a white Mercedes which knocked the woman down. 3. Where are the scissors that I bought last week. 4. It must have been Mary who left the note. 5. The Government, which has a large majority, might not win. 6. The meeting, which I thought was going to be really boring, was very interesting. 7. The bomb blew up a car which was near the bank. 8. I wish I knew the name of that man who spoke to me again today.

64.1

1. from 2. at 3. by 4. about 5. for 6. for 7. at 8. about 9. at 10. by 11. by(or at) 12. at 13. with 14. for, for (or about, about — can you see the difference of meaning?) 15. by, by 16. by

64.2

1. with 2. at 3. for 4. from 5. about 6. from 7. from 8. by 9. for 10. at, at 11. from 12. with 13. by, about 14. with 15. from, about 16. from, for

65.1

1. at 2. for 3. in 4. since 5. on 6. in 7. on 8. on, in 9. on, at 10. at

65.2

a. in 1990 b. at Easter c. on Thursdays d. at night e. in the morning f. in July g. on July the thirteenth h. on Christmas Day i. at five o'clock j. at lunchtime k. in the afternoon l. in the twentieth century m. on Sunday night n. at midnight

65.3

1. in, till(or until) 2. during(or in, after, from) 3. at, in 4. on 5. at, in (or during) 6. in (or during) 7. in, for 8. at, till (or until 9. in, in, at, in 10 in, in

65.4

. . . on Saturday morning . . . for two months . . . in 1975 . . . since then . . . for a while . . . on Sunday afternoon . . . for the past two days . . . till 2 in the morning . . . for two months . . . for the last 12 years . . . at night . . . from 9 till 6 . . . at weekends . . . during the day . . . on Friday 15th . . . in the morning . . . after 7 any evening . . .

65.5

1. . . . three weeks ago . . . for six weeks . . . for another three weeks . . . in a month . . . for a week . . . for another two weeks
2. . . . on Friday evening . . . in the afternoon . . . at lunchtime . . . in the afternoons . . . at the weekends . . . in the evening . . .

65.6

Look back at the drawings to check your answers and ask your teacher to look at them, too.

66.1

The treasure is hidden under the number 2 on the line third from the bottom and second from the right . The key is hidden under the number 5 on the bottom line, third from the left.

66.2

Karen lives at number 3. Carol lives at number 2. Maria lives at number 5. Steve lives at number 1. Abdul lives at number 6. Razi lives at number 4.

66.3

1. at 2. in, in 3. on 4. on 5. under, on 6. in (or among) 7. beside (or next to), on, on 8. on, opposite 9. above, under 10. in, between 11. behind 12. below, above

67.1

1. into 2. out of 3. off 4. over 5. down (or along) 6. across 7. under 8. round

67.2

1. over(or across) 2. past 3. over 4. across 5. through, up (or down!) 6. back to 7. off 8. round and round 9. along, out of 10. Around

68.1

Only one person caught the train — Alex.

68.2

1. and 2. but 3. but 4. because 5. but 6. and 7. because

68.3

1. if 2. because 3. although 4. although 5. if 6. because 7. if 8. Although

68.4

Other answers are possible to individual examples, but there is only one unique solution: 1. while 2. as soon as 3. when 4. until 5. before 6. so that 7. after 8. since 9. so 10. although

68.5

The only unique solution is the order the words are printed in the practice: or at 7, but it might be half past etc.

68.6

although the accuracy . . . because their husbands . . . if you have . . . then you should . . . as it gives . . . not only about giving . . . but also about kissing . . . when you leave

68.7

whoever you are . . . wherever you live . . . whether you are a conservationist or not . . . as if this beautiful . . . suppose that were the case . . . even though the world . . . in case you think . . . once you wake up . . .

68.8

1. when 2. until 3. as soon as 4. since 5. as 6. while 7. before 8. after

69.1

1. Mick never apologises if he is late. 2. You can't be a first-class athlete if you smoke. 3. Water freezes if it's below zero. 4. I always arrive early if I come by bus. 5. My teacher is annoyed if I don't do my homework.

69.2

1. The plane will be late if it's very windy. 2. Zoe will pass her exams if she works hard. 3. We'll be very tired if we go to London. 4. I'll meet you at 3 if I finish in time. 5. Mick will be famous if he appears on TV.

69.3

1. Andrew wouldn't be happy if he lived alone. 2. He would visit New York if he had enough money. 3. He wouldn't be late so often if he bought a watch. 4. He would speak better English if he visited Britain. 5. He wouldn't be so tired if he went to bed earlier.

69.4

1. d 2. e 3. b 4. c 5. a

69.5

The following are suggested answers. Ask your teacher to look at your answers.
1. . . . she wouldn't have got wet. 2. . . . she would have taken a raincoat. (. . . she might not have gone shopping at all.) 3. . . . she wouldn't have fallen on the stairs. 4. . . . her purse might not have been stolen. (. . . she would still have her purse.) 5. . . . she wouldn't have been so late. 6. . . . her family wouldn't have been annoyed.

69.6

The following are suggested answers. Ask your teacher to look at your answers.
1. If aid does not arrive very quickly, lots of poeple will die. 2. If more doctors don't arrive soon, lots of children will die. 3. If the people don't have tents, they will have nowhere to sleep. 4. If food does not arrive, the people will starve. 5. If the rain does not stop, the situation will get worse.

69.7

The following are all possible sentences: 1. a, c, d, e   2. a, c, d, e   3. a, c, d, e   4. d   5. b
(Were you surprised at how many of these were possible?)

69.8

The following are suggested answers: 1. .If the weather gets warmer, everyone will have to stop work. 2. If this weather continues, there will be a shortage of water. 3. If it doesn't get cooler, old people will die. 4. If it doesn't rain soon, the harvest will be ruined. 5. If the harvest is ruined, the farmers will lose money.

69.9

. . . I'll lose my holiday pay . . . if I lose that, I won't be able to afford to buy a car . . . if you don't have a car . . . if I don't get it, I don't know what I'm going to do . . . if we gave a car to you, we would have to give one to all . . . everything would be all right . . . If you are sure that . . . I'm sure that will be fine.

70.1

1. a hundred and one 2. five hundred and sixty three 3. nine hundred and ninety nine 4. one thousand four hundred and eighty seven 5. two hundred and fifty thousand (or a quarter of a million) 6. five and a quarter 7. three and an eighth 8. three point one four two 9. a half 10. seven tenths

70.2

Most of the examples in this practice are idioms and worth learning.
1. three 2. eleven 3. sixes and sevens 4. nine times out of ten 5. two and two 6. Two's company, three's a crowd. 7. one hundred 8. four 9. fifty-fifty 10. forty (do you agree?)

70.3

1. Third 2. second 3. fourth 4. twentieth 5. tenths 6. first 7. first come, first served 8. eighteenth (perhaps twenty first, and in some contries twenty fifth and fiftieth)

71.1

Thirty days hath September, April, June and November. All the rest have 31, except February alone, which has 28 days clear, and 29 each Leap year. (**hath** is an old form of **has**)

71.2

1. a quarter past two 2. eleven twenty (or twenty past eleven) 3. five past four 4. eleven forty five pm, a quarter to midnight, a quarter to twelve at night, twenty three forty five

71.3

1. Libra is from the twenty fourth of September to the twenty third of October. 2. Taurus is from the twenty first of April to the twentieth of May. 3. Cancer is from the twenty second of June to the twenty second of July. The other signs are Capricorn(22.12-20.1), Aquarius(21.1-19.2), Pisces(20.2-20.3), Aries(21.3-20.4), Gemini(21.5-21.6), Leo(23.7-23.8), Virgo(24.8-23.9). Scorpio(24.10-22.11)

72.1

1. long time ago 2. the day before yesterday 3. the day after tomorrow 4. in a few days time 5. eighteen months 6. the other day 7. a couple of years ago 8. in a few weeks time

72.2

1. years ago 2. some years ago 3. eighteen months ago 4. last June 5. the other week 6. the other day 7. in an hour or two 8. the day after tomorrow 9. in a couple of months 10. in a few years

73.1

1. unequal 2. unlocked 3. disagree 4. unfriendly 5. dishonest 6. unbreakable 7. unkind 8. dislike 9. misunderstood 10. disorder 11. dissatisfied 12. uncooked 13. helpful 14. disorganised 15. disqualified 16. dissimilarities 17. unpack 18. unnatural

73.2

1. childless 2. hopeless 3. powerless 4. fearless 5. thoughless 6. friendless 7. careless 8. meaningless

73.3

1. impossible 2. incomplete 3. irresponsible 4. indirect 5. insincere 6. illegitimate 7. immature 8. incorrect 9.. irrelevant 10. inaccurate 11. invisible 12. illogical 13. inexperienced 14. impractical 15. incapable 16. insensitive 17. illegal 18. incovenient

73.4

1. anti-nuclear 2. non-driver 3. re-do 4. pre-1900 5. mis-placed 6. over-enthusiastic 7. ex-king 8. post-1980
9. pro-war

73.5

Ask your teacher to look at your answers. Here are some ideas:
1. anti-Apartheid, anti-political, anti-abortion, anti-war
2. pro-Russian, pro-American, pro-modern, pro-anything-new
3. ex-wife, ex-husband, ex-President, ex-Prime Minister

73.6

1. kindness 2. happiness 3. smoothness 4. weakness 5. sadness 6. darkness 7. illnesses 8. roughness
9. cheerfulness

73.7

1. loveable 2. laughable and unacceptable 3. recognisable 4. unbreakable 5. washable 6. unbelieveable
7. uncontrollable

74.1

Group 1: breaks, costs, drinks, eats, hurts, rests, talks, walks
Group 2: begins, buys, enjoys, feels, flies, goes, leaves, remembers
Group 3: catches, chooses, freezes, reaches, rushes, passes

74.2

The following are suggested answers. Ask your teacher to look at your list.
arrived(d), borrowed(d), cleaned(d), divided(id), exploded(id), fitted(id), glanced(t), helped(t), increased(t),
jumped(t), killed(d), laughed(t), motored(d), named(d), opened(d), picked(t), queued(d), rested(id), searched(t),
tried(d), undressed(t), viewed(d), wished(t), x-rayed(d), yawned(d), zipped(t)

75.1

1. John's 2. men's 3. boys' 4. wife's 5. parents' 6. Minister's 7. lady's 8. town's 9. birds' 10. Pete's brother's

75.2

1. boxes 2. ladies 3. tomatoes 4. flies 5. lilies 6. potatoes 7. bosses 8. matches 9. babies 10. speeches

75.3

1. permitted 2. written 3. swimming 4. putting 5. bigger 6. livelier 7. happily 8. getting 9. stopped
10. hoping

76.1

1. I'd take it back . . . if I were you. 2. So do I. 3. Excuse me, could you . . ., please . . . — I'm afraid,
I've got no change. 4. I'm afraid I haven't. (or I'm sorry . . .) 5. Could I . . . please. 6. Would you mind
helping . . . please. 7. Would you mind opening the window, please.

76.2

1. So can I. 2. So am I. 3. So can I. 4. So do I. 5. So would I. 6. So do I. 7. Neither am I. 8. Neither do I.

77.1

1. mind 2. I have asked . . . I'm sorry, Sir. 3. I think it's ten to. 4. Would you like to come . . . I'd love to.
Thank you very much. 5. Would you like to come with me? . . . That's very kind of you, but I'm afraid I
can't. 6. Have a biscuit. 7. Let me hold . . . It's all right, thank you. I can manage. 8. Why don't you . . .
9. Why don't we meet . . . That's a good idea. (or what a good idea) 10. I'd rather go . . . 11. I am sorry
to hear that. 12. Thank you very much. 13. Don't forget your umbrella.

78.1

1. What does this mean, please? 2. Excuse me, could you tell me where the police station is, please?
3. Excuse me, what time do you make it? 4. Have a good trip. 5. Hello, I don't think we've met before.
6. Sorry. I've got the wrong number. 7. Give my regards to your parents. 8. Many Happy Returns. (you can
also say Happy Birthday) 9. Happy New Year! 10. Congratulations! I hope you'll be very happy.

78.2

1. Have you the time, please. 2. How do you spell address? 3. Have a good holiday. 4. Is this correct,
please. 5. Could I speak to . . ., please? 6. How do you do.

INDEX

This index gives the most important references to each point. Where there are two or more references, the first is the main one. We hope you will find the index easy to use. This means we have not included any unnecessary or unusual items.

INDEX

INDEX